ADOBE®
PHOTOSHOP® LIGHTROOM™ FOR
DIGITAL PHOTOGRAPHERS ONLY

ADOBE® PHOTOSHOP® LIGHTROOM™ FOR DIGITAL PHOTOGRAPHERS ONLY

Rob Sheppard

1807
WILEY
2007

Wiley Publishing, Inc.

Adobe® Photoshop® Lightroom™ for Digital Photographers Only

Published by
Wiley Publishing, Inc.
111 River Street

Hoboken, N.J. 07030
www.wiley.com

Copyright © 2007 by Wiley Publishing, Inc., Indianapolis, Indiana

Published by Wiley Publishing, Inc., Indianapolis, Indiana

Published simultaneously in Canada

ISBN: 978-0-470-04723-1

Manufactured in the United States of America

10 9 8 7 6 5 4 3 2 1

For general information on our other products and services or to obtain technical support, please contact our Customer Care Department within the U.S. at (800) 762-2974, outside the U.S. at (317) 572-3993 or fax (317) 572-4002.

Wiley also publishes its books in a variety of electronic formats. Some content that appears in print may not be available in electronic books.

Library of Congress Control Number: 2006939437

about the author

Rob Sheppard has had a long-time and nationally recognized commitment to helping photographers connect with digital imaging technology. He was one of the small group of people who started *PCPhoto* magazine nearly ten years ago to bring the digital world to photographers on their terms. He is the editor of *Outdoor Photographer* magazines (second only to Popular Photography in circulation), group editorial director of all Werner Publication photo magazines (*PCPhoto, Outdoor Photographer*, *Digital Photo Pro* and *HD Video Pro*) and is the author/photographer of over 18 photo books, including *Adobe® Camera Raw for Digital Photographers Only.*

He also writes a column in *Outdoor Photographer* called Digital Horizons and teaches around the country, including workshops for the Palm Beach Photographic Centre, Santa Fe Photography and Digital Workshops, BetterPhoto.com and the Great American Photography Workshop group. His Web site for workshops, books, and photo tips is at www.robsheppardphoto.com.

As a photographer, Rob worked for many years in Minnesota (before moving to Los Angeles), including doing work for the Minnesota Department of Transportation, Norwest Banks (now Wells Fargo), Pillsbury, 3M, General Mills, Lutheran Brotherhood, Ciba-Geigy, Anderson Windows, and others. His photography has been published in many magazines, ranging from *National Geographic* to *The Farmer* to, of course, *Outdoor Photographer* and *PCPhoto.*

credits

Acquisitions Editor
Kim Spilker

Project Editor
Cricket Krengel

Technical Editor
Michael Guncheon

Copy Editor
Lauren Kennedy

Editorial Manager
Robyn Siesky

Vice President & Group Executive Publisher
Richard Swadley

Vice President & Publisher
Barry Pruett

Business Manager
Amy Knies

Project Coordinator
Adrienne Martinez

Graphics and Production Specialists
Stacie Brooks
Jennifer Mayberry
Rashell Smith

Quality Control Technician
Jessica Kramer

Proofreading
Jeannie Smith

Indexing
Estalita Slivoskey

Cover Design
Mike Trent

Wiley Bicentennial Logo
Richard J. Pacifico

foreword

In thinking about how to begin this foreword for Rob's latest book, an old Chinese proverb comes to mind: *A teacher can lead you to the door; learning is up to you.*

That proverb popped into my head for two reasons. First, Rob is a wonderful teacher, as well as a great photographer. Second, he will not only lead you to the door through which you will begin your exploration of Lightroom, but he'll guide you along the way, into the "classroom," so to speak, as you mentor in the learning process — thereby making mastering Lightroom fun, easy and fast. What more could you ask from an author/teacher?

Actually, if you are a serious photographer, there is, indeed, something more you could request from an expert on Lightroom: not just a book about Lightroom's tools and features, but a book about how to use Lightroom to expand your photographic horizons and vision — and yes, how to improve workflow! Rob does all of the above in his well-organized chapters, which cover everything you want to know about Lightroom.

The scope of the information in this book, however, is not limited to Lightroom. You'll also get some valuable tips on Photoshop, RAW files and printing.

As you read the following pages, you'll also learn a bit about Rob. His passion for photography, digital images and teaching is evident in his writing style. Speaking of which, back in May 2006, Rob and I were teaching at a photography seminar in beautiful St. Augustine, Florida. The weather was ideal and photographic subjects were everywhere. Me? I was out shooting from dawn to dusk. Rob? He was glued to the desk in his hotel room, working on this book using two laptops (so that he could write and work in Lightroom easily at the same time). His work and his readers are that important to him.

Rob is a dedicated, talented, teacher — someone who takes you beyond "the door." So much for the old Chinese proverbs.

Rick Sammon
www.ricksammon.com

preface

When I first started working with the early beta versions of Lightroom, I was impressed with the program. It was far better than Adobe Bridge or Camera Raw for dealing with lots of RAW photos. Since then, the new version of Photoshop, CS3, has incorporated some of Lightroom's innovations into Bridge and Camera Raw, improving both of them as well. Still, Lightroom's ability to give photographers a totally integrated program from editing and organizing to image processing to photo sharing is unmatched by any other Adobe program. Plus it offers some amazing processing capabilities, as you will soon learn, that no one else is doing.

The official name of the program is Adobe Photoshop Lightroom — a bit unwieldy, don't you think? So you will often see it referred to simply as Lightroom in this book. Most people commonly call it Lightroom anyway. Adobe wanted to include Lightroom as part of the Photoshop brand which is how it got its official name.

Since this started as a totally new program, I first came to it as most photographers will, knowing little about its capabilities. Then Adobe decided to do a public beta, which really did refine the program, yet it also kept changing it! For months, I'd get a new version of the program and discover fun new tools . . . but also new things to learn and understand. I really did want to understand what Lightroom could do for me as a photographer so I could translate that for you as a photographer, too.

I admit to a bias in doing this book. I am uninterested in programs like Lightroom or Photoshop as software programs with a big list of features. I really only care about what they can do for the photographer. They both do a lot, but Lightroom has very obviously been designed more specifically for the photographer than Photoshop ever has been.

So in this book my goal has been to explain features to the reader and give some perspective on how photographers can use them. As in my other books, I wanted to produce a book that addressed photographers needs and concerns, one that made photography as important as the technology. It's easy to be wowed by cool features in Photoshop or Lightroom, but it's a different thing altogether to make that cool feature really fit in a photographer's workflow.

You can find additional information about Lightroom and Photoshop as I find new things to work in them on my Web site at www.robsheppardphoto.com.

acknowledgments

There are so many people who really helped me understand and adapt to new technologies that I can't mention them all. I thank everyone who has ever given me information or challenged me to do better in communicating to readers about digital photography, including the great editors at Wiley. I do need to give a special thanks to George Jardine at Adobe who was instrumental in helping me get through all the new tools in Lightroom and clarifying what they could do and how they worked.

I also have to really thank all of the great folks who have been at my workshops and seminars who have taught me what photographers really need to know about digital photography and Photoshop. Without them, I would never have known the nuances of what photographers with a great range of knowledge and skills really understand and don't understand about digital photography. I especially thank the workshop participants at BetterPhoto.com who constantly challenge me to come up with better ways of explaining things.

I want to especially acknowledge my supportive parents who often wondered what the heck this photography business was all about when I was growing up, but supported it anyway and now understand the beauty of it all. I have to especially thank my family, particularly my wife, Vicky, a terrific partner, who tolerates me photographing all over the place and, when home, saying I will just be a minute (but rarely am) then spending much time in my office working at the computer.

contents at a glance

contents

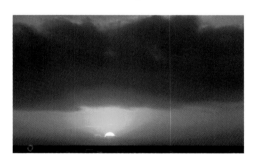

chapter **2 The Basics of Lightroom**   **15**

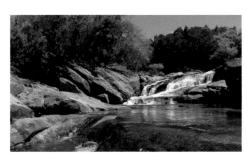

chapter **3 Lightroom Starts with the Camera**   **39**

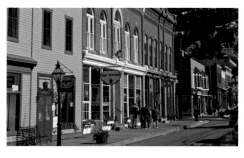

Part II Using Lightroom Modules 55

chapter **4 Library Module Basics** 57

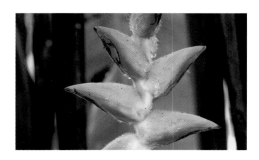

chapter **5 Organizing Images in the Library Module** 81

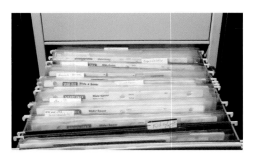

chapter **6 Image Processing in the Develop Module   99**

chapter **7 Added Processing in the Develop Module   129**

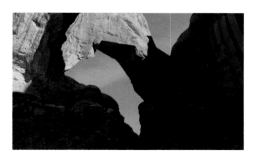

chapter **8 Presentation Possibilities in the Slideshow
         Module   151**

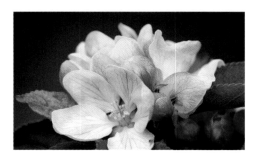

chapter **9 Making a Better Show in Slideshow   179**

chapter 10 Making Sense of the Print Module 201

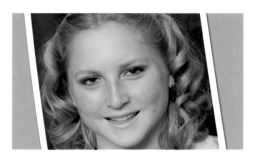

chapter 11 From Good to Great Printing with Print 223

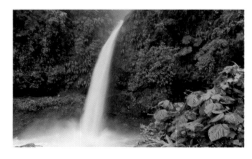

chapter **12 The Web Module   245**

Part III The Photoshop Partnership   273

chapter **13 Going Between Lightroom and Photoshop   275**

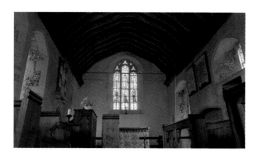

WHAT IS LIGHTROOM ALL ABOUT?

Part I

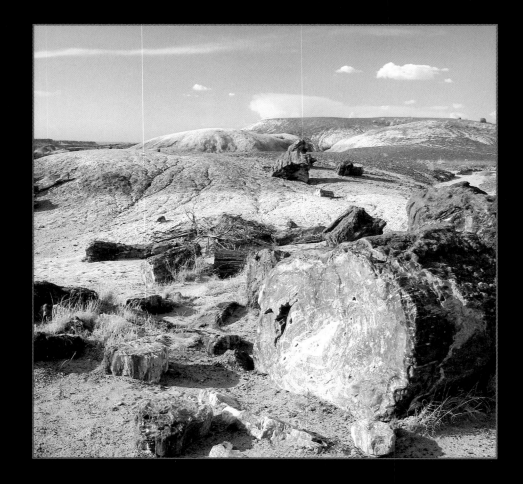

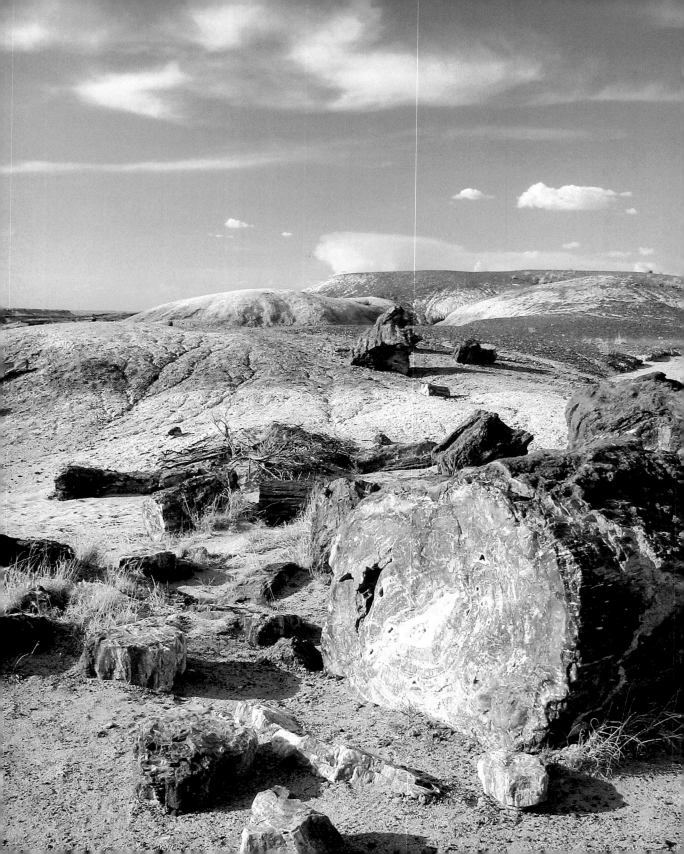

Chapter 1

INTRODUCTION TO THE PHOTOSHOP LIGHTROOM CONCEPT

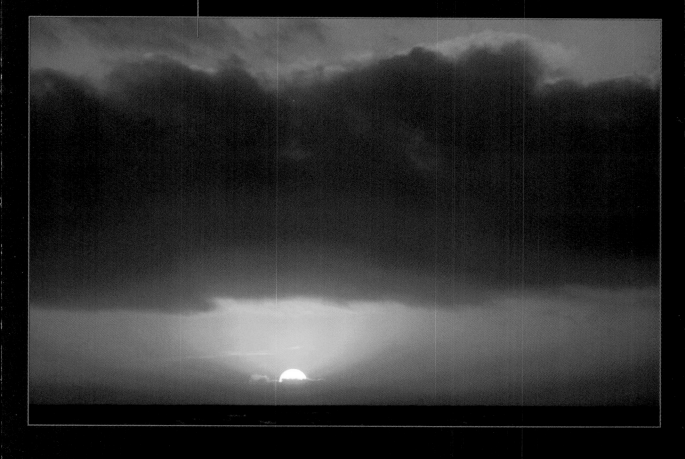

You have embarked on a voyage of discovery. Adobe Photoshop Lightroom is a whole new program that offers you a very different way of working with photos in an Adobe product (and it is influencing the design and functions of other Adobe software now, too). It does not have a decade of history or a wealth of books, videos, and such things about it.

However, I believe it is well worth the effort to learn Lightroom. The program, as you can see in figure 1-1, makes some very powerful tools readily available in a context that you will quickly understand. In this chapter, you discover what makes Lightroom different and how that difference is important to you as a photographer.

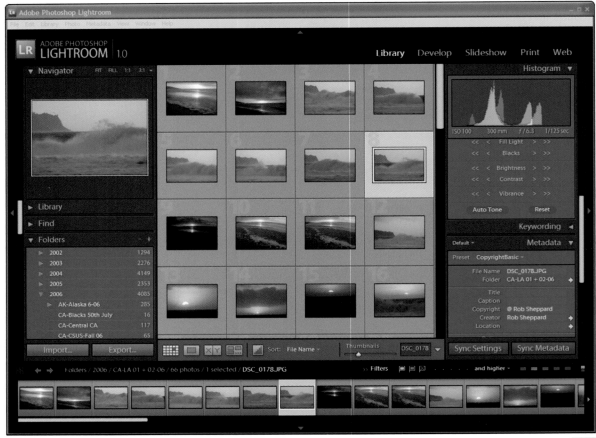

WHAT IS LIGHTROOM ABOUT?

Photoshop is the premier image-processing software available today. But it was never designed specifically for photographers. There are many things about Photoshop that make photographers crazy!

Lightroom is not designed to replace Photoshop (it is even considered part of the Photoshop family of products), but it is made specifically for photographers. Adobe's first effort to make the Photoshop processing "engine" (all the algorithms and high-level computer engineering that happens behind the scenes, under the hood) more accessible to the average photographer was Photoshop Elements. (You may remember Photoshop LE, but that was a butchered version of Photoshop, not a product made for photographers.) Photoshop Elements introduced many photographer-friendly ideas that influenced later software. Just

compare the interface of Photoshop Elements interface shown in figure 1-2 with Lightroom's.

Photoshop Elements was a great effort, to be sure. Lightroom goes far beyond that. It is a program built from the ground up for photographers, and more specifically professional and advanced photographers. It was developed to enhance the photographer's experience with working with RAW and other image files so that the photographs are as important as the program.

Lightroom is not about designing fancy graphics, creating wild composites, or prepping images for the printing press — all things that Photoshop does very well. It is about organizing digital images to make them more accessible, processing them quickly, and then getting them to an audience through slide shows, prints, or Web galleries (and of course image files).

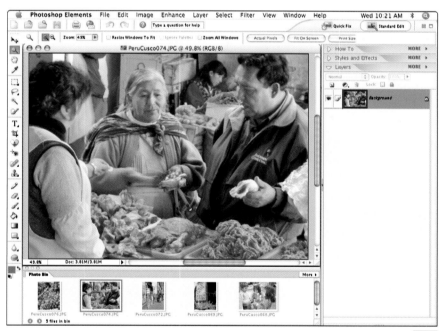

1-2

Designed for RAW

RAW is an important format for photographers because of its depth of information. It offers a great deal of flexibility in its use and processing so that very high-quality images can be consistently achieved. High-quality (low-compression) JPEG is absolutely capable of excellent, professional-level images, but it has much less flexibility before problems (or image artifacts) start showing up. For the early part of digital camera history, RAW was a bit esoteric for photographers. It demanded more in its processing, required special software, created larger files than many photographers' computers were able to handle well, and so on. In short, it was a pain to use.

Lightroom was designed to make RAW processing an easy, integrated part of image work on the computer.

Adobe Camera Raw first changed how RAW could be integrated into a Photoshop-oriented workflow, as shown in figure 1-3. Other RAW conversion software programs offer excellent results and their own workflow advantages, plus they process colors slightly differently, so they do have advantages for some photographers. However, the fact that Camera Raw fit the Photoshop workflow really made quite a difference for most photographers.

Adobe software engineers had long wanted to make RAW file processing easier, more efficient, and better integrated with how a photographer works. Lightroom does exactly that. In fact, if you compare the features of Camera Raw to Lightroom, you'll notice that a good part of Lightroom's Develop module is based on Camera Raw. And now, with Photoshop CS3, which includes Camera Raw 4, you can see Lightroom influencing Camera Raw! The Adobe engineers are using what they learn from photographers using one product to refine the others.

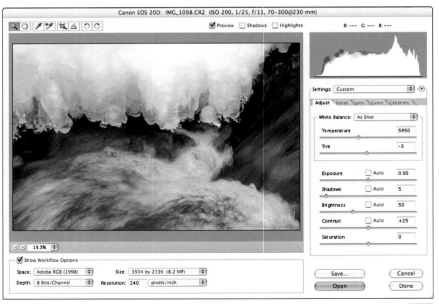

1-3

With all the talk about RAW files and Lightroom, it is worth noting that Lightroom also works quite well for other formats. It will do its magic with well-crafted JPEG files, which makes organizing, processing, and using them more efficient and more effective than ever. In addition, the actual JPEG files are not altered by Lightroom — all adjustments are saved as instructions and not actually applied to the files until the image is exported from Lightroom.

Non-Destructive Processing

Non-destructive processing is a really big deal. This is something unique to Lightroom in that it deals with ALL files non-destructively.

You may have heard about non-destructive processing before. It means that you can adjust a file without damaging its original data. The look of the image changes, but no pixels are harmed. What happens is that the program creates a set of instructions on how to process an image, but does not apply those instructions to that file until a new file is needed.

RAW file processing is non-destructive simply because of the nature of a RAW file. A RAW file is basic data from the sensor — you can convert it to another format, but the original data cannot be altered in any way through processing. However, JPEG files have been traditionally processed in a way that changes pixels. That's how Photoshop works, though Camera Raw 4 processes JPEG files non-destructively, too.

Changing pixels is not how Lightroom works. It affects JPEG, TIFF, and RAW simply with instructions for adjustments. You can adjust and readjust any file as much as you want without affecting its quality. It is only when you export the file that it finally changes, with the adjustments actually applied to the pixels.

There is another advantage to non-destructive processing in Lightroom that is often missed — it reduces the number of image files you have to keep. For example, you don't need multiple files at different resolutions for printing — you simply print directly from the Lightroom file. You don't need a whole new set of image files for a slide show — you just work on the slide show in Lightroom. And you don't need to make up a whole series of file sizes for clients — you can always get exactly what you need from the Lightroom file.

Why Lightroom and Not Aperture

Originally, I thought about putting this section later in the chapter, but I know this is a big deal for a lot of photographers. Lightroom came along just after Apple's Aperture (shown in figure 1-4). It seemed like Adobe was just copying Aperture, using its power with Photoshop to create a me-too program.

If you think a bit about that, you will quickly discover that this was simply not possible. Developing a program like either Aperture or Lightroom takes a lot of work and time. It is not something that developers can throw together overnight in response to a competitive product. Adobe undoubtedly changed its plans for how to continue its development of Lightroom after Aperture was announced, but it did not change its original concept.

Both companies developed programs for photographers because they recognized a frustration that a lot of photographers had. Photoshop is great, but it doesn't fit cleanly into a lot of digital photographers' workflow needs. Photographers wanted a complete solution, especially something that integrated RAW image workflow into the process, from getting images onto the computer's hard drive all the way through producing the print.

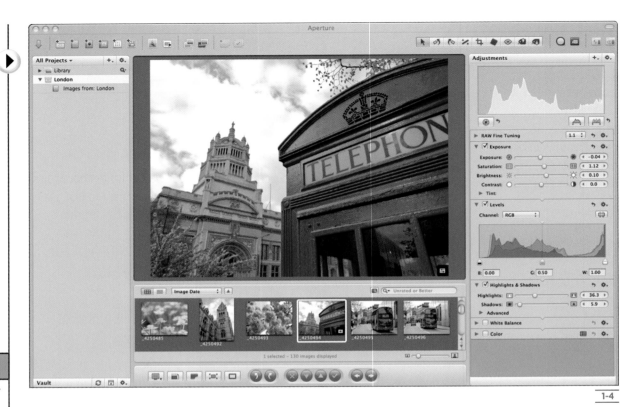

This driving force, strong photographic needs that Photoshop or any other program was not meeting, stimulated some very bright people at both Adobe and Apple. Because both companies saw the same needs, the programs they developed offer similar functions to meet these needs.

Yet Aperture and Lightroom are very different programs. There are some things that Aperture does better (its light table is phenomenal) and some things it lacks (it has no threshold screens for black and white tonalities). Both programs also deal with filing and organizing images, processing, slide shows, and prints in different ways.

A big difference, however, is in how the programs are used by photographers and their computers. Aperture is a highly processor- and RAM-intensive program. There is no question that Aperture is not simply a program for Apple to sell for its own sake, but it also

sells computers. Though Apple claims Aperture can run well on low-powered machines, it really doesn't do all that well. You need a computer with some power.

Lightroom, on the other hand, has a much smaller footprint on its host computer. It will run, and run quite well, on older computers without requiring as much processing power or RAM. In addition, Lightroom works well on both Mac and Windows computers. Aperture is Mac only.

PRO TIP

RAM is still important for any image processing software. With too little RAM, your computer slows down as it uses the virtual RAM or memory it creates with your hard drive. Have at least 1GB of RAM for Lightroom (2GB is better if you are also running Photoshop at the same time).

THE LIGHTROOM DEVELOPMENT PROCESS

Lightroom was developed in a very different way from any other Adobe product because it was first released in a public beta program, as shown from an early stage in figure 1-5. This means that anyone (and maybe you) could have downloaded the early version of the software, tried it out, and given Adobe feedback on what was right or wrong for the program.

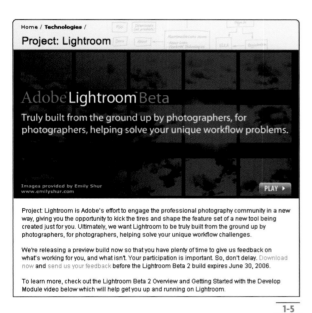

Home / **Technologies** /
Project: Lightroom

Adobe**Lightroom** Beta

Truly built from the ground up by photographers, for photographers, helping solve your unique workflow problems.

Images provided by Emily Shur
www.emilyshur.com

PLAY ▶

Project: Lightroom is Adobe's effort to engage the professional photography community in a new way, giving you the opportunity to kick the tires and shape the feature set of a new tool being created just for you. Ultimately, we want Lightroom to be truly built from the ground up by photographers, for photographers, helping solve your unique workflow challenges.

We're releasing a preview build now so that you have plenty of time to give us feedback on what's working for you, and what isn't. Your participation is important. So, don't delay. Download now and send us your feedback before the Lightroom Beta 2 build expires June 30, 2006.

To learn more, check out the Lightroom Beta 2 Overview and Getting Started with the Develop Module video below which will help get you up and running on Lightroom.

1-5

Software generally goes through a series of stages of development. After the company establishes the initial idea, sets goals, and puts a development team into place, the team creates a program. Early versions are called alpha software as features come and go. The program is very fluid and not at all stable at this point.

After a bit, the team determines the main features and interface design, thus reaching a more stable, less fluid part of the development. At this point the program becomes the beta software. It goes to beta testers, which include folks inside the company and special testers outside the company, who try out the program in their specific situations. They look for problems, mistakes, shortcomings, and so forth.

As developers refine the software, they distribute new beta versions called *builds* to the testers to test again. This way the software developers get input from a variety of people in a lot of different situations to be sure the final program is as good as it can be. These people all work very hard to catch all the bugs they can and look for program limitations, though individuals may still later use the software in a way no one thought of and find new issues later when the program is actually released as a saleable product.

With Lightroom's beta free to the public, anyone could literally be a tester of the software. Instead of a limited group of testers evaluating and commenting on the beta software, thousands of people could see it and help make it the best program it could be.

This really affects photographers because it means that Lightroom was not only developed specifically for photographers, but it was also refined by photographers on its way to a final product.

However, there is sort of a good news/bad news element to the public beta. On the one hand, lots of great ideas came into the Lightroom development team, who worked furiously to incorporate a lot of new features into the program before it was a final product. But on the other hand, the program did become more complex with less simplicity and ease-of-use compared to when it was first announced.

LIGHTROOM COMPARED TO PHOTOSHOP

Here's something I need to clear up right away. There is little in Lightroom that you can't do in Photoshop (including Bridge). Lightroom is not some amazing new approach to processing images in the computer. In fact, a lot of Camera Raw shows up in Lightroom, as well as ideas from Bridge and Adobe Photoshop Elements programs (and Lightroom is now showing up in Camera Raw, Bridge, and Photoshop, too).

Lightroom is not a new program that bumps Photoshop out of the top position in image processing. It is, as I've explained, one that responds specifically to photographers' needs for working on images in the computer. It is about making a process easier, more convenient, and more intuitive for photographers.

To be more explicit:

> **Lightroom is a program designed to include features optimized for photographers.** Photoshop is a high-featured program designed to meet a great deal of users' needs from graphic artists to art directors to video artists to photographers and more.

> **Lightroom offers a flat hierarchy of controls you can access quickly.** Photoshop offers hierarchies of controls with different levels of access to meet the diverse needs of its users.

> **Lightroom has a small RAM footprint and boots up very quickly.** Photoshop has a large RAM footprint and loads slowly.

> **Lightroom is designed for fast work by a photographer.** Photoshop is designed for complex work by many types of users and speed is not the primary goal (although Photoshop CS3 does have speed refinements built into it).

> **Lightroom offers a targeted set of controls to deal with images.** Photoshop gives you an infinite amount of control over how you deal with images.

> **Lightroom only offers tools that affect the photographer.** Photoshop offers text, special effects, high-level commercial printing controls, and other specialized tools.

> **Lightroom has no compositing or manipulation tools.** Photoshop includes advanced compositing and image manipulation tools.

> **Lightroom integrates the workflow process into a linear and photo-centric process that can be used nonlinearly as needed.** Photoshop separates parts of the workflow process into nonlinear (and often illogical for photographers) patterns.

I could compare the two for a long time. My point is not that either program is arbitrarily better, but that they are different and offer different processes for the user.

Photoshop has a huge number of tools that you can use in a great number of ways. That is definitely true and all of its tools just can get a little overwhelming, as shown in figure 1-6. Lightroom takes a very different approach. Its tools are aligned in a way that matches photographer workflow needs.

Bottom line: Lightroom is a highly capable program that helps photographers organize and process images faster and more efficiently. It offers a better and more photo-centric workflow than Photoshop. For some photographers, Lightroom offers a complete and effective way of working with digital images and they will need nothing else.

Introduction to the Photoshop Lightroom Concept

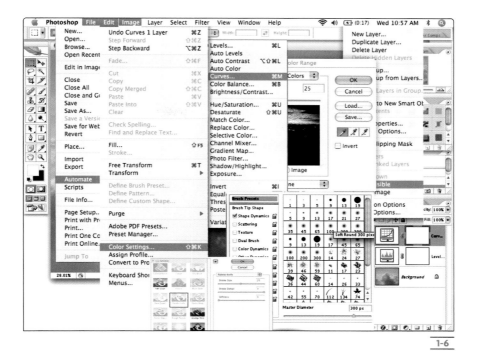

1-6

CAN PHOTOGRAPHERS FORGET ABOUT PHOTOSHOP?

Some photographers will be able to give up Photoshop. If Lightroom does everything you need, why bother with Photoshop? But I'm afraid that I can't tell you if that is something for you or not. You'll have to see how well Lightroom meets your needs.

I love Lightroom. Lightroom is far better than Bridge for organizing and storing images. It is also much, much faster (though the latest version of Bridge does try to address this issue in how it deals with pre-views). Lightroom makes working with RAW files a real pleasure, and the Slideshow and printing modules simplify those processes and include a great deal of power.

However, because Lightroom cannot do everything that Photoshop can do, I am not about to give up using Photoshop. Image processing includes making overall adjustments to an image, but very often, you need to make local or small area changes. Photoshop, with its selection tools, layers, layer masks, and history brush, offers a wealth of power for adjusting an image in quite precise and defined areas. Lightroom is not made for that.

For folks who like special effects, from image-warping filters to composited images, Photoshop is the place to go. And if your work involves going beyond working an image for slide shows or printing, you may need the added color- and graphics-oriented tools you'll find in Photoshop.

WHO BENEFITS FROM LIGHTROOM?

Lightroom is for digital photographers, obviously. Any digital photographer will find it useful. It is aimed at pros, yet anyone who shoots a lot of photographs, needs to organize and access them readily, and needs a way of processing them quickly and easily through to a saved file, slide show, print and/or Web gallery, will find Lightroom a great way to go. You can see one photo's progression through the modules in Lightroom in figures 1-7 through 1-11.

Lightroom is for serious photographers who don't need the full-featured options of Photoshop or its price. And it is for photographers who want to work quickly and efficiently with most images, while retaining the ability to use Photoshop in a more targeted way for specific images that need its power (and its more detailed workflow).

It is definitely for the photographer who doesn't want to deal with the learning curve of Photoshop or is intimidated by all the tools Photoshop offers the user. Yet it is also for the sophisticated Photoshop user who wants a simpler approach to working with large numbers of photos more quickly, especially RAW files.

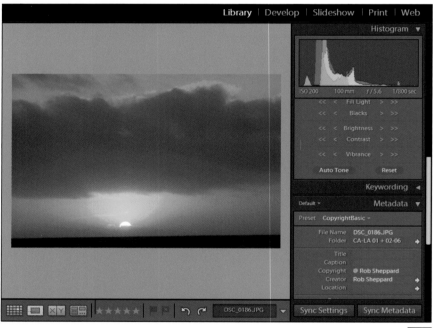

1-7

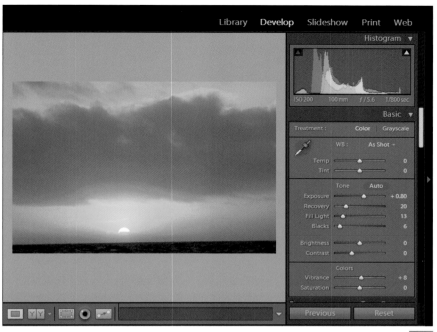

1-8

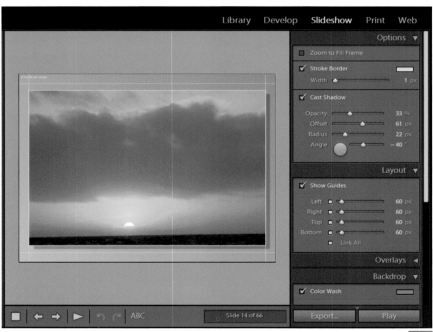

1-9

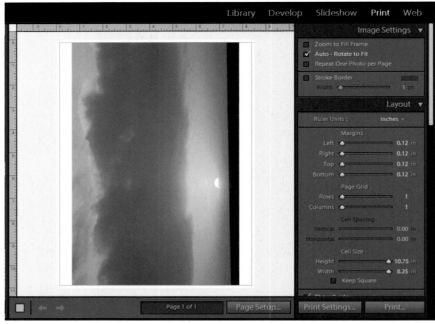

1-10

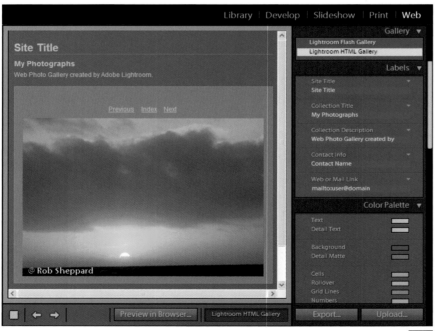

1-11

Chapter 2

THE BASICS OF LIGHTROOM

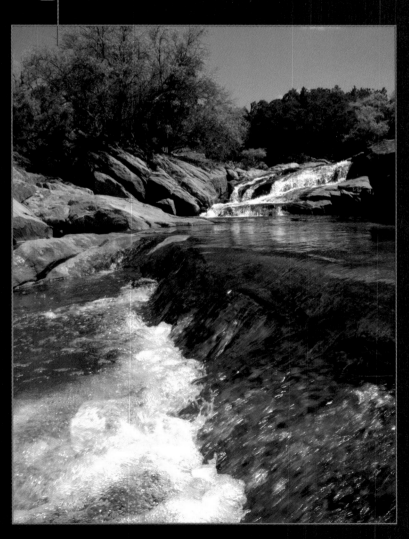

A new program ... where do you start? This is always a challenge for anyone working with the digital darkroom. Adobe Photoshop Lightroom has no long history of books, workshops, seminars, or just a lot of people using it over time. Yet this program is laid out in such a way that if you understand some basic concepts about it, you can learn to use the whole program very quickly.

As you see when you open the program, Lightroom is based on modules, so once you have images in it, you can jump around within the program as much as you want. Some people need to think very linearly, others need, just as much, to think nonlinearly. Lightroom works for both mindsets, but I do think it helps to understand the basics of the program first, which is what this chapter is all about.

How Lightroom Is Organized

Lightroom takes a very different approach compared to most image processing programs in how a photographer accesses its features. The interface is arranged spatially into four distinct regions or panels, while the program is organized linearly around a set of four work modules.

Panels

The four regions are panels that identify and contain ways of dealing with an image, as shown in figure 2-1 and figure 2-2. Each panel changes depending on the module (compare figure 2-1 with figure 2-2); however, work panels appear at the right and left that offer you adjustments and controls over your images. The center panel is photo-based, and highlights the image (or images) you are working on. It can include one or multiple images. The final panel is the filmstrip at the bottom that lets you go quickly through a selected group of photos.

You can turn panels on and off so to better see the photo (or group of photos) at the center in two ways. First, you can just press Tab and the two side panels disappear, as shown in figure 2-3. They return when you press Tab again.

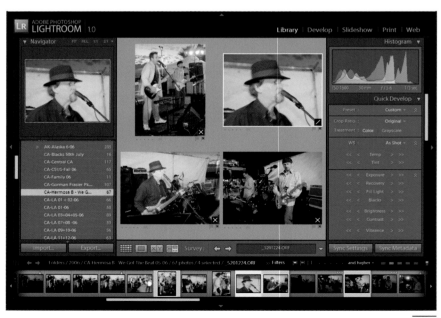

2-1

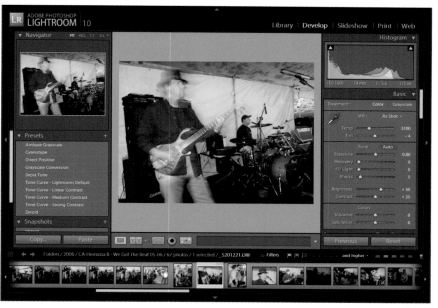

2-2

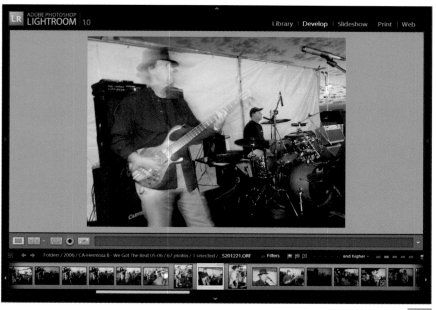

2-3

Second, you can hide them one at a time by clicking the small arrows at the far sides of the panels (in reality, the arrows are just reminders — you can click anywhere near them on the bars where they reside). The arrows are dark gray until you mouse over them.

Then they turn a lighter gray as they become active. Figure 2-4 shows Lightroom with the left panel hidden (and the top/menu is hidden too). The panels come back temporarily if you move your mouse to the far edge of the interface where the panel is, and are

hidden again if you move the mouse over the middle of the photo. They remain visible if you click again on the arrow.

You can hide the filmstrip panel, too. Click the little arrow at the bottom of the interface, below the filmstrip, and the strip of photos hides, as shown in figure 2-5. It comes back temporarily if you mouse over the bottom of the screen or stays on if you click the arrow again.

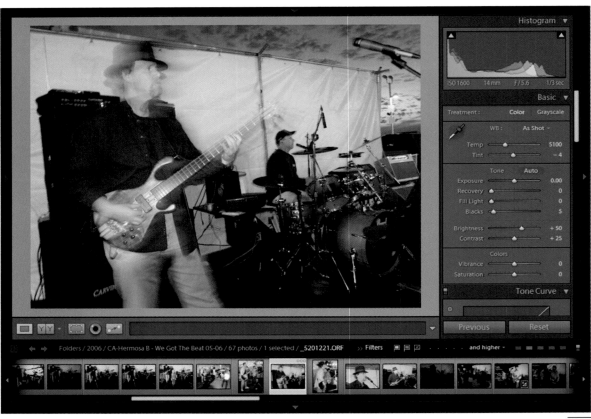

2-4

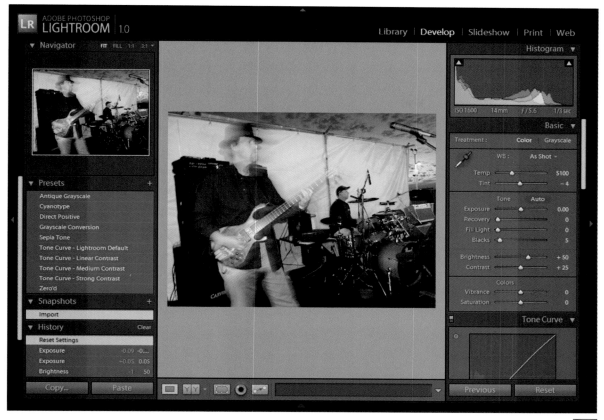

2-5

When the filmstrip is hidden, you can press Tab and the side panels become hidden, leaving you with just the image you are working on, as shown in figure 2-6. Pressing Tab does not bring back the filmstrip, just the side panels.

If you don't like the way the panels are sized on your computer, you can adjust how big each one is by moving your cursor over the dividing bar between the panels. This changes your cursor to a bar with arrows and allows you to make a panel larger or smaller by clicking and dragging.

PRO TIP

The larger the monitor you can work with, the easier it is to work with all of the panels at once. Using smaller monitors, especially those on laptops, often means you have to hide certain parts of the interface so the part you are working with is large enough.

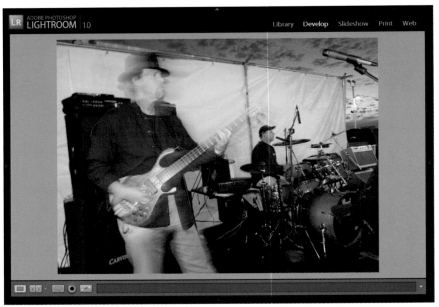

2-6

MODULES

The other important thing to understand about Lightroom is that it is organized linearly into modules that you can access in any desired order. Consider these modules workrooms that let you make changes to an image, and the controls in each workroom all relate to a specific function. According to Adobe, modules can be added or subtracted from the program, so the company may add more in the future (or you may be able to add special modules created by independent software developers).

The modules are

> Library

> Develop

> Slideshow

> Print

> Web

They appear at the top right of the Lightroom interface in figure 2-7. I am going to keep the same photo in the interface for each module so you can better see how the modules change the interface. These are all images of a local baby-boomer rock band made up of business professionals performing in Southern California.

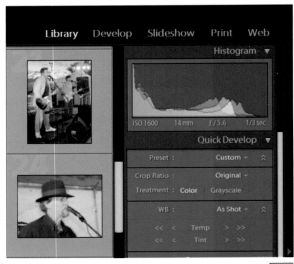

2-7

You select any one module by just clicking on it. You can use them in order, starting at Library and finishing with Print, or you can select any one of them at any time. You always have access to photos with the filmstrip at the bottom of the screen. You will learn more about using each module in later chapters.

Library

Library is where you "keep" your photos for Lightroom to work on, though most photographers don't actually file images through Lightroom (it is possible to file images through Lightroom, though this might not be the best choice for you). They typically use the program for its organizing capabilities that keep a reference as to where images are on the hard drive or other media. Library is the place to systematize and sort photos. This module (shown in figure 2-7) gives you image import and export options, folder editing and organizing capabilities, labeling and other information options, and even a chance to quickly process images.

Develop

Develop is where photos are processed, as shown in figure 2-8. This is where you adjust and optimize images, using some controls that are just like those in Camera Raw and others that are completely new. Develop has controls from basic exposure to color tuning, cropping, and even lens aberration correction. You can see the control groupings as shown in figure 2-9.

X-REF

For more information on color tuning, see Chapter 6.

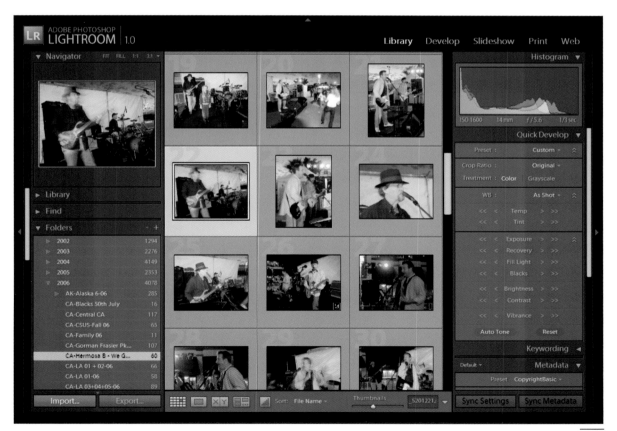

2-8

This module also introduces a very useful way to work quickly with images: the Presets Browser panel on the left, shown in figure 2-10. All the other modules include something similar, offering pre-made adjustments for images.

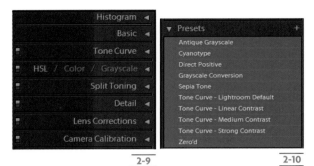

2-9   2-10

Slideshow

Slideshow (seen in figure 2-11) introduces something possible in Photoshop (Bridge) and Photoshop Elements, but ramps up the capabilities considerably.

This part of Lightroom gives you some great capabilities for showing off groups of images, just like the old slide shows from the days when most people shot film. If you have a digital projector, you can even project these images like the "old days." Slideshow gives you a great deal of control over how the images are displayed, including the ability to add some very cool image enhancements such as borders and drop shadows.

Print

The next module is Print (as seen in figure 2-12). This is the first time in any Adobe product that all printing related functions are put into one place. Adobe engineers knew that photographers like to make prints, so they created a module to gather together printing options. You actually have a lot of control here for the print, yet because Lightroom groups the adjustments and settings in a manner that is logical for printing, you can truly focus on what matters in printing and not be distracted by a lot of unrelated stuff.

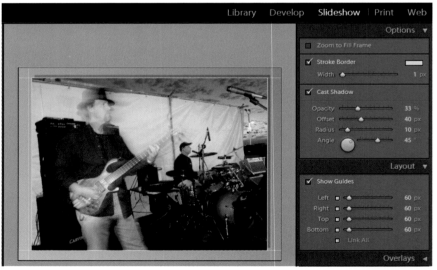

2-11

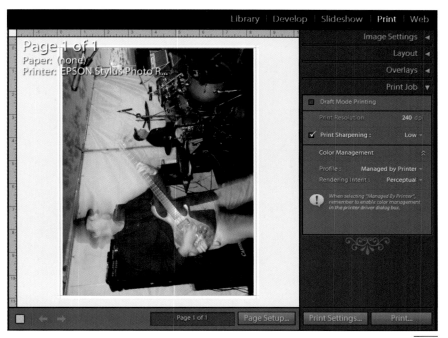

2-12

Web

The last module is Web (as seen in figure 2-13). This offers you an easy way of making Web galleries for a Web site. This is a fairly simple module with two basic forms of galleries, one HTML, the other Flash. You control the text you need and how the galleries display the work.

A really great thing about Lightroom is that you can skip back and forth among these modules as needed. If you test a slide show, (shown in figure 2-14) for example, and find one image is off in exposure compared to others, you can immediately go to Develop (shown in figure 2-15), fix that exposure, and then go back to the slide show. That is a really cool feature. I can tell you that working with images for slide shows or printing has been annoying at times when I had to go back and readjust an image, and then start over with it for the slide show or print. This totally changes how you work with images in that way.

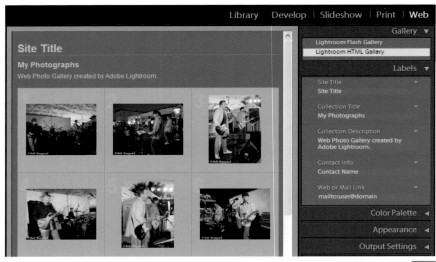

2-13

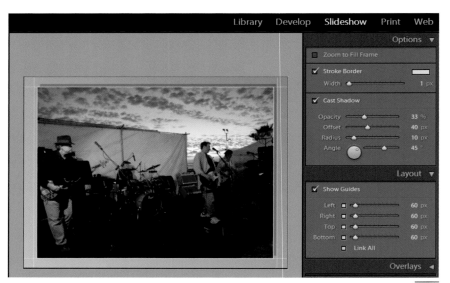

2-14

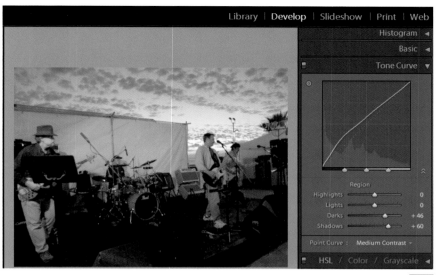

2-15

ADOBE'S FIVE RULES FOR LIGHTROOM

I have no idea who came up with this idea at Adobe, but it is a great one — a set of five rules for using Lightroom. These are not rules as in absolutes or laws you must follow, which makes them very usable. They are really guidelines that direct how you can work with Lightroom, but they are also obviously guidelines that the program developers used to guide their work. Adobe's five "Rules for Lightroom" are

> Work by modules

> Look to the panels for controls

> Use the filmstrip to work with your photos

> Know important key commands

> Enjoy the process

WORK BY MODULES

As you've seen, Lightroom is structured into modules. It is not done that way simply to keep different functions separate; it also makes it easier for photographers to work through images in an intuitive way.

This is a framework to constantly keep in mind as you are learning Lightroom. If you have trouble remembering where a certain control is, think about the modules and where that control might logically be. Any time you click to activate a module, a new set of controls and choices appears in the panels at the left and right sides of the screen.

These modules are also a great framework for a workflow:

1. Start with the Library module, do library (organizing) sort of work there.

2. Process the image or images in Develop.

3. Next use the image in presentations, either as a slide show, a print, or a Web gallery from the respective modules.

LOOK TO THE PANELS FOR CONTROLS

Everything you need to do with an image you can find in the panels at the sides of the central work area. All controls and adjustments are grouped into sets of similar functions. This makes them much easier to use than the menu structure of Photoshop. While you can use the menus at the top of Lightroom, you won't be using them much.

You can find nearly every standard photo adjustment you need here. Each panel has controls and adjustments appropriate to the task the module defines. Panels at the left hold preset browsers, while panels at the right hold the actual tools. The panels also include section headers to group controls by category. You open a category by clicking on the section header (for example, see Basic in the Develop module in figure 2-16) or close the choices to make the interface simpler by clicking again on the category.

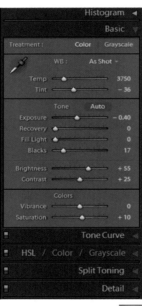

2-16

USE THE FILMSTRIP TO WORK WITH YOUR PHOTOS

Lightroom is designed to have images always accessible to you. You don't have to constantly open an "open" dialog box and search for images on your hard drive. All photos from a particular group (folder, keyword search, or collection) are in the filmstrip. This is a linear view of the current images in the Library group that you have selected.

You can change what is in the filmstrip whenever you need by going back to the Library and choosing a different group of images. The Filmstrip, as shown in figure 2-17, provides all the other modules images you can work on within that module.

KNOW IMPORTANT KEY COMMANDS

You can work with Lightroom more quickly and efficiently if you learn a few key commands that you access directly from the keyboard. More than a few keystrokes make the process of working an image go more smoothly, but start with these important key commands:

> **L.** The lights out mode. This is really a cool key command to remember. Press L once and the screen turns black except for your photo. Press L again and the whole interface dims except for your photos in the center work area, as shown in figure 2-18. This is a very quick and useful keystroke that lets you better examine your photo without any distractions around it.

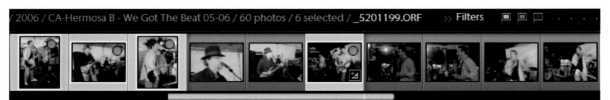

2-17

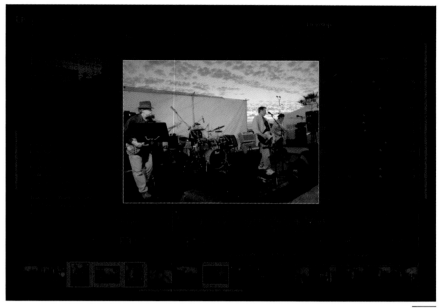

2-18

> **Tab.** Hides side panels. This is a quick way to simplify the interface (see figure 2-19). The side panels of controls are hidden, shifting the focus to just your photo, and the Filmstrip remains available. See either panel instantly by moving your cursor to the sides; hide them again by moving the cursor away. Press Tab again and the panels return. Shift+Tab hides/unhides both side panels and the Filmstrip panel as seen in figure 2-20.

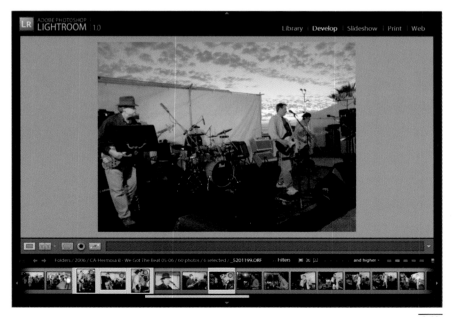

2-19

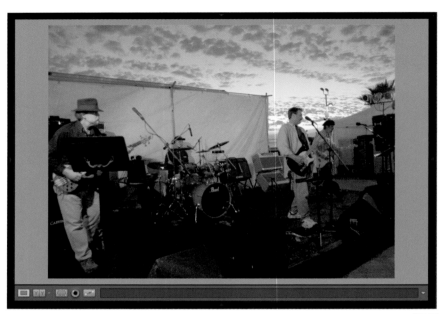

2-20

> **C and G and E.** The Compare, Grid, and Loupe views. These are used in the Library module and let you shift quickly among the Compare (C), Grid (G), and Loupe (E) arrangements of images in the center workspace.

> > **Compare.** This view lets you look at two or more images at once for comparison.

> > **Grid.** In this view you see all images in the group you are working with.

> > **Loupe.** This view is of just one photo.

> **T.** The cycle Toolbar mode. This only affects the Toolbar below the central photo area as seen in figure 2-21. It simplifies the view as shown in figure 2-22.

> **Left and right arrow keys.** Enable you to move through the filmstrip. Using these keys rapidly takes you through the images on the filmstrip, starting with the selected image showing in the central panel.

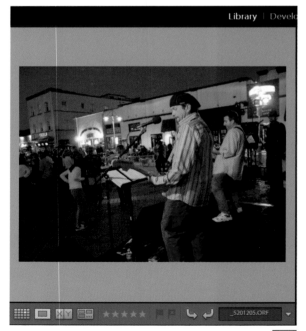

2-21

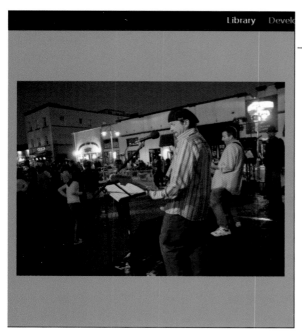

2-22

THE CRAFT OF LIGHTROOM AND PHOTOGRAPHY

One thing that I like to stress in all my workshops and books is the craft of photography and the digital darkroom. Craft is the learned skill of doing something well; it suggests the idea that someone is making or constructing something in a way that requires care and ingenuity. Photography is definitely a craft — an art and a science developed with practice by using and learning the many tools involved so that through trial and error, one masters the skills needed through a period of apprenticeship.

While it is true that most photographers don't have a true, traditional apprenticeship (though some do, becoming assistants to top photographers while they hone their craft), one cannot pick up a camera and immediately become an excellent photographer. You need to learn how to control the equipment, from f-stops to shutter speeds, and how to deal with the medium. You need to learn how to make a photograph with care and ingenuity. Most pros and advanced amateurs understand that. They know that it takes some time to master exposure and composition, for example, as demonstrated in the scene shown in figure 2-23 and figure 2-24. Figure 2-23 is an over-exposed, amateurish composition of a waterfall taken at Inks Lake State Park in Texas. Figure 2-24 shows more control and mastery over both the exposure and composition.

Just as it took you some time to master f-stops and shutter speeds, it will take some experience with Lightroom until you really master its capabilities. Yes, it is set up for photographers; yes, it is designed to be intuitive for the pro and advanced photographer. However, this does not mean that once you know the basics of this program, you have mastered its craft. You must spend some time with the program, playing with its controls and working on a lot of images to really know how to benefit from its power.

ENJOY THE PROCESS

I really like this little rule. I'm glad the Lightroom developers included it. Some folks treat Photoshop so very, very s-e-r-i-o-u-s-l-y. I think that having a fun, playful attitude toward Photoshop helps you in that program, too, but it is especially important in Lightroom. Lightroom is made to encourage experimentation and trying out features. You can quickly go from one thing to another, make comparisons, try new tools, and so forth. Treat Lightroom as a fun way to deal with your images and look for the fun in the process. You are likely to discover many new ideas that way.

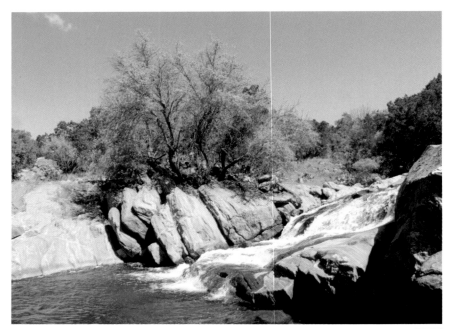

2-23

I also stress the idea of craft because Lightroom is especially made to make RAW file processing easier and more efficient. There is still a serious and problematic misunderstanding about RAW — that is very dangerous for any photographer: If you shoot RAW, you can always fix image problems in the software. The idea that RAW makes it so easy to correct poor shooting technique so that you don't have to worry about being as careful when shooting is, to put it bluntly, wrong. It is not the best way to use Lightroom or any other image processing software. Crafting a fine image starts when you first pick up the camera, which is what the next chapter is all about.

CUSTOMIZING LIGHTROOM'S IDENTITY PLATE

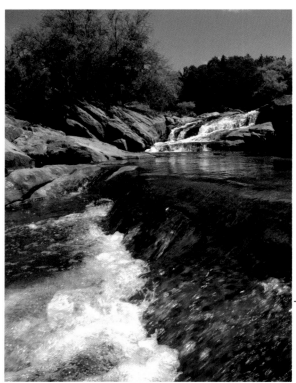

2-24

Lightroom has a neat little feature that will appeal to many pros who use the program with clients, for example, on a laptop while in the field. This is the ability to change the identity plate, as Adobe calls it, which is the program identity part of the interface at the top left where it says Adobe Photoshop Lightroom. You can actually put in your own name (or studio name).

To do this, follow these steps:

1. **Choose Edit ⇨ Identity Plate Setup in Windows (shown in figure 2-25) and Lightroom ⇨ Identity Plate Setup on a Mac.** The Identity Plate Editor dialog box appears.

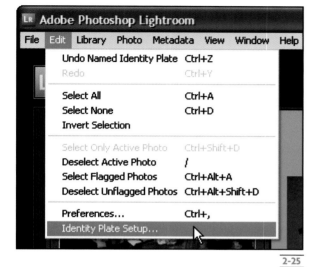

2-25

2. **Select the Enable Identity Plate option and type in your name in the name space at the left (with the "Use a styled text identity plate" option selected).** There is a drop-down menu that has a default of custom at first — this menu lets you save or remove specific Identity Plates. Your name appears in the identity plate area at the top left, as shown in figure 2-26. The default is an interesting font, but it is not particularly consistent with the rest of the interface. Also, the letters start right at the very left edge of the interface by default — I find that is too close so I like to add a space or two before the letters start.

However, this does bring up something you may find gives you a really cool interface — you can change the font for both your name and the module picker buttons, as shown in figure 2-27. You pick the name font with the font drop-down menu after selecting the letters, and then match it to the module word fonts by using the drop-down menus below that area in this

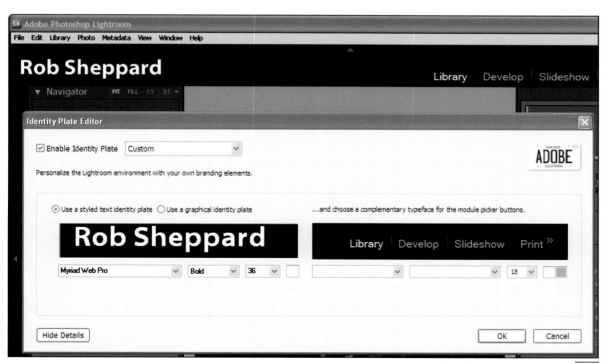

2-26

...and choose a complementary typeface for the module picker buttons.

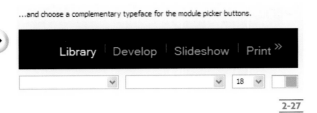

2-27

dialog box, as shown in figure 2-28. The font choices are obvious: from left, the typeface, thickness or italic, and size. Color is not as obvious — you click the square box to the right of font size to get the color picker shown in figure 2-29 (the Mac color picker has a different look than seen here).

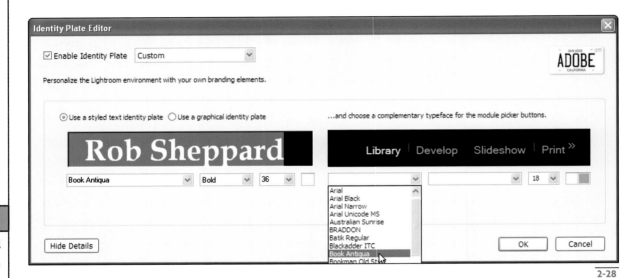

2-28

2-29

To enhance your Identity Plate and make it more graphic, you can even select parts of the name and change just that font and color, as shown in figure 2-29. This gives the Lightroom interface a very custom look, as shown in figure 2-30.

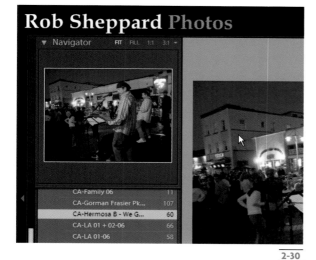

2-30

The ability to add your name and change fonts and colors gives you a lot of personalization capabilities, but if you have a studio with a graphic, you can add that, too, after you have sized it up to a maximum 60 pixels high (that is all Lightroom can use). You simply select the Use a graphical identity plate option and then use the Locate File button that appears to navigate directly to the image you need. The result is the Lightroom interface with a custom logo.

A caution on the Identity Plate. Watch your colors and bold logos. They can be distracting from your actual photos. This can be a real problem when working with the Develop module because strong colors, for example, can affect how you see colors in the image you are processing. Notice that Lightroom has an overall very neutral interface — this was done for just that reason, avoiding color and tonal distractions.

PREFERENCES

Unlike Photoshop, Lightroom has few preferences to set. I have found that using Lightroom with its default preferences rather than going in and setting new ones is fine for my use, and I suspect, many other photographers. However, you should know where Preferences are and how to set them.

Preferences are found in the main menu. Choose Edit ⇨ Preferences on Windows (see figure 2-31), and Lightroom ⇨ Preferences on a Mac. This gives you the dialog box shown in figure 2-32, with General Preferences displayed first.

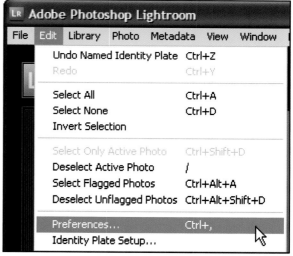

2-31

PRO TIP

Remember the F key. If you can't see the menus or other parts of your computer screen beyond the basic black interface of Lightroom, just press F once or twice and you reveal and hide those elements.

2-32

Mostly the settings and choices are set up to work well with photographers' needs, so you can leave most of them as is. If you don't like seeing a brief splash screen as Lightroom starts up, uncheck that choice. Many photographers don't like their computer to go to the Internet and check for updates to Lightroom, so they leave that choice unchecked.

Completion Sounds are simply alerts to tell you when certain processes are complete. Some people like their computers to beep when certain actions occur, some don't. Your choices are to hear no sound or a variety of beeps, chirps, and so on, depending on your operating system. You can also reset all prompts and presets if you find you are missing things through working in the program for a while.

For External Editors shown in figure 2-33, you set up how images are exported to Photoshop in terms of file format, color space, and bit depth. For most

photographers, I recommend PSD, AdobeRGB (1998), and 16 bits, respectively. You can see that the Adobe engineers have included a paragraph about these choices — the information in it is true, but I think is overly negative (as is they had to use full disclosure) and not all that helpful.

In the Additional External Editor, you can select whatever other image processing software you might use. You use the Choose button to navigate to that application and select it for this then choose format, color space, etc.

If you then click the File Management tab, you get the choices shown in figure 2-34. I really don't like Lightroom to do anything when it detects a memory card is attached to the computer, so I select Do Nothing from the When a memory card is detected drop-down menu. The other choice in the menu is Show Import Dialog, which allows you to import directly to Lightroom. The import directly function does offer some very good automatic capabilities for adding metadata, but it is very limited as to how you name folders. I also recommend selecting the option telling Lightroom to ignore camera-generated folder names.

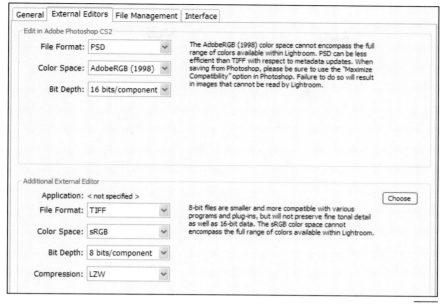

2-33

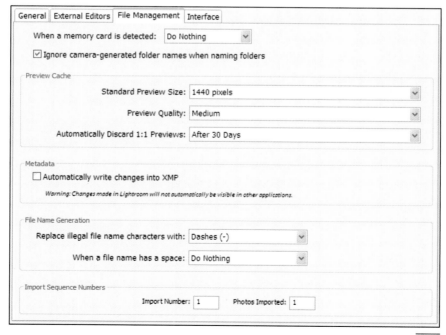

2-34

In general, I would imagine most photographers will leave the rest of the page at the defaults.

In the Interface tab, shown in figure 2-35, you can generally leave all these settings at their default settings, too, although this is an area for some interesting personalization. For Panels, you can decide if you want to keep the decorative flourish below the last controls in any panel (Panel End Mark). Personally, I think this little design touch gives Lightroom some personality, but you can turn it off. Panel Font Size makes the fonts larger and more easily read, but that does change the spacing of the panels (this can be helpful on high-resolution monitors where the fonts start to be hard to see).

In the Lights Out section, you can change how dark the dimming level is and its color. I can see making it a little brighter, but I would not suggest other colors unless you have a specialized need. Other colors affect how you see colors in the image itself. I'd be wary of making Background changes, too, unless you have a very specific need for that. The Tweaks section simply adjusts how certain actions occur in the interface.

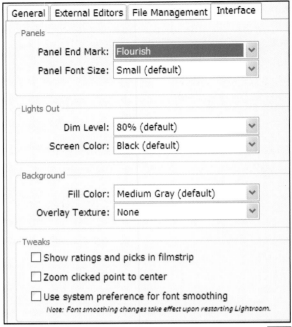

2-35

Q & A

What if I don't use all the modules? Can I turn any off in order to simplify the program even more?

That's an interesting idea, though at the moment, all four modules are always available. Adobe has made it possible for independent developers to create new modules (sort of like plug-ins for Photoshop), but the company has not given users the flexibility to turn modules on or off.

The templates/presets browsers seem like an interesting way to apply standard effects to an image. They seem like they might be similar to Actions in Photoshop. Are they? And can I create my own?

That is very perceptive. You might consider Photoshop Actions to be the inspiration for these templates and presets. They basically set up the controls in Lightroom to create certain effects or do typical adjustments in standard, repeatable ways. These are not auto functions like Auto functions in Photoshop — those examine an image through program algorithms and apply changes based on them. Presets and templates are like Actions because they use a precise set of adjustments to create an *effect*, a set that will always be duplicated once you choose that template or preset.

As you will see later in the book, you can indeed set up your own presets. This can make your own work in Lightroom more efficient and let you consistently apply adjustments that you need all the time.

There seem to be an awful lot of options for setting up how you work with Lightroom. I thought this was supposed to be a simple program. How can I know which functions to use, turn on or off?

That is true. Lightroom has a lot of adaptability. The Adobe program designers knew that photographers tend to be an independent lot who have very specific ways of working that often don't match other photographers' choices. They wanted to make a program that would adapt to these needs.

You really have to play with the program a while. That is, perhaps, one reason why Adobe designers suggest you enjoy the process, that you experiment with the program. Find what works for you. You may or may not do everything the way I do, or any other photographer, but if it works for you, then that is the best way to handle Lightroom. But that takes a bit of time working with it. You will know which functions work best for you after you have worked in the program for a little while.

Chapter 3

LIGHTROOM STARTS WITH THE CAMERA

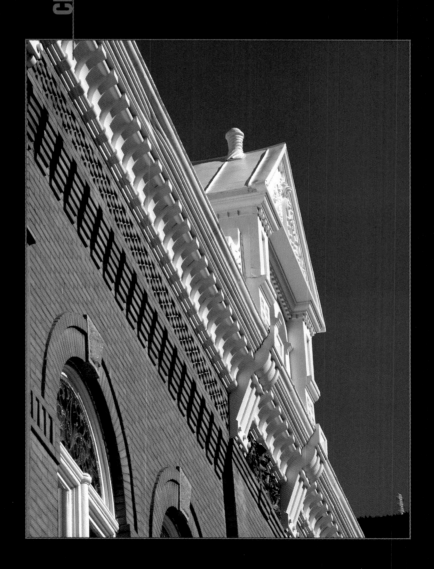

Adobe Photoshop Lightroom is about photography. As I have noted in the previous chapters, it has no text capabilities, no compositing features, and no image manipulation potential. It doesn't have the extreme adjustment capabilities that Photoshop has.

Lightroom works best when the original image comes into the program as good as it can be from the start. It is true that the program has some amazing features such as highlight recovery that can help with problem images, but still, those images are best served if photographed well from the start. Lightroom is made to integrate with your photography, not to be an extra program used to adjust or "fix" images after the photography is done. This chapter is about getting the best photos possible for Lightroom right from the start of your photography.

It is important to understand that Lightroom is not a graphics program. Photoshop is both a photo and a graphics program. In Photoshop, you can create vector-based shapes, distort images, and make a designed page with graphic elements, text, and photos. You can also create montages of images that become something different from their original intent and change images into graphic and artistic forms that may or may not relate to the original intent of the photographer.

AVOID TRYING TO "FIX IT" IN LIGHTROOM

Lightroom is definitely not a "fix-it" program. You cannot do extraordinary adjustments with amazing techniques and pull interesting images out of poorly shot photos. In this book, you learn how to get the most from any photograph you bring into Lightroom, but you won't learn how to repair bad images. Lightroom just is not made for that.

So you can get a better idea of how to approach photography when you are working with Lightroom, here's an example. In figure 3-1, you see a scene in San Francisco. It has problems.

The smoke at the right and top left is burned out — it has no detail. There is no color to the light. Highlights on the bus are washed out. These are things that were

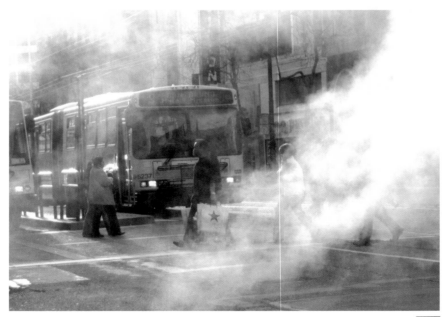

3-1

recorded (or not recorded) by the camera. No amount of work on a RAW file helps these areas. You can probably improve the image in Lightroom, but not really fix it. Strive to shoot the best possible image to begin with — don't rely on Lightroom to "fix" a mediocre shot.

PRO TIP

Lightroom is a powerful program, but it needs image detail to work on. Both under- and over-exposure are challenges. This doesn't mean you have to make every highlight and shadow an exact value. Some images demand washed out highlights or totally black shadows. You do need to be sure important bright and dark areas in your photo are exposed properly.

In Photoshop, you can do a number of things to this image. You can try adding a layer with smoke detail created with the program's cloud filters and some adjustments, and then use that to fix the blank areas that should show smoke. You can add a selected area of color at the upper left of the image to build on the little bit of color that appears in the smoke up there. You can add some noise to the highlights of the bus in order to knock its brightness down and not have it look simply gray when darkened. You can add additional color and tonality to areas that need it. Even though it is always important to shoot your image as best you can when you're working with Photoshop, too, you are able to do some things to fix problem images.

Such fixing is simply not possible in Lightroom. Lightroom was not made for beginning photographers still learning their craft. It was made for pros and advanced amateurs who know how to control things like exposure shown in figure 3-2. This means you must pay attention to how the photo is shot from the beginning in order to gain the most from Lightroom.

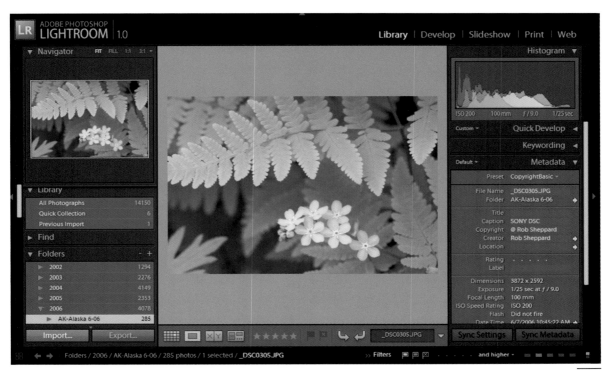

3-2

I don't mean to imply that you can't make mistakes or that every single shot you ever make will be perfect. That's not possible. I have made most mistakes that photographers can make, even while working for a client! I have attached the wrong size filter and vignetted edges, shot a new camera that had an underexposure problem without testing, used flash at the wrong sync speed, and so on. But making mistakes and learning from them is part of the craft of photography. With experience, you make fewer mistakes and your images are more consistent. That's when Lightroom works its best.

GETTING WHAT YOU PAID FOR FROM YOUR DIGITAL CAMERA

There is far more discussion about digital workflow today than about how the photo is shot. Workflow is a hot topic among digital photographers, and for

good reason. What is the best way to work through an image in any software program? How can you make the best use of your time in Lightroom and other software in the digital darkroom? These are all workflow issues.

As I note in this book, and others I have done, I believe that this workflow process starts when you press the shutter on your camera (or even before, when you pickup the camera) — in other words, right from the start. If workflow is just about what to do in Lightroom (or any other software), then you can be trapped by things like poorly exposed images, demonstrated by figure 3-3, that take far more work than necessary in the program. And even then, the image may be compromised from what it could have been. Lightroom will not let you retake a picture when it wasn't quite right from the start.

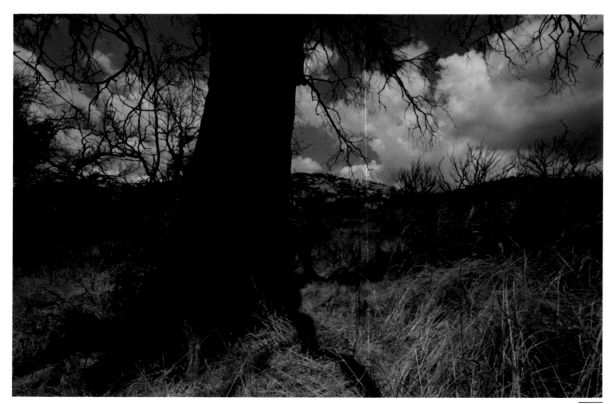

3-3

It is important to bring your images into Lightroom with a range of tonalities that are appropriate both to the subject and the sensor in your camera. Given Lightroom is optimized for working with RAW files, that old "urban legend" about RAW has returned that you don't have to be as careful shooting because RAW has so much power, or perhaps an even more damaging myth is underexposure helps because highlights don't get too much exposure.

Before I even get into the details involved with exposure, consider this: you paid a lot of money for your digital camera. A great deal of those dollars went toward the sensor in the camera ... and for good reason. The designers of that sensor put in an awful lot of work to get a great tonal range, excellent color response, and low noise characteristics. If you do not use the sensor fully by exposing properly, you are wasting your sensor's capabilities, wasting your money, and in essence, getting a cheap version of the original, yet you paid full price.

TONAL RANGE, SENSOR CAPABILITIES, AND LIGHTROOM

A sensor has a certain capture range from black to white, and no matter what format you use, that range is finite. Now what happens with RAW is that there is additional information within that range. While this is helpful in the midtones, it is most useful at the low and high ends of tonalities. This affects how you expose an image to get the best image file for processing in Lightroom.

With a JPEG image from a camera, for example, tonalities jump from a certain very light gray to pure white faster than with RAW. The pure white is the same maximum for light hitting the sensor, but RAW retains more steps in those highlights, giving what appears to be a greater exposure range. This is represented by figure 3-4 and figure 3-5. (These are not made to the scale of how grays are actually represented by JPEG and Raw files, but are meant only as illustrations.) In figure 3-4, light grays skip rapidly to pure white compared to the extra gray in figure 3-5. Figure 3-4 is more like a JPEG format, while figure 3-5 is more like a RAW format.

Something similar happens for the darkest tones and black. For all practical purposes, this aspect of RAW gives the photographer more capabilities with an image at the brightest and darkest tonalities. This is one of the great benefits of RAW. But still, pure white and pure black are restricted by the sensor's capabilities, not the file format used, and that affects what Lightroom can or cannot process.

This becomes especially important when exposure is restricted so the full range of the sensor is not used.

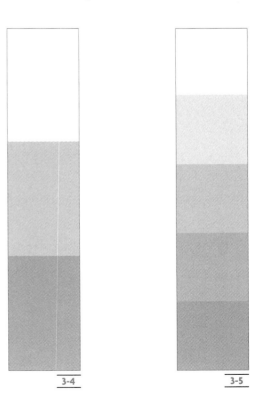

3-4   3-5

GETTING THE BEST TONAL RANGE FOR LIGHTROOM

The best tonal range for Lightroom comes from getting the best tonal range possible from a scene based on the potential and limitations of any sensor. Unless you are a character on the television show *CSI: Crime Scene Investigator* with Hollywood-powered software, you cannot process an image in Lightroom (or any other image processing program) to get something out of nothing. If you don't have detail in the file, no trickery will develop it.

Understanding how to read a camera's histogram and using highlight warnings helps. However, I have recently seen a trend toward some misguided advice to underexpose digital images in order to protect highlights. While it is true that overexposing highlights can be a problem, I have seen images from pros who should know better, images that have been significantly underexposed just to be sure highlights weren't overexposed.

I've also heard photographers say that as long as there are no *blinking highlights* in the frame, the exposure is okay (the blinking highlights indicate possible overexposure on the LCD review). This can also lead to serious underexposure, and serious underexposure both stresses Lightroom and ensures that you are not getting what you paid for with your sensor.

PRO TIP

For really critical work where you want to be sure how specific tones are translating into brightness values in an image, consider using a spotmeter. Many higher-level cameras include true spotmeter capabilities. Handheld spotmeters can also be very helpful for evaluating exposure for a scene. The spotmeter requires some experience to get the most from it, but it lets you better judge exposure on small areas in the image.

Look at figure 3-6. This is a graphic representation of a range of tones (it is an illustration — the real range of tones would vary depending on the sensor and in-camera processing) that could appear in a scene. These are even steps from pure black to pure white. If you took a picture of this with a sensor that captured the same tonal range and exposed properly, you would get an image that would match, as demonstrated in figure 3-7. Think of the left set of tones as those captured by the sensor, and the right as those in the original scene. The two bars are identical.

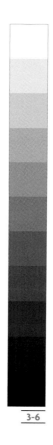

3-6

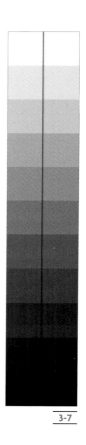

3-7

Figure 3-8 shows the tonal range for an image that is underexposed sitting to the left of the proper tones, with arrows going from the original tones on the right to the new ones in the underexposed image. This is an example of an underexposure made well under the highlight brightness "for security." There is no pure white in the left bar, the tones captured by the sensor. In fact, true light grays are not captured correctly at all because the whites of the scene were underexposed by three steps. The result is that white is now seen incorrectly as a light gray. This is not a problem yet because it is pretty easy to move a light gray to a pure white in Lightroom.

The problem is in the darker areas. Notice that the darkest grays in the original scene were not captured, period. They are now in the pure black area. In fact, the four darkest tones, black to a dark gray three steps up, cannot even be "seen" by the sensor as different. They all register as pure black. This is significant if you need those dark tones. It is a big problem with JPEG format because there will be no tones there at all. With a RAW format, it is possible there are faint hints of tone that might register, so you might be able to salvage something from at least the brighter dark grays. But there are other problems with that salvage job.

Suppose you went into Lightroom and stretched the underexposed image so that the light gray representing white actually became white. You can see what would happen in the left side of figure 3-9. There is now a range of tones from black to white in the top bar, the underexposed image. Notice, however, that this range is missing steps. It had to be stretched from incomplete tonalities. If those missing tones are important to the image, then you are just out of luck. You can't manufacture them in a real photo.

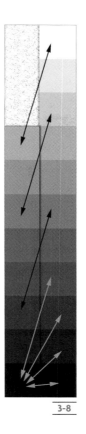

3-8

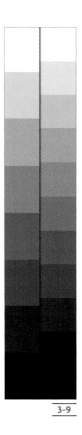

3-9

Another problem is noise. No matter how good a modern sensor is, noise will show up in the darkest areas of the photo. If you make the darkest areas much brighter, which had to happen to get to figure 3-9, the noise rises up out of the shadows and becomes visible.

Does this apply to a real photo? You bet it does. Check out figure 3-10 and figure 3-11. This actually represents a real example of a situation that I have heard photographers talk about. Figure 3-10 is exposed for the winter scene in central Minnesota, but uses a graduated neutral density (ND) filter to knock down the brightness of the sky. This allows for more exposure in the rest of the scene yet detail in the sky can be retained (highlights are not lost).

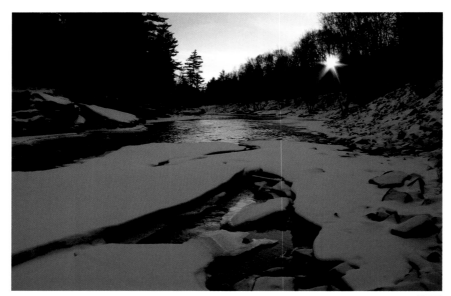

3-10

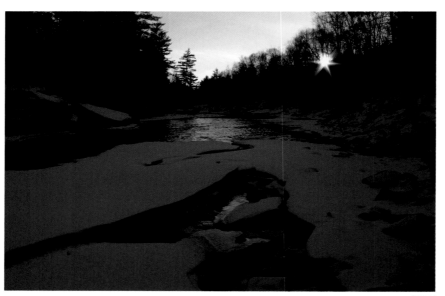

3-11

In figure 3-11, the overall scene has less exposure, this time without a graduated ND filter (notice the detail that shows up in the upper trees because of this).

However, the exposure had to be reduced so that the sky would not be washed out. This makes all of the tones in the water, snow, and trees much darker, shifting them down on the capabilities of the sensor.

In figure 3-12, the scene in figure 3-11 has been brightened to match the snow tones in the middle of the image to those in figure 3-10. You'll notice a color shift immediately, which is pretty common, plus the sky starts to wash out. I shifted all tones to match the snow, which did increase brightness in the sky. Elaborate use of the Tone Curve in Lightroom can reduce that change to the sky, but other things can be affected adversely when you do this.

PRO TIP

A graduated ND filter is a great asset for workflow in Lightroom. This filter enables you to balance light levels in a scene as you shoot, giving you an image for the computer that will take less effort to adjust.

Figure 3-13 and figure 3-14 really tell the story. These are cropped, enlarged details of 3-10 and 3-12, respectively. You should immediately see a rougher looking image in 3-14, from the shot I brightened to match figure 3-10. It just did not have the tonalities needed to give the smoother tones that appear in the water and snow of the detail in figure 3-13. In addition, the dark areas of figure 3-14 are starting to look a little ratty because of noise, and the color is not as good. This is, I think, a pretty clear indication that to get the best results from Lightroom, you need to bring in the best exposure, the best use of your camera's sensor.

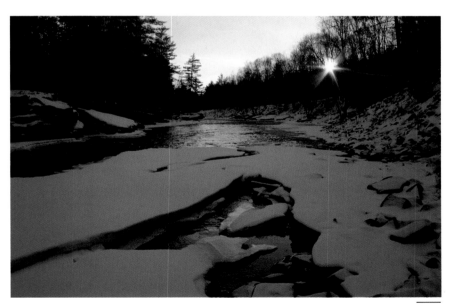

3-12

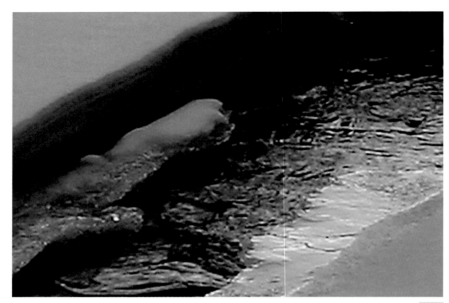

3-13

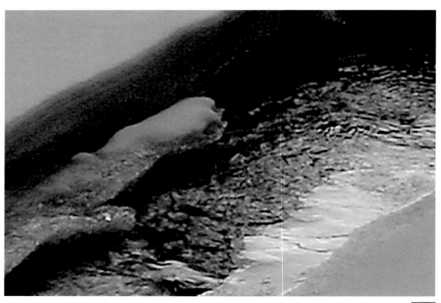

3-14

Getting the Best Color for Lightroom

In the previous section, you saw the color shift when I brightened the underexposed image to match the photo with better exposure. There are several reasons for this, but realize that no matter what the reasons are, you are going to either have to settle for different color or take additional time to work on the image in Lightroom in order to get the right color.

Here's an example of one color problem you can avoid by proper exposure. Look at figure 3-15. It shows a set of color tonalities from black to white. These were created when I added a certain red to the scale seen back in figure 3-6. In this case, the red is most intensely red (best saturation) in the darker tones.

In figure 3-16, I placed an underexposed strip to the left of the full range of color tones, similar to what you saw in figure 3-8. Once again, arrows go from the original tones on the right to the new tones as exposed. This again represents underexposure well under what is needed for the highlights.

Right away you should see a big problem in the dark areas. Notice that the rich, saturated color in the original scene is not captured, period. It is now pure black! True, you do see some saturated color coming from what were brighter colors, but these are, in a sense, false colors, because they were not in the original scene. Even if you worked very, very hard in Lightroom (or even Photoshop), you would not be able to get the great dark colors of the original scene to look right.

3-15

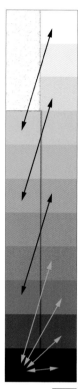

3-16

Okay, so now you go into Lightroom and stretch the underexposed image so that the light pink representing white actually becomes white. You can see what would happen in figure 3-17. While a complete range of tones from black to white shows up in the top bar, this range is missing colors.

NOTE

Some readers may recognize that it is possible to adjust pure colors like these differently in the computer than colors in a photograph, so these figures are only meant to illustrate what happens in a photograph.

There is a further problem dealing with how color changes with exposure. Suppose in this case, the bright, saturated color in position number four from the bottom (see figure 3-18) was not as badly underexposed. Suppose it showed up in the file looking like the color in figure 3-19. What has happened is that the color has gotten darker, but it has also lost some of its *chroma,* or color quality.

Making it lighter doesn't match the original color, as shown in figure 3-20. It loses the quality of the original color (which is also apparent in the winter scene in figure 3-12) because the chroma of each color is not the same.

Can you get to a better color in Lightroom? In this case, yes, but at the minimum, it is going to take you much more work to get there than if you start with a photo that is properly exposed for color. If, however, a color is too dark, with too little of its original color, it will be very difficult to make it look its best.

3-18

3-19

3-20

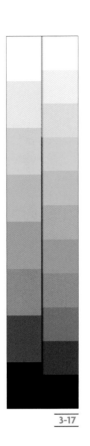

3-17

JPEG Shot Right or RAW Shot Sloppily?

You might be wondering if Lightroom will do better with a JPEG file that is shot right or a RAW file that has sloppy technique. The answer, like so many in photography, is that it often depends on the subject and the scene involved. However, in most situations, you will probably find better colors and tonalities with a JPEG file that is shot right. The reason for this is that inside your camera is a very smart RAW processing engine. If the photo is shot right, it goes right to that engine looking good from the start.

The answer, however, should be to shoot better JPEG and RAW files. Lightroom is optimized to work very, very well with both JPEG and RAW files. Many photographers shoot RAW+JPEG to gain the advantages of both. Regardless of the format you choose to save your images, photograph with optimum technique from the start. Lightroom does its best when the files come into the program shot their best, too.

WORKING THE SUBJECT

One way that most pros photograph a subject is to "work the subject," as it is called. This is a way to get the most from your interaction with the subject so that you have the photographs you need when you go to the computer and Lightroom. It can mean changing exposures, or bracketing, so you capture the needed tonal and color range. If you are unsure at all of how a particular scene will record certain tones or colors, try different exposures.

Some photographers get into a mode that their technique is so perfect in camera and computer that they don't need to do such bracketing. I am not that perfect, nor do I want to do a lot of extra work in Lightroom if I don't have to, so having some choices to work with can be a big help.

Working the subject also means taking more than one photograph to explore how the subject looks and responds to the camera, beyond simply exposure, which is a very common technique among photojournalists, annual report photographers, and magazine photographers. It is almost the only way fashion advertising work is done, though its use varies quite a bit with other types of advertising photography. Food and automobile photography, for example, is often done as a single approach to the subject based on a specific ad design.

In figure 3-21, you can see a group of images from working the subject, the main street of a small town, Georgetown, in the mountains west of Denver, Colorado. You can see the variety of images in Lightroom, both in the main, central work area as well as the lower filmstrip. Working the subject is perfect

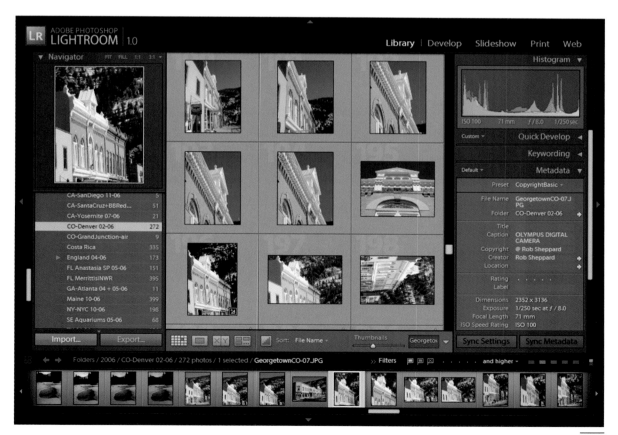

for Lightroom because this program allows you to see groups of images so nicely, plus it is set up to work that group, from one to all images, very well.

To clarify the concept of working the subject, I have included four very different versions of the subject from this group in figure 3-22 through figure 3-25. While you can do repetitive work on such images in Photoshop (and Camera Raw), Lightroom is set up in such a way that it makes it very easy to adjust such images consistently, and then tweak individual shots

as needed. You can quickly select the images you need in the Library module, process one in Develop, and then apply those adjustments to the rest of the selected group. You can go in and finesse any adjustments done to the photos to enhance the look of individual shots, too. When your exposure and technique are consistent, the ability to group process also helps by allowing you to do one set of adjustments for a whole group of images.

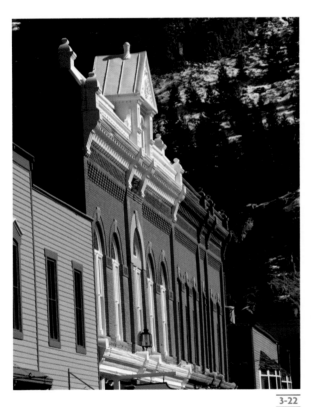

3-22

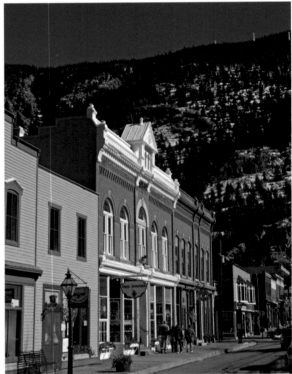

3-23

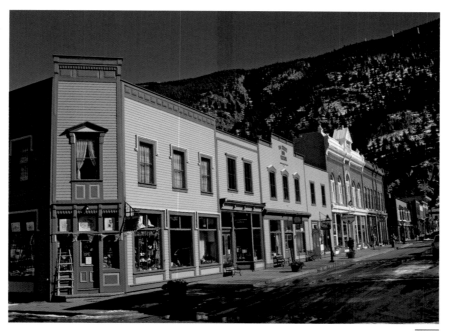

3-24

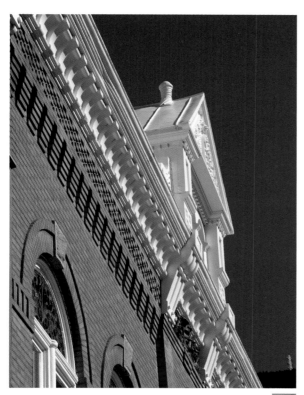

3-25

Lightroom also includes some excellent tools for comparing images, from composition to exposure. This example I've presented here only shows a few images from working a subject, but Lightroom is ideal for working much larger groups, too. Still, I can guarantee you that if your photo technique gets sloppy, the time you spend in Lightroom will increase dramatically as you need to deal with more images. Lightroom doesn't do you any favors if your images are not well done to begin with.

I am a little confused. I had always understood that RAW provided more latitude for photography, so that you can relax a bit, especially for digging out detail in dark areas. Is that wrong?

If you think about the extra bit-depth or tonal steps in the bright and dark areas, you can understand why RAW might be seen as having more latitude than JPEG. You do gain more exposure points in the lightest and darkest parts of the image. This results in giving you more flexibility in adjusting a RAW file to show more detail in those areas, which in effect, gives the appearance of more latitude. There is no question that you have more adjustment potential within the full range of tones that a sensor can capture, but you cannot go beyond its capabilities.

Similarly, you can definitely find good detail in the dark areas that Lightroom can mine for tonalities. The problem comes if you expect that you can always do that and are not careful with exposure. If dark areas need to show good tonal detail but they have been squashed into the darkest tones of the image, then there will be tone and contrast problems when they are unsquashed — plus the potential for noise increases dramatically in those areas when these adjustments are made.

What if I want my image to be dark? Should I keep the tones dark from exposure or give them more exposure so color is better preserved?

If you are careful with exposure, you can certainly expose to keep the dark tones in the image so they match the dark tones in the real scene. However, if you are not careful and their brightness drops even a little, you can lose important tonalities and colors in those dark areas.

With dark scenes, it can be helpful to actually give a little more exposure than is appropriate, making those dark tones a little brighter in the image than they are in the real world. As long as this causes no problems with important highlights, this can help you get better tonality and color in dark tones. Except for very light tones and colors, it is always easier to make a tone or color darker than it is to make it lighter. Slight overexposure of an overall dark scene is very easy to correct, plus you will have no noise problems.

But what if I messed up when taking a picture and it really isn't exposed optimally for the scene? That photo might be really important to me. Can't Lightroom fix it?

Lightroom has a lot of power to adjust an image because it is working in the data intensive 16-bit space, though JPEG images do not have the full capabilities of the space. You can really do quite a lot to the image to get it looking the best it can be, so yes, you can fix problem images in Lightroom. However, you typically cannot get what you had expected from the scene — colors can be off and noise increased, for example.

Lightroom has its limitations for dealing with extremes when an image is not exposed properly. There are additional things that can be done in Photoshop, such as the application of Healing tools, the Clone Stamp tool, and careful use of layers. Photoshop has more capabilities for "fixing" problem photos. You can start the processing in Lightroom and finish in Photoshop.

Part II

USING LIGHTROOM MODULES

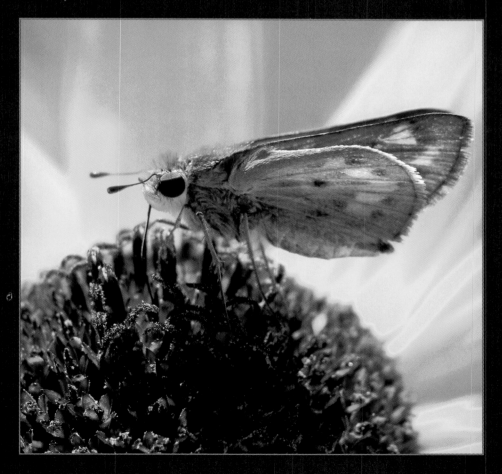

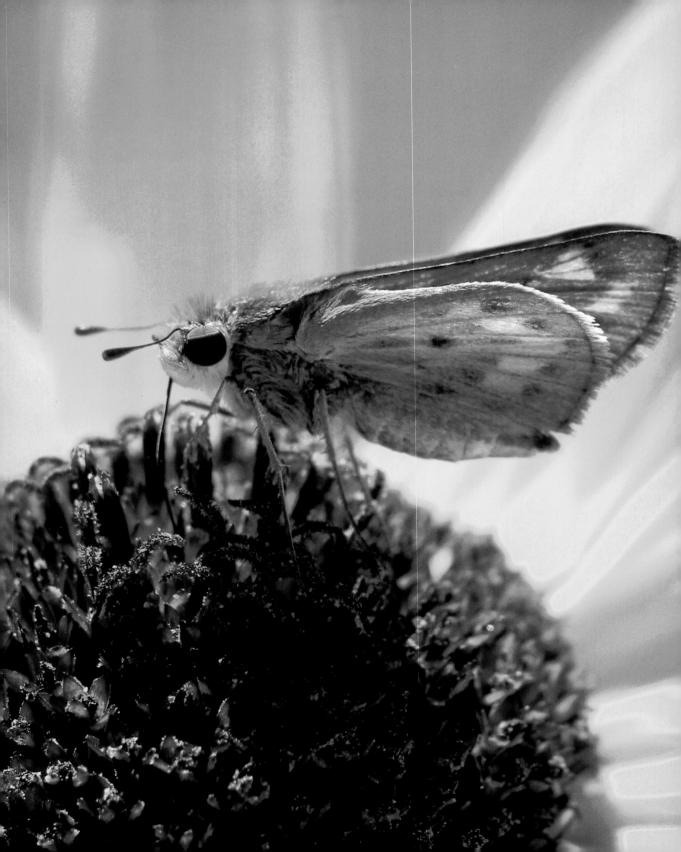

Chapter 4

LIBRARY MODULE BASICS

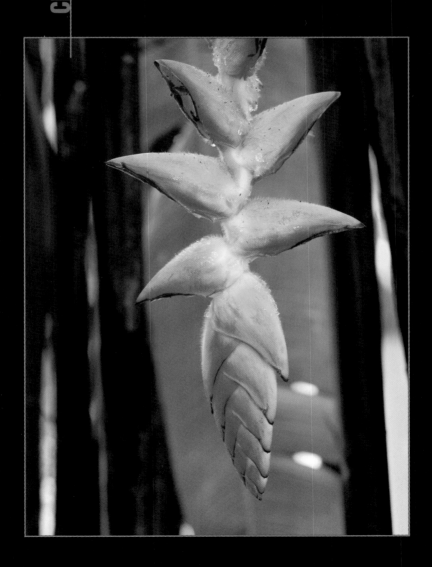

As digital photography expands, so do image files. Anyone who has had a digital camera more than a few months and shoots regularly has a lot of image files to deal with. Heavy shooters, whether they are serious amateurs or busy pros, can have thousands to sort and organize.

Adobe Photoshop Lightroom's Library module has some excellent tools to help you edit and catalog your photos. It is important to keep in mind that every organization program has certain ways it works best, and that is true of Lightroom. In this chapter, you learn what the basic capabilities of Library are. The next chapter walks you through actually using Lightroom's Library with specific examples.

AN OVERVIEW OF LIBRARY

In figure 4-1, I have collapsed all the submenus on the left and right panels so that you only see the main categories.

The main organizing functions are in the left panel, and are shown alone in figure 4-2:

> Library

> Find

> Folders

> Collections

> Keyword Tags

> Metadata Browser

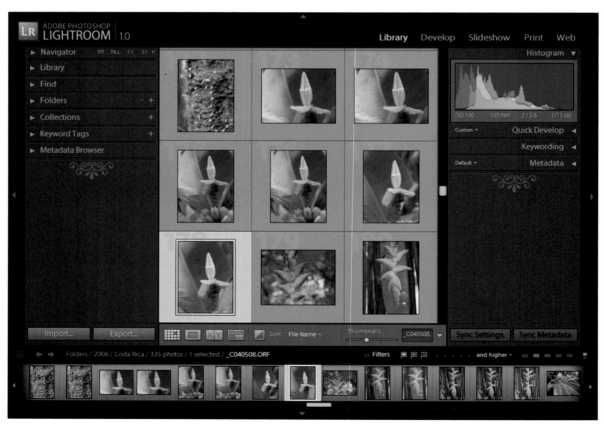

4-1

Navigator, while at the top of the organizing function list, is not an organization function, which is why you don't see it in figure 4-2 or listed as part of the organizing functions. The Navigator part of the panel, shown expanded in figure 4-3, is a key control that affects how images are viewed in the central viewing area, plus it allows you to find a specific location on an image when it is enlarged. It offers four quick-access magnifications of the image (Fit, Fill, 1:1, and 3:1) plus a drop-down menu for additional choices. When you have an image enlarged in the central area, you can move the view around by clicking or clicking and dragging the white box over the image in the Navigator as shown in figure 4-4. It is also part of the Develop panel.

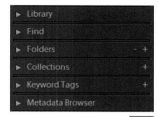

4-2

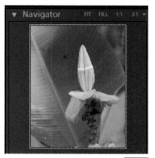

4-3

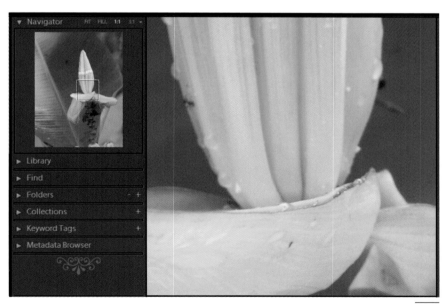

4-4

It is important to understand that Lightroom's organizing capabilities are simply tools for image organization, not requirements for your workflow. Some photographers will use more tools than others, and they will use each function differently. It is very important to use Lightroom in ways that work for you. It really is designed to be flexible.

Below these organization functions are two important buttons whose functions are intuitive (they are described in detail toward the end of this chapter):

PRO TIP

If you get mixed up by any of the features of the Lightroom interface, you can often find what you need by going to the menu bar at the top of the interface. These menus repeat the functions imbedded in the interface and are logically organized by topic, such as Library or Photo. Plus, there is an excellent Help menu accessed by the far-right menu category.

> **Import.** For importing images into Lightroom from a memory card or a location on your hard drive.

> **Export.** For exporting images from Lightroom to another program (such as Photoshop) or to save a processed image to the hard drive. Export applies the non-destructive settings used for the adjustments to the photo.

The central work or viewing area is used to view, edit, compare, and review photos. A toolbar below this area affects how you see images displayed in the image work area. There are a series of important commands accessed by clicking the appropriate icon in the toolbar (shown in figure 4-5) or by using a keyboard command.

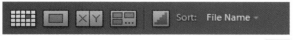

4-5

From the left, these controls are

> **Grid.** Click this grid-like icon or press G and your images show up as as a grid in the central work area as shown in figure 4-6.

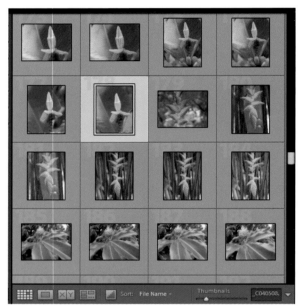

4-6

PRO TIP

You can use the toolbar to help you edit your images. Notice that it changes with the views. You get additional controls for each view.

> **Loupe.** Click this single-image icon and you change the screen to show one image in the work area (shown in figure 4-7), which can be magnified (like using a magnifier or loupe) by clicking on the image or pressing the Spacebar. You can also use E to get into the Loupe view.

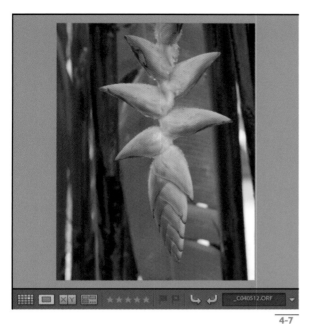

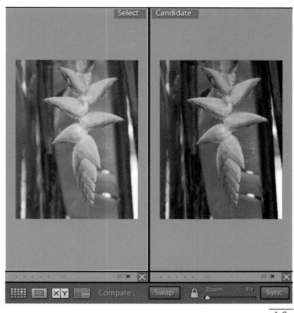

4-7

4-8

> **Compare.** This X/Y icon takes you to a view that shows two images for direct comparisons — a selected image (Select) that you want to compare to another (Candidate) for precise editing of your photos as shown in figure 4-8. You can choose two or more images from the Filmstrip or Grid view (Ctrl/⌘-click to select), but only two show at once. As you click the X at the lower right, images are deselected from the group. You can magnify images here by using the controls in the Navigator control group in the left panel or the Zoom control in the toolbar. Swap, an additional X/Y button at the right that has arrows, changes the Select image with the Candidate image. The last X/Y button at the right is "Make Select" and changes the selection from the Filmstrip.

> **Survey View.** Looking like a small group of images, this icon changes the screen to a comparison mode similar to Compare, though this time you can compare two or more images at once as shown in figure 4-9. The image with the / is the active one and its file name shows in the box on the toolbar. Any of the images can be removed from consideration by clicking the X or / box. The drop-down menu at the far right of the toolbar changes how information is displayed in the Toolbar (look for this in other central area views, too).

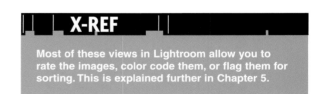

X-REF

Most of these views in Lightroom allow you to rate the images, color code them, or flag them for sorting. This is explained further in Chapter 5.

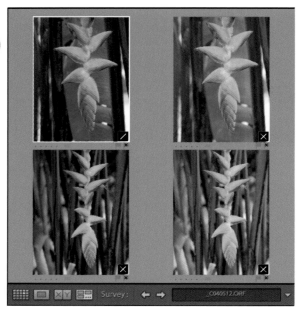

4-9

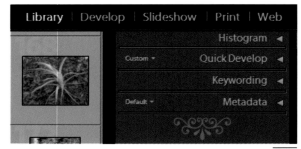

4-10

> **Sort Direction.** This icon doesn't actually give you a new view, but is used with the other views to change the order of the images seen in the central work area.

On the right panel, shown in figure 4-10, you gain some insight on any photo you have selected, plus the ability to adjust images, changing them in some way. These functional groups are

> Histogram

> Quick Develop

> Keywording

> Metadata

These items are explained later in the chapter.

When you look at the overall Library interface, you can see it is pretty simple and laid out in such a way that you can easily and quickly find things. Click any of the control or adjustment bars, such as Library, and you get a group of adjustments or controls specific to that category. You can leave any of these collapsed so there is not a distracting set of choices that you don't need at any given time.

THE LEFT LIBRARY PANEL REVEALED

In figure 4-11, I hid the right panel and the Filmstrip. Now the left panel is emphasized with its functional categories plus a lot more space is dedicated to the images themselves. This setup can be very useful when you are editing images and need to see a lot of them at once. That can almost be a necessity if you are working on a laptop or a smaller monitor. Having more space in a bigger display for the Lightroom interface makes it easier to leave all the panels in view.

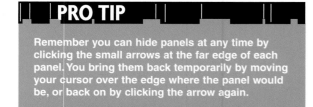

PRO TIP

Remember you can hide panels at any time by clicking the small arrows at the far edge of each panel. You bring them back temporarily by moving your cursor over the edge where the panel would be, or back on by clicking the arrow again.

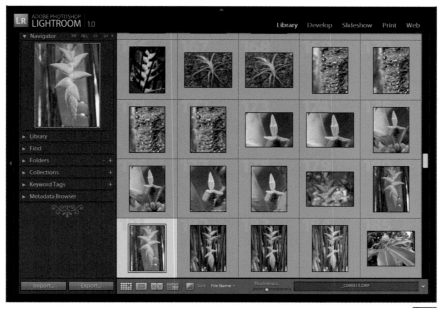

4-11

Here's what those left-side functions do:

> **Navigator.** This was described in detail earlier in the chapter in the overview of Library. Essentially it controls how images are viewed in the central viewing area.

> **Library.** This gives you a quick overview of all images that have been brought into Lightroom. It contains three options, as shown in figure 4-12.

> **All Photographs.** This view shows you every single photo you have in your collection that you have assigned to Lightroom to track. Use this function whenever you need to get back to all images that Lightroom is handling, especially when you have restricted its view by using a specific keyword search. I am not sure I can recommend it to most photographers unless you have a very powerful computer, as this view can take a long time to load.

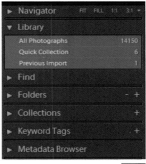

4-12

> **Quick Collection.** This view is a useful way of very quickly making a selection of images that you want to separate from all the rest for a slide show, some prints, a Web gallery, or maybe selects for a client. You simply select a group of photos (Ctrl/⌘+click them or click on the first one in a series and then Shift+click the

63

last one) and drag them over this category. Then every time you click Quick Collection, you only see those photos. You can also instantly put images into Quick Collection through the Filmstrip. If you run your cursor over an image there, you see a faint circle appear. Click on that circle and the image is put into Quick Collection.

> **Previous Import.** This view is a way for you to quickly go to the last group of images you brought into Lightroom.

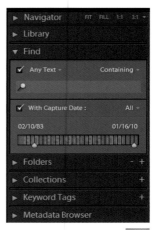

PRO TIP

You can quickly and easily change the size of all images displayed in the Grid mode for the image work area. At the bottom right of the work area is a small slider in the toolbar (labeled Thumbnails). Move the slider back and forth to change the size of the thumbnails in the work area, which you can see if you compare figure 4-1 with figure 4-6.

> **Find.** This function, shown in figure 4-13, gives you the ability to quickly search for images by file name, keywords, and more by using the Any Text section. This is a feature of Lightroom that gets you quickly to photos — assuming, of course, that you have given them names or keywords. There is a little quirk to this feature, however. It will only show you the find for the view you are in. However, you can see where other images reside by checking the numbers to the right of your folders in the Folders section — these numbers denote images that fit the Find criteria and you can see them by clicking on the appropriate folder. You have to clear your Find text by clicking the X to the right of the text in order to go back to the whole folder image set, though. Click on the Containing drop-down menu for options to control this search. The With Capture Date section lets you find photos taken on a certain date or within a range of dates. Click on the All drop-down menu for options to control how the dates are searched.

> **Folders.** Lightroom calls all imported groups of images Folders (as shown in figure 4-14). This could be images downloaded directly from the camera or memory card. Or the Lightroom Folder could reference the actual folder where you have placed your images on your hard drive (this is how I like to work and is seen in figure 4-14).

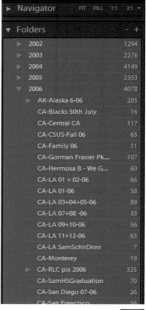

You can rename any folder whatever you would like by double-clicking the name and typing in something else (I would be very careful about keeping names consistent with how you have your images filed on your hard drive — Collections and Keywords are better places to use unique names to classify and organize your photos). The minus and plus signs allow you to quickly add or subtract folders from the list; however, minus does not remove photos from your hard drive, just from Lightroom's view.

> **Collections.** Collections is where the real organization of Lightroom begins. You get to pick your photo categories here, as shown in figure 4-15 (the list you see here is just a beginning of what is possible). You use it for any sort of category that enables you to group common types of photos together across multiple folders. You can pick anything that fits your interests and needs, from client-based subjects such as ABC Corporation Warehouses to personal themes such as family members. I think it would be very interesting to see various collections on diverse photographers' computers — there are bound to be some very interesting groupings!

The Collections area is very easy to use. You simply set up a collection by clicking the plus sign at the right of Collections and give the new collection a name. Next you select a group of photos from a folder (Ctrl/⌘+click them or Shift+click through a series) and drag those photos onto the collection name. If you start to get a lot of Folders in Lightroom, they shove the Collections group down so it can't be seen. Click and drag on the light gray navigation bar directly to the left of the collections to move the panel groupings up and down.

> **Keywords Tags.** Keywords are a common way of tagging photos so that they can be searched for specific topics. You can create keywords by clicking the plus sign to the right of Keyword Tags to get the dialog box seen in figure 4-16. This dialog box allows you to put in specific keywords for tagging images as well as tell Lightroom what other words act as synonyms in a search. In addition, you can select a group of photos and tag them all at once and export keywords with the image.

Some photographers heavily implant a lot of keywords with every image. Then a search by keywords locates those photos almost instantly. On the other hand, it takes time to put in a lot of keywords, so other photographers just use a minimal number (I admit that I am not the keywording type, though I do understand its value — it is just a bit too tedious for my personality). Adding keywords to a photo is very easy; just click and drag appropriate photos onto the word to give them that keyword. This way you don't have to do a lot

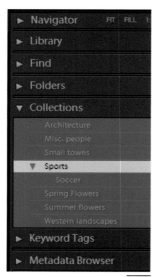

4-15

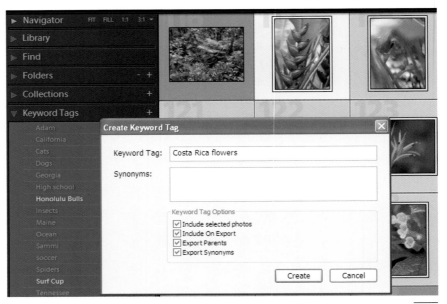

4-16

of typing. Lightroom also lets you add keywords to photos as they are imported and to the metadata that can be accessed with the right panel.

> **Metadata Browser.** This section of the organizing panel is really going to have mixed use by different photographers. I don't find it all that useful for my work, but I know folks who do. This section allows you to find certain images based on the metadata, as seen in figure 4-17. For example, you can locate all images shot with a particular focal length of lens, a specific camera, a particular person (if you are using Lightroom with different photographers' images, all identified in the metadata), date, file type, and location.

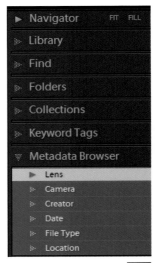

4-17

VIEWING IMAGES IN LIBRARY

Lightroom gives you a lot of power when you are browsing, editing, and reviewing your photos. I like to start by hiding the side panels (use the Tab key) and the Filmstrip (click the bottom arrow) to get to what you see in figure 4-18. This makes Lightroom act like a light table used for editing slides.

I really like this form of Lightroom for editing photos, because it really lets the photographer focus on the photos for editing. You don't think about making collections or processing them at this point.

PRO TIP

You can display many things with each image in Grid mode. The default is a set of dots that can be used to give images 1–5 star rankings. However, if you right-click on the dots, you will get a context menu that allows you to display all sorts of things with the image. This, once again, is another reason why Mac users need to have a right-button mouse.

Using Lightroom Modules

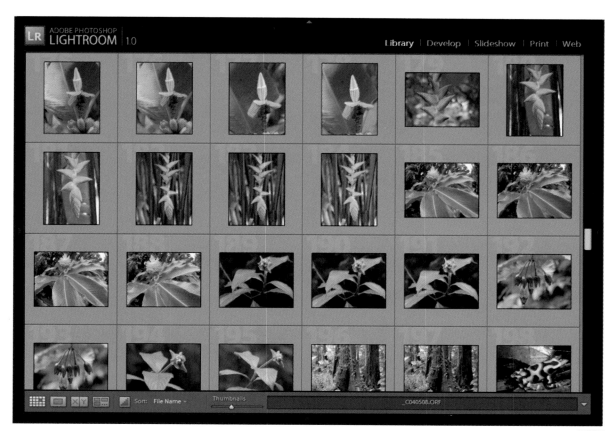

4-18

There are several important things that you can do with your photos in this full-screen image mode. First, I like to rotate all verticals to vertical so I can better evaluate all the photos. You do this by clicking on an image; then rotate arrows appear at the lower left and right of the image. Click the arrow pointing in the direction you need to rotate the shot. You can do multiples by Ctrl/⌘+clicking the images and then clicking the rotate icon again.

Next, you can remove the shots you don't like, either just from Lightroom or from your hard drive as well. How you approach this editing phase is very personal. One way to do this is to click (or Ctrl/⌘+click for multiple selections) anything you don't like in Lightroom, and then press Delete. A Confirm dialog box appears that asks if you want to delete the file from the hard drive or just from Lightroom.

You can also rate images by stars according to whether you like an image or not (and how much) as shown in figure 4-19. Simply select an image, and then click on the little dots below it for the appropriate star rating. Or use the keyboard numbers 1 through 5 for the number of stars rating. You can go through a lot of images very quickly this way.

Two other ways of marking images are through the use of flags and colors. Colors can be selected with keyboard numbers 6 through 9 or right-clicking the image and choosing Set Color Label. Flags are basically on or off and can be used by clicking the flag that appears to the upper left of the image when you hover your cursor over the thumbnail.

To evaluate an individual image, double-click it. This shows you a single image in the Loupe view, as shown in figure 4-20. Now click once on the photo and it is louped, or magnified, so you can check details, as shown in figure 4-21. You move the view around by clicking and dragging. Click again and you get the whole image. If you want to check the same area for detail in another photo, you can use the filmstrip at the bottom of the interface to select a different photo.

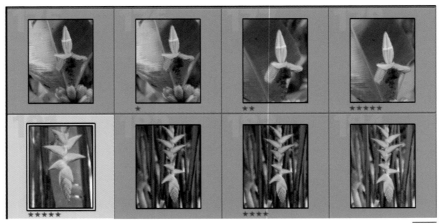

4-19

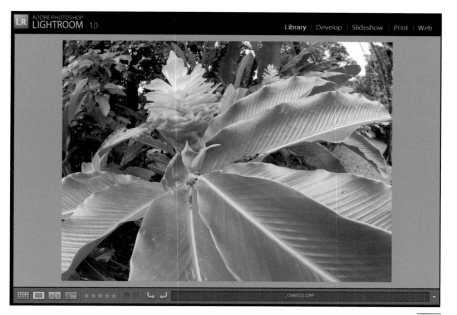

4-20

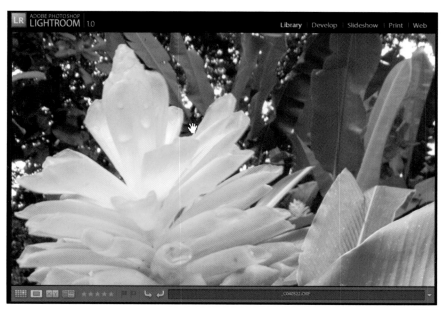

4-21

You will often want to match up specific photos with each other to see how the composition or focus compares. This is the purpose of the Compare and Survey modes. If you select a few images in the Filmstrip, you automatically get to the Survey mode shown in figure 4-22. You can see that it is really helpful to keep the side panels hidden when using the Compare mode. If you double-click any image, it goes to the magnified Loupe view. Double-click again and you return to the Survey mode. I do a lot of my editing work this way. I find the Compare mode is useful when checking critical focus, but usually, I like to see multiple images as seen in the Survey view mode.

NAVIGATING THE FILMSTRIP

Filmstrip is a very useful tool for finding and acting on images. You will find it an increasingly important resource as you work through Lightroom's adjustments, controls, and other features.

Navigating this strip is pretty easy and important for you to understand. The main slider underneath the images (shown in figure 4-23) moves the whole Filmstrip back and forth so you can find the photos you need. At the left and right sides of the strip are small arrows. Clicking either arrow moves the images in that direction to allow you to see more on the Filmstrip. You can use the arrow keys to do the same thing. If you click and hold, the images move continuously as if you really were watching a filmstrip in action — helping you get to photos faster.

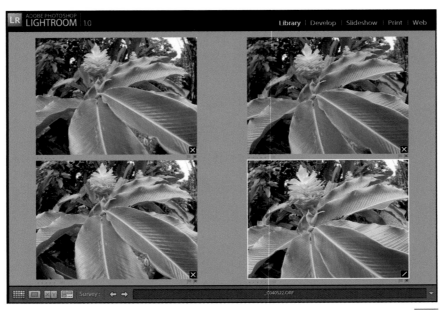

4-22

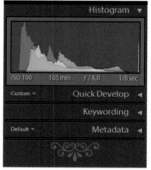

Right above the Filmstrip is a set of controls related to image organization. You can go to the Library grid at any time by clicking the left icon. The arrows are used to toggle back and forth between the view you are looking at and your last view. Next in line on the Filmstrip is a section showing you the directory structure of where the image is located. Then you have sorting filters based on flags or on star or color ratings.

THE RIGHT LIBRARY PANEL REVEALED

The right panel shown in figure 4-24 includes some specific things you can do to single images or groups when multiple photos are selected in the multi-image views and the changes are synced. If you have done your main organizing and need to do some quick developing work on multiple photos or apply keywording to a specific group of images, it is helpful to hide the left panel so that you have a larger area for the Grid mode. This arrangement lets you work more easily with many images at once when you are using the controls of the right panel.

4-24

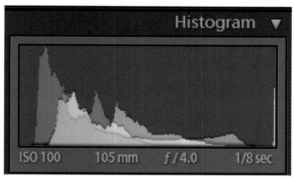

4-25

Here's what those right-side functions do:

> **Histogram.** At the top of the right panel are key bits of information about the photo. You can see an RGB histogram of the image and some important metadata for the shot (ISO setting, focal length, f-stop, and shutter speed) as shown in figure 4-25. This is mostly helpful, but RGB histograms are harder to read than simple brightness or luminance histograms, and to use them fully, you have to know more about color channels than most photographers actually need to know.

> **Quick Develop.** This set of options, shown in figure 4-26, is an interesting add-in to the Library that really has little to do with Library functions. It enables you to do some quick processing of images. Some photographers might find it useful for quick adjustments, but in general, I can't really recommend it because the controls are quite limited compared to the power of the fully realized controls in the Develop module. Quick Develop does allow you to do everything from adjust white balance to change the brightness and contrast of the image by clicking the arrows to either side of the controls.

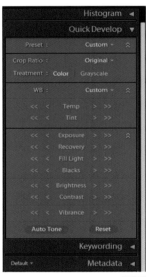

4-26

X-REF

Because all of the controls in the Quick Develop options are repeated in expanded form in the Develop module, they are explained in Chapter 6 where the Develop module is covered.

> **Keywording.** This category seen in figure 4-27 is a very useful part of the right panel and one you will quickly become very familiar with if you like to use keywords. In Keyword Tags, you describe elements of your photographs so you can find those photographs again later. You can add keywords to individual images or a selection of them in the Grid mode. You can also click on any keywords in the section below to add them to the images. In figure 4-27 this area is seen as Recent Keywords; however, Lightroom does include some preset keywords that can be accessed if you click on keywords or the arrow to the right of Set in order to access a drop-down menu. Any existing keywords on an image show up in this category, too.

As I mentioned before, photographers use keywords in very different ways. Some use a lot of descriptive terms and isolate every different composition to add new ones. Others use just a minimum of words that might only really describe a shoot, while still others do something in between. There are no rules here. You have to find what works for you. You are creating keywords that are logical for you, words you can later search for.

> **Metadata.** *Metadata* is data about data or information about your image file. You actually have several choices as to what is displayed here. The data shown in figure 4-28 are the defaults and some entries can be changed, such as Caption. If you click the Default drop-down arrow, you get other choices for metadata. You can check camera settings in the Exif data or you can input IPTC data. IPTC stands for International Press Telecommunications Council, and *IPTC data* is a standard for attaching specific, contextual information about a photograph that many programs can easily read.

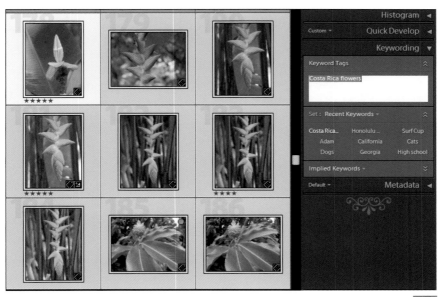

4-27

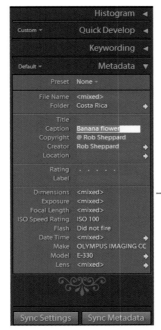

4-28

> **Sync Settings and Sync Metadata.** Sync Settings and Sync Metadata buttons are also shown in figure 4-28. These are used when you have multiple images selected and you want to make processing adjustments or metadata details consistent across all of them. When you click either button, you get a self-explanatory dialog box asking you what you want to sync among the images.

IMPORTING PHOTOS

Of course, to use all of the organizing and other features of Library, you need photos. At the bottom of the left panel are Import and Export buttons, as shown in figure 4-29. These are essential to Lightroom, as they enable you to bring photos into the program (Import) and send them out for use outside the program (Export).

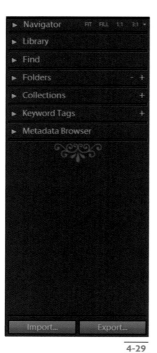

4-29

Click Import and you immediately begin the process of importing photos to Lightroom. Your operating system's File Open dialog box appears, as shown in figure 4-30. After finding the folder with your photos (that you have already downloaded to your hard drive), click Choose Selected (you can also select individual photos by opening folders and clicking on the ones you want).

The Import Photos dialog box shown in figure 4-31 appears. This is an important box to understand, as it offers you a number of capabilities that give you more flexibility in handling your files, plus make your organizing and sorting photos workflow easier.

> **File Handling.** At the top, you have several choices available from the File Handling drop-down menu as shown in figure 4-32, starting with Import Photos at their Current Location. The next three choices place files into a new location, which Lightroom sets up and controls, either by copying or moving files, on your hard drive.

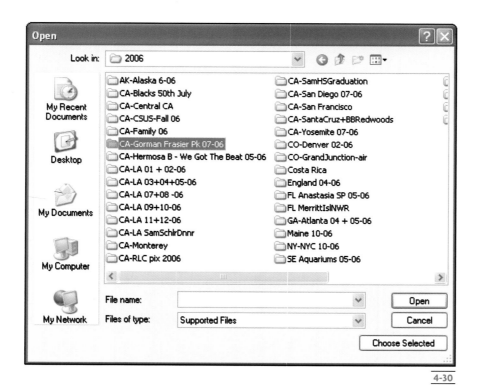

4-30

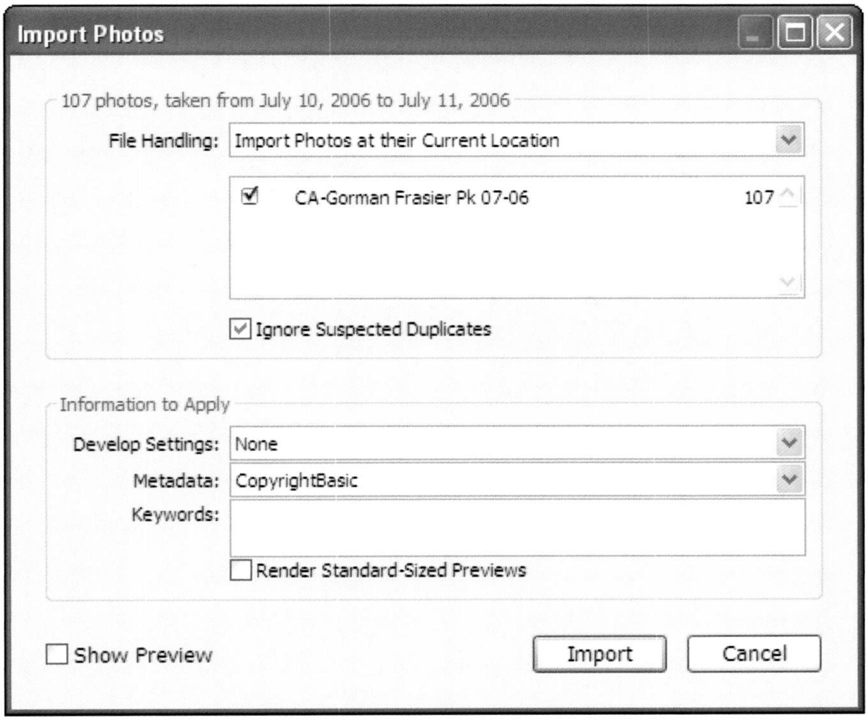

4-31

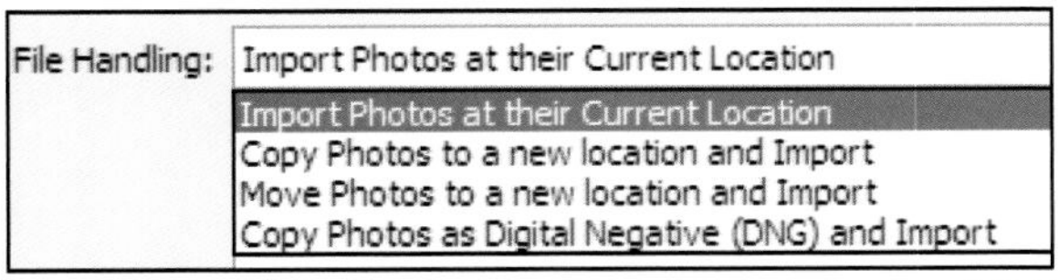

4-32

I don't know about you, but I really don't need the same photos in multiple locations, so copying has no appeal. Moving doesn't help me because it messes up my filing structure. Finally, although there are some good reasons to copy important images as DNG files (Adobe's RAW file format), doing an entire import this way wastes hard drive space. The only advantage that I can see to doing all of this is if you want to place image files into one location on the hard drive. If that appeals to you, then choose a copy or move option. If you

chose a copy or move files option from the drop-down menu, an additional section for file naming appears in the dialog box. You can rename the photos in the Name box. Type whatever name works for you.

The next section of the Import Photos box deals with how the files are separated into groups when they're brought into Lightroom. Lightroom segments Folders by default, so if you have subfolders in a folder, your photos are separated by those subfolders. If you want everything in a folder to come in en masse, then uncheck the checked boxes that define this by your subfolders. I recommend that you import directly from folders you have already set up on your hard drive rather than trying to sort it all out here.

> **Information to Apply.** The Information to Apply section is next and is great if you are a working photographer because it lets you add important metadata to all photos as they move into Lightroom control.

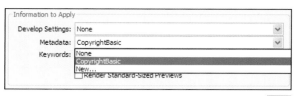

4-34

> The Develop Settings, shown in figure 4-33, are based on Develop module presets, which are be covered in Chapter 6. However, this is really a specialized use of Import — for studio and commercial photography where the image type, exposure, light, and so forth does not change, this can be useful. For most other photography, it is rare that you would apply the same adjustments to all of them.

4-33

> From the Metadata drop-down menu, you can apply preset metadata information (such as copyright) or choose to create a new metadata preset, as shown in figure 4-34. If you choose New from the menu, the New Metadata Preset dialog box shown in figure 4-35 appears. You can add information in all of the blank areas (scroll down in your dialog box to see all the options) and the information is applied to the metadata of each imported image. If you are doing a regular series of shoots related to a specific client, for example, you can type the client's name in the Preset Name box, and then fill out the form so it's specific to that client and the work for them. This way you always have a unique set of information automatically connected with all photos from your shoots (as long as you select that preset).

4-35

> Below the Metadata field is the Keywords field. You can add keywords here that are specific to the imported images, such as client, subject, location, and so forth, and these keywords are automatically applied to all the photos being imported. If your shoot is very specific and is basically all about one subject, then you can be as detailed as you want. However, if you have a variety of subjects, then you are likely to have fewer keywords that fit all the photos.

> **Show Preview.** You can quickly review (as well as select or unselect) all the images in a preview image, at the right of the Import Photos interface by selecting the Show Preview option as shown in figure 4-36. I find this slows down the process so I don't use it.

Now just click Import in the dialog box and Lightroom imports all of the photos into its system and lists them in the Folders area. It may take Lightroom a little time to do its thing, depending on the power of your computer and the size of your import.

PRO TIP

You can also import photos directly to Lightroom from your memory card or camera. You can tell Lightroom to automatically recognize your new card or camera connection in Preferences (Edit ⇨ Preferences on Windows and Lightroom ⇨ Preferences on a Mac). Lightroom opens a dialog box that's basically the same as the Import Photos dialog box, but has some additional choices to tell Lightroom where to put the images on your hard drive.

EXPORTING PHOTOS

Export is the second button at the bottom of the left panel, shown in figure 4-29. Using the Export feature in Lightroom is fairly straightforward. It simply structures the traditional Save As command found in most programs for exporting one or more images. You cannot save over your original files in Lightroom (unless you really work at it with a TIF or JPEG file, and you cannot affect a RAW file), so Export always acts like Save As.

Click the Export button to open the Export dialog box, shown in figure 4-37. From the top of the Export dialog box, the first two sections are as follows:

> **Preset:** This drop-down menu choice has some preset options for how you might want to export images as DNG RAW files or e-mail sized files, for example.

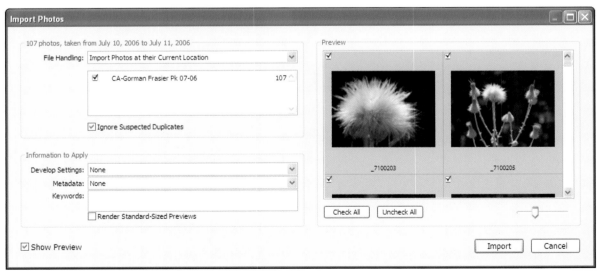

4-36

4-37

> **Export Location.** This is simply the folder you want to put the photo into. Choose gives you a traditional file structure dialog box that looks similar to the Save dialog for most programs (dependent on your operating system). You can also create and put this image into a subfolder by checking Put in Subfolder.

> **File Naming.** This section gives you a number of choices in the Template box as seen in figure 4-38. Each choice gives unique options for automatically naming your image or images if you have selected a group of them.

The rest of the choices are pretty familiar.

> **File Settings.** This section has options for format and quality. From the File Format drop-down menu, you can choose JPEG, PSD, TIFF, or DNG as appropriate to your needs.

> **Image Settings.** Here you can choose a Color Space (sRGB, AdobeRGB (1998), or ProPhoto RGB), Bit Depth (8 or 16), and Resolution. You can even add a copyright watermark. Other options here include constraining the size to a specific need.

> **Minimize Embedded Metadata.** This is not used by most photographers, which is why it is not checked by default. This simply attaches a minimum amount of metadata to the file rather than everything possible in the IPTC and EXIF data.

> **Post-Processing.** This section offers some post-processing specifications such as Show in Explorer.

When you have selected all the appropriate conditions for your file, click Export and the photo is saved to your hard drive.

PRO TIP

If you want to export a photo directly to Photoshop, the easiest way to do that is to right-click on the image in Lightroom's central work area. This lets you send the image to Photoshop with the processing applied. I highly recommend a right-click mouse for Mac users for this reason (and for the usefulness of context-sensitive menus that come from right-clicking most programs).

Q & A

I am not sure I follow this Export concept. In Photoshop, you just save a photo. How is Export different from Save or Save As in Photoshop?

Once an image is in Lightroom, it is never actually changed at a pixel level, and no layers are added to it. Everything that is done to an image is done by only adding instructions, making the adjustments "nondestructive" in that nothing is actually changed. Small accessory files record the instructions Lightroom automatically creates to accompany the images.

In Photoshop, on the other hand, as soon as you make adjustments, something changes in that file. Even if you use an adjustment layer, which is nondestructive to pixels, you change that file with that addition of a layer. None of those changes are recorded to the Photoshop file unless you save them.

So, in order to make adjustment instructions in Lightroom "stick" to an image, or become permanent, you have to process the image file and save it as a new file. That is essentially what exporting does. With Photoshop, any changes to the file have already occurred while that image was inside Photoshop, so the file does not need to be processed, only saved. You can simply save the file as it is. It is basically just a difference in the way the two programs handle the preservation of changes in an image.

How much metadata that is already connected with a file can I actually change?

Some metadata, such as Exif data, is embedded with the file as you take the picture. This is camera information and, in general, you cannot change it. Usually, you want this to be consistent so that you know what your camera was or wasn't doing with a particular shot.

On the other hand, you can change all IPTC data. Lightroom lets you set most of this when you import images into the program. You can then readjust this information with the Metadata control on the right panel. There is a lot there, but rarely do most photographers need it all. Use what is appropriate. If you are changing a lot of IPTC data (besides the caption or description info that is specific to an individual photo), you might reconsider what you are applying to the original photos as they come into Lightroom. You should be able to do quite a bit of this work there.

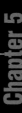

Chapter 5

ORGANIZING IMAGES IN THE LIBRARY MODULE

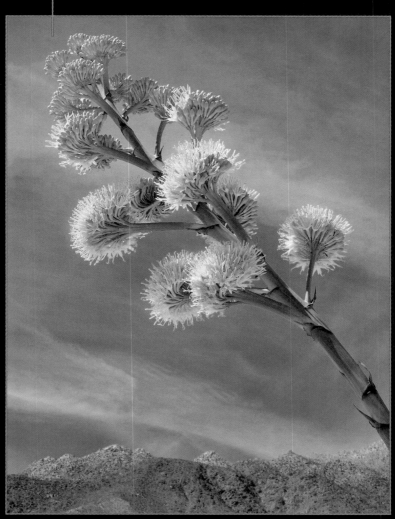

Lightroom's Library module has some easy-to-use features that are quite powerful. I like the way they help you organize your images. However, using those features requires a bit of thought and work on your part. You need to decide how best to deal with organizing images. Lightroom just provides a place; it's up to you to determine how to use that place.

This has become a major issue among photographers today: the best way to file and organize digital images. There are even experts promoting one way to work as the way, which has led to multiple experts touting their approach as "the way." In a sense, they are all right. When it comes to handling image files, different photographers respond differently to what is best for them, so there will be multiple "bests."

So, as a photographer, how do you know which approach is best for you? How can you use Lightroom optimally for your purposes? In this chapter, I offer some ideas on doing just that.

A Mental Transition

Let's be honest. No photographer ever got into photography because he or she wanted to work with the computer. Photographers become photographers because they like taking pictures, capturing images of their world, and, even, because they like this interesting merger of technology and art. For me, sharing what excites me in nature, such as shown in figure 5-1, is a prime mover of my photography. For you, perhaps it is sports, people, travel, or some specialized type of photography (I recently read in National Geographic about a photographer working to capture every species of hummingbird in photos). One of the real challenges photographers face with the computer is how to focus on images and not get overwhelmed by the technology. There is a need to make a mental transition away from focusing on technology for its own sake and toward harnessing that technology for your photography's benefit.

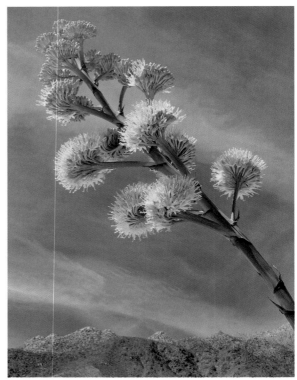

5-1

However, I have discovered from my classes and workshops around the country that many photographers are looking for help in making that transition. I want to help you with that, and this chapter is designed for that purpose. I can tell you that if you have not made that switch, you will not gain the most benefit from Lightroom's image file management capabilities.

Managing Physical Image Files in the Past

It is important to first look at how you filed photos in the past because that can help you better work out a system for filing images on your computer. You may hear the argument from some computer gurus that how you filed in the past is dead and gone. You should be working "the new way," and paying attention to your old habits simply computerizes old, and perhaps outdated, habits.

There is good logic to that. After all, the computer does provide capabilities that one could not even imagine as recently as a few years ago. It is a waste to not use a computer's modern capabilities to gain new possibilities in working with images.

However, I have found that if photographers ignore how they worked with images in the past and simply adopt a new system because someone else says it is "best," they struggle with it; at best, they will not use it to its full capabilities, and at worst, they use it in a minimal and superficial (and not very helpful) way. On the other hand, if photographers look a bit at how they filed images in the past, and what worked or didn't work for them, they can apply some of those ideas to image file management in the computer, creating a system that is more appropriate for their specific needs.

With film, you had to have a physical place for the photos. For many amateurs (and even a few pros I knew who did not shoot stock images), old images were "filed" by sticking them into boxes and tucking them away in some storage space — the old "shoe-box in the closet." This was never a very efficient way of dealing with photos, but it did store them for potential (albeit difficult) access at some point. These boxes were organized, in a way, because they were kept in bags or boxes that related to a trip, a job, or, possibly, just a date. You could search for an image if you had an idea of where or when you took the picture.

For photographers who shot stock, they needed a much more organized system. They needed to find specific photos to fill requests for images from potential clients. Typically, they would use many filing cabinets with categorized drawers, then further refine categories for folders or binders (the actual physical "holder" varied), and then even further refine information on specific images based on the filing names for them as shown in figure 5-2.

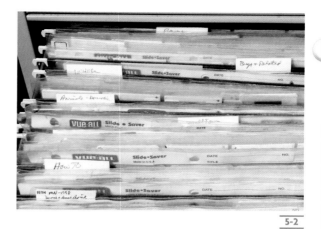

5-2

Photographers who shot commercial work (such as annual reports or advertising images) used something similar, but they had very specific needs based on clients. They would have the same sort of filing cabinets, but the drawers and folders would be organized first around clients, next by shoots for that client, usually in chronological order (often with the most recent at the front of the drawer), and then labeled by specific elements of a job (such as subject, selects, and so forth).

Photojournalists had somewhat different needs (whether they personally filed their images or their publication did). They needed to find photos specific to news events, sports competitions, unique days, and so forth. Still, they needed a place for these images and a way of accessing them in folders, cabinets, and other filing places.

In all of these situations, photographers were not even consistent within a specific group. This is actually a very important element of image filing to take note of, because it often revealed some things that were core to how a photographer worked and thought. Some photographers filed very broadly, for example, and simply took all images from a specific shoot, put them into a folder labeled by that shoot, and then did nothing else other than place that folder into the appropriate file cabinet or box.

Other photographers filed to a far greater extent. They would document very specific information about each and every photograph, including labels for slides that had tiny type that challenged even young eyes, but had everything you needed to know about those images. Typically, this sort of filing would include very specific, detailed file names that affected how the images were organized.

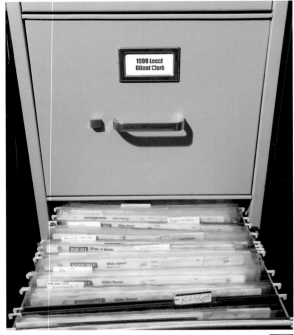

MANAGING FILES ON YOUR COMPUTER

Many photographers get into trouble with image filing on the computer when they figure they have to forget all they learned about their likes and dislikes regarding image filing of film. The computer seems so alien and different from filing cabinets and folders. It offers none of the physical contact that film filing does.

This is exactly what not to do. To make the most of Lightroom and your computer, you have to see the Library module as a way of accessing file cabinets, drawers, and folders. While they aren't physical locations, they act the same way — they are simply places to hold your photos. Look at figure 5-3 and figure 5-4. You see two different things, a filing cabinet and some of the folders recognized by my version of Lightroom, yet they truly do represent the same things. If you can hold that idea when working with managing image files, you can use many of the ideas you had in the past, and then modify them to better use the capabilities of the computer.

Lightroom's Library module is not some magical search program that somehow manages to look through an amorphous group of images so they can be more easily found. It is just the same as filing slides in a cabinet. The better organized your filing system (based on your needs) was, the easier it was to find photos. The better you set up and manage your filing system with Lightroom, the easier it is to find your digital images.

5-3

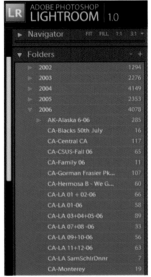

5-4

I want to re-emphasize, though, that I do not advocate any one way of setting up these files. I am offering you some ideas and possibilities to consider, but you must look at how you have worked over the years and what seems to best fit your personality as well as professional and personal needs for filing and image access.

LIGHTROOM, FILE CABINETS, AND SUCH

In Chapter 4, you learned how Library was set up and organized. If you compare it to a traditional filing cabinet, I believe you get good ideas on how best to use this module.

Your computer's hard drive is basically your room full of filing cabinets as shown in figure 5-5. Lightroom can put images directly into that room if you download them through the program. It then sets up its own way of putting those files into folders and cabinets, all done behind the scenes, so to speak — you just have to be sure you have enough space on the hard drive to always be able to contain them.

Or you put the photos directly into folders in those "filing cabinets" yourself (before you import to Lightroom). This is what happens when you download a shoot into a folder on the hard drive. The folder sits inside other folders (months or years, clients, location, etc.), which can be seen as the equivalent of drawers and cabinets in that hard drive "room."

Lightroom then sets up its own file folders in its own cabinets to reference your folders on the hard drive. One "cabinet" is the Folders section. There, it places all of your images into folders based on a specific shoot or download. It does this with references to the images in their original locations — it doesn't move the actual images. In the Collections section, unique groups of images are copied (virtually, not in reality) into new folders based on special categories commonly used and labeled by you, with your specific needs based on how and what you photograph.

Photos are assigned additional organizational capabilities based on such things as how they are named, the caption information associated with them in the

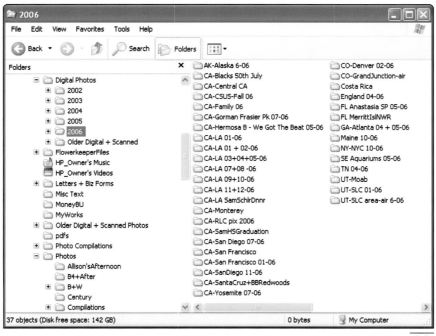

metadata, and keywords. The naming process is the same as the one you might have used to name film images; metadata and keywords convey the information that often went into little labels on the slide mount. A big deal for all this extra information is that you can quickly and easily search (using the Library Find function) all images with the power of the computer. It is like having a Harry Potter–esque assistant who can quickly go through all your cabinets, folders, and labels to find you exactly the photos you need.

SETTING UP AN ORGANIZATION SYSTEM

The power of a digital search is what makes the computer so helpful in dealing with image files. You can find photos faster than you ever could with a physical filing system.

However, the analogy of the physical system is very much applicable here. If you did not put your slides, for example, into the "right" folders (that is, ones with names you could readily use), you would never find those images. You might have the world's greatest photo of an American eagle catching a fish in the river, but if it is filed in the Travel cabinet in the Mississippi River folder and not in some bird folder, it might be difficult to find. The same thing happens in Lightroom. You might have a stunning photo of a young soccer player, but if it is filed under an obscure shoot, such as Trip to Cleveland, and is not included in a soccer collection or not connected to keywords such as soccer, youth, and goalkeeper, you might never find this photo again.

To avoid problems finding filed images and enable you to make best use of your photographs, you need to do some preplanning to decide on a consistent way to name your folders and collections, plus determine some conventions on how you will apply names, keywords, and captions to the photos. Use your personality, personal preferences, and past experiences with film to determine what and how much information to include in each area, but it is worth making some consistent choices to set up a system that works well for you.

It's important to be consistent because if you keep changing the way you name images, for example, you increase your work and complicate your workflow (because you have to figure out a new system every time) and make them harder to search and find successfully. Plus, if you don't have a consistent set of terms to use for keywords, the search process is frustrating: What do you search for? Baby, babies, newborns? Eagle, birds of prey, symbol of America? Sure, you could include all of these, but most people don't. You are best served with a list that you can use again and again, and to search images based on that list as well.

Keywords, folder names, and so forth are going to be personal, unique choices for each photographer. Photographers who work for a stock photo agency may find that the agency asks you use a specific list. Otherwise, you need to create a list of words that work for you and that you can use in a consistent way. For example, a nature photographer might have categories broken down like this:

Birds

Specific categories of birds (shorebirds, hawks, owls, thrushes, etc.)

Locations for birds (NE birds, SE birds, Midwest birds, etc.)

Flowers

Specific categories of flowers (sunflower family, lily family, mint family, rose family, etc.)

Timing of flowering (spring flowers, summer flowers, fall flowers, winter flowers)

Locations for flowers (NE flowers, SE flowers, Midwest flowers, etc.)

And so on. It is important to remember that you need to find what kind of keywords work best for you, or if they even work with your workflow.

All this organization work might seem a bit overwhelming — after all, Lightroom offers a lot of power to do this — but I want to emphasize again that you need to choose and use what works for you and your image needs. To be honest, I often get a bit over-whelmed by the projects I am involved with and don't have time to follow all the ideas I discuss here. That doesn't make those ideas less valid; it's just that real-istically, life sometimes gets in the way of optimum organization. Plus, some folks are more detail ori-ented than I am and can sit down for hours and fill in keywords, whereas I get tired of it long before that.

Still, it helps to envision an ideal way of working. I'm going to explain an approach that I use. It works, but I recognize it doesn't work for everyone. Use it to stim-ulate your own methods for using your computer and Lightroom to file and organize your images.

BRINGING IMAGES INTO THE COMPUTER

I like to set up folders in preparation for receiving dig-ital images. This fits the Lightroom workflow quite well, even though this portion is not done in Lightroom. I set up my hard drive so that there is a specific folder for digital images (this is like a filing cabinet). Then I create main folders in the digital images folder for each year (these are like cabinet drawers). I do all this separately from actually setting up of folders for a specific shoot, though, usually, I

set up a new year folder when I have the first shoot from the year. You can see how this might look on your computer in figure 5-6.

Now every time I have a new shoot, I open the year folder and create a new folder for that shoot. Put some thought into how you name these folders. They should represent your photography and how you shoot.

Given I do a lot of travel and nature photography, I mostly name these folders based on location by state (or country) and month (the location fits both my travel and nature needs) as seen in figure 5-7. Now when any folder is imported into Lightroom, it shows up with the same name in the Shoots area, a name that makes organizational sense, and also one that is easy to search. If I go to a specific location many times, then I simply set up new folders with the same location but different months.

PRO TIP

In both Windows and Mac, an easy way to create a new folder is to right-click in the opened folder space and select New Folder — another good rea-son to have a right-click mouse for Mac!

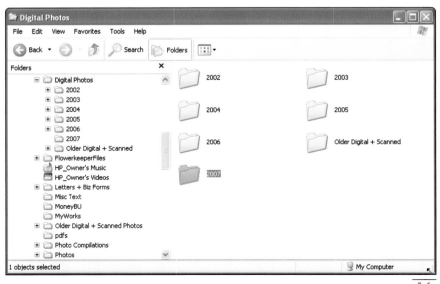

5-6

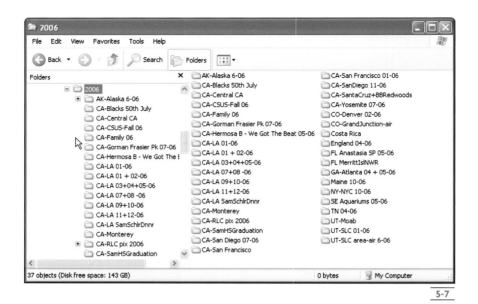

5-7

I often have sublocations, places within the state or country that need to be separated. I create new folders for them within the bigger folder as shown in figure 5-8, using those specific locations, the larger location, and a date. This way that particular folder goes into Lightroom with a solid naming scheme for folders. Again, this is all searchable, so I am starting my organization from the start.

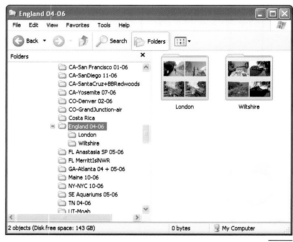

5-8

PRO TIP

You can download images to your computer either from the camera or from a memory card reader. I highly recommend a card reader. With the camera, you have some distinct problems: you have to find a place to put the camera, the camera must have a fully charged battery (or be plugged into an AC adapter), and you need to keep track of your camera cord. With the memory card reader, you have some definite advantages: it's usually faster than the camera, it requires no additional power, you can keep it attached to the computer, it has a very small footprint, and you can keep it plugged in and in place, ready for use.

I do all this before downloading any memory card. Once I have a folder (or folders) ready for photos, I put my memory card into a card reader and open its folder. I see a lot of photographers just downloading the over-riding or top-level DCM (digital camera media) folder that holds the actual images. To me, that creates extra work later because you end up with folders and names you don't need. I go to the actual photos inside the folders, select them all, and drag them to the new folder or folders I have created for them on my hard drive as described previously.

ORGANIZING THE IMAGES

Once the photos are on the hard drive, you have access to them in the computer, but only in a very generic sense. You need to be able to see them for editing, renaming, sorting, and so forth. You do all this in Lightroom.

I start by importing the folder or subfolders within a folder from the shoot I just downloaded to the hard drive. Simply go to the Import button or File ➪ Import and browse to find the folder you need. If you put all of the images into one folder, this process is relatively simple. Choose a folder and select the button, Choose Selected. The Import Photos dialog box opens and you include whatever information you can, including copyright and basic keywords as shown in figure 5-9. Adding copyright information here can be very helpful in ensuring this is always included with your images. If your group of images has a consistent subject or location, you can add that information in the Keywords section and have that included on all of them. Then, when you click Import, you get a new entry listed in Folders with the same name as your file folder's name.

I recommend keeping Folders solidly grounded in how you file your images. Most of the time, Folders should reflect how your images are filed on your hard drive (grounded in how you file your images) — don't create some new naming system for Folders that does not reflect how your images are filed. That, in turn, is based on the way you photograph. Like most photographers, when I get certain shoots that don't fit the norm, I also create special Folders for them.

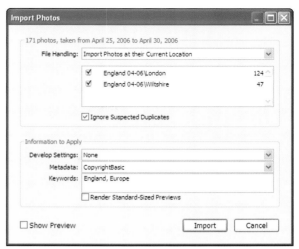

5-9

However, you can also use Folders as a way of organizing distinct groupings of your photography, such as client. You can create a folder directly in Lightroom that is a client name, and then import all jobs for that client into that folder, so each job shows up as a subset of the overriding Folder category. Do this by clicking the + button to the right of Folders. The Browse for Folder dialog box appears. Find the folder you want to create a subfolder within, and then click Make New Folder as shown in figure 5-10. This is just a way of keeping the Folder section a bit tighter when you have a lot of individual folders that still belong to a larger grouping.

You could also use Collections for this purpose, but I don't find it as useful for tracking specific shoots, which goes back to the file cabinet analogy. I consider the Folders category as my file drawer and use the subfolder based on a shoot within it. I like to use Collections more for subject matter that cuts across folders.

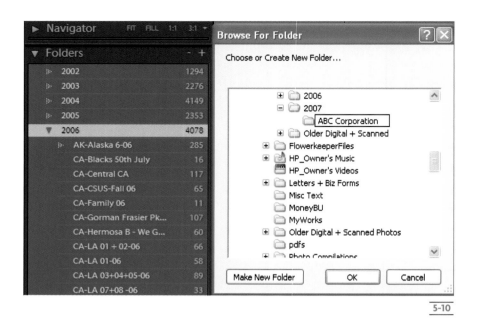

EDITING THE SHOOT

At this point in the process, you generally want to spend a little time editing your photos down to get rid of the junk and sort out your better images. Again, how you approach this is very personal. Some photographers like to keep everything they shoot, some like to keep only the very best images, and both will argue that the other is doing this process wrong! I think they are both right — for their own work, but not necessarily for others.

I like to remove photos I really don't like and know that I will never do anything with. I just have no desire to see mistakes, experiments that didn't work, and so on, plus I don't like needlessly using hard drive space — but that is my preference.

I also find the actual process of editing is very helpful to my photography — I can really examine what my photography is doing or not doing as I work. Here's how I like to edit:

1. **Remove the junk.** I really don't like keeping the junk around. So I go through the images very quickly in Grid mode. I rank the photos I don't like with one star by clicking on the small star ratings under each photo (which appear when the cursor moves over the image). I select a group of images by Ctrl/⌘+clicking or Shift+clicking from first to last, then rate all of them with one star if I don't like them (shown in figure 5-11). I then sort to show just the starred images by clicking the one-star bullet in the sorting row of the Filmstrip (seen to the right of Filters). I select all of them (Ctrl/⌘+A) as shown in figure 5-12 and press Delete to remove the photo(s) from Lightroom and off the hard drive. You get a second chance at choosing to delete or not with the Confirm dialog box that appears, shown in figure 5-13. I know there are readers who will react in horror to deleting photos, but it works for me (fear not, you can also just choose to remove them from Lightroom). It lets me clean up a file to only the good images.

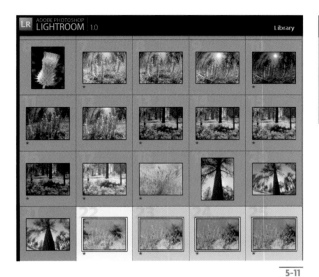

5-11

PRO TIP

If you are not sure about certain images, remember that you can always enlarge them by double-clicking into the Loupe view. You can also compare selected photos at larger sizes in the Compare and Survey modes.

ADOBE PHOTOSHOP LIGHTROOM 1.0

Library | Develop | Slideshow

Custom ▾

Default ▾

Preset
File Name
Folder

Title
Caption

Copyright
Creator
Location

Rating
Label

Dimensions
Exposure
Focal Length
ISO Speed Rating
Flash
Date Time
Make
Model
Lens

Sync Settings

Sort: File Name ▾   Thumbnails   _7100203.ORF

Folders / 2006 / CA-Gorman Frasier Pk 07-06 / 14 photos / 14 selected / _7100203.ORF   » Filters   ★ . . . . and higher

5-12

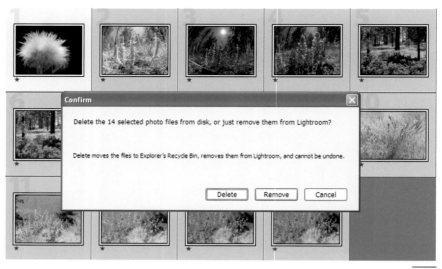

5-13

2. **Choose selects.** Selects are those images that I consider the best. You can use all of the five-star rating system that Lightroom gives you, giving photos a range of ratings. You simply go from photo to photo and press a number from 1 to 5 depending on how many stars you want to give each one. I find that confusing for my work. So I typically just edit for the key images that are most important to me at this point. I go through images one by one and press 5 or photos I like or click on the fifth dot in each image area, which also gives a 5 rating as seen in figure 5-14. Use 0 to unrank any image or just click again on the stars. I use the Compare and Loupe modes as necessary to better evaluate photos in larger sizes. Also, at this point I rotate any images that need rotating to vertical as I go through the shoot.

3. **Edit selects.** Again, using sort to show just the starred images by clicking the 1-star bullet in the sorting row of the Filmstrip (seen to the right of Filters), I can tell Lightroom to only show me the 5-star selected photos as shown in figure 5-15.

I can decide if these really are all worth 5 stars. If I find some aren't, I can downgrade the rating to 4 or press 0 to remove any rating. Again, I typically do not use the whole range of ratings because it isn't that useful to me. Many photographers do find the additional ratings helpful for sorting images into different groups.

At this point, I have a much cleaner collection of images. I have gotten rid of the junk and tagged my best images so I can sort them for further use as needed.

PRO TIP

Lightroom offers a number of ways of rating or ranking images. Besides stars, you can also use colors. Colors choices do not show up the way star rankings do on the info area around the images in Grid. However, they are very easily used by using numbers 6 through 9 for red, yellow, green, and blue. You can also right-click an image for these options in the context menu. This context menu also gives you other options on how to work with images in the Grid view.

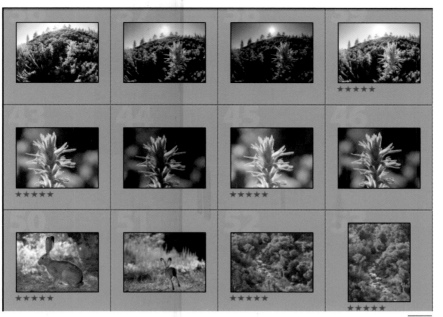

5-14

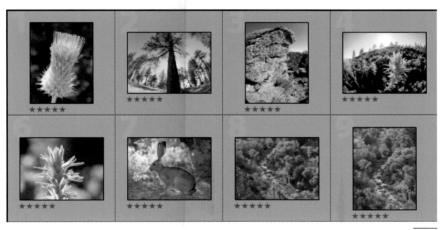

5-15

RENAMING IMAGES

After the initial edit, I find it helpful to rename digital images to something related to a specific shoot — at least something that makes more sense to me than the names that come directly from the camera, such as IMG00982. You can rename files in Lightroom very easily. Simply select the photos you want to rename and choose Library ⇨ Rename Photos or press the F2 function key. The Rename Photos dialog box, shown in figure 5-16, appears. If you click the File Name drop-down arrow at the far right, you see a series of templates for renaming as shown in figure 5-17.

But how do you actually name your files?

This is an extremely personal thing. I believe you must create some sort of naming convention that works for you and gives you information you need. You want to create a way of naming so that you can look at a file name and learn something about it without even seeing the photo. You don't want to overdo this, though, as really long names can be very unwieldy and won't always display properly when you are looking for them.

I like to create a file name based on the File Naming template, "Custom Name – Original File Number," that works out something like this: *CA-FrasierPark-AtlasMtn-7100205.ORF*, as shown in figure 5-18.

My chosen name translates as follows and may give you some ideas:

> **State or country.** Given most of my images are based on locations, I start with the two-letter state abbreviation or something similar for a country. The sample file name was a shot from California.

> **Specific shoot info.** I then add some abbreviated information that usually refines the location; this photo was taken in Frasier Park. And it might also refer to a specific subject matter I was shooting; this example is a photo of Atlas mountain.

> **Original file number.** By keeping the numbers of the original file name for when I shoot RAW+JPEG, I can reference the RAW and JPEG files if needed (for example, I might use the JPEG file for a quick e-mail and now want to process the same image as RAW). If you are shooting only RAW, you probably don't need this information and can use the template, "Custom Name – Sequence."

PRO TIP

At some point in your filing and organizing images, you need to back up your images. This is extremely critical. I have several external drives that duplicate all of my photo files, and as I bring new shoots into the computer, I also copy them onto the back-up drives. I use automated back-up software called Save-N-Sync from Peer Software, but there are others that do equally well. The important thing is to do it.

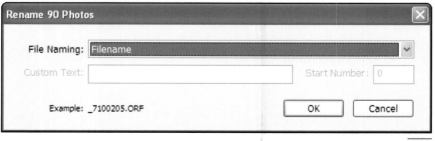

5-16

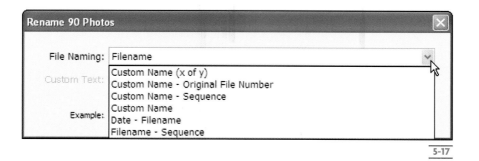

5-17

Rename 90 Photos

File Naming: Custom Name - Original File Number

Custom Text: CA-FrasierPark-AtlasMtn-   Start Number: 0

Example: CA-FrasierPark-AtlasMtn--7100205.ORF   OK   Cancel

5-18

USING COLLECTIONS

At this point in my Lightroom workflow, I can start using Collections and Keywords, which provide more ways to organize your photos. I can use Keywords when the images are imported into Lightroom, but it's only very generic at that point.

Collections are a great way of grouping images from many shoots into categories that you use regularly. You can add categories as you go, but use Collections for large numbers of images with subjects that go across Folders. For me, that includes things such as spring or summer flowers, regional landscapes, bugs, travel scenes such as architecture, and so it goes, as shown in figure 5-19.

I create both overall collections and subcollections within the larger group. To do that, click on a collection, and then click the + button, which gives you a simple dialog box, Create Collection (shown in figure 5-20), where you type in the name of the collection.

Then check the box about "Create as a child of [the original collection]." If you decide to change where a particular collection resides, you can simply click and drag it into another collection at any time.

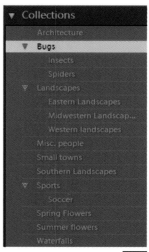

5-19

95

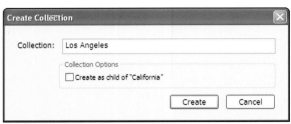

5-20

Once I am satisfied with the organization of my Collections, I go through the new shoot in Grid mode with thumbnails that are pretty small. I have already seen the images in a larger format when I was editing the shoot (enlarging as needed with Loupe), but, usually, seeing the big version doesn't matter for Collections. If you can't see the photo subject clearly

when it's small, then use the Loupe view as needed. If you stay in Grid as much as possible, the organizing process is much faster.

In the Grid view, I select images in groups by Ctrl/⌘+clicking each, and then dragging the images onto the collection name.

PRO TIP

As a collection increases in size, it is a good idea to split it into new subcollections. For example, you might find a collection, Waterfalls, gets too large and needs to be split into waterfalls by region, such as NE Waterfalls, SE Waterfalls, and so forth. How large you go before splitting it up is really up to you. At what point are you having trouble with the size? Make a subcollection by clicking the + button to the right of Collections, naming the new subcollection, checking the box that tells Lightroom to create this subcollection as a child of the root Collection, and then clicking Create.

Q & A

I am not sure your approach to keywords will work for me. I have a staff that sometimes has to find images and just going on a visual search doesn't necessarily work for them. You're the expert, so should I try to simplify my use of keywords?

No, not at all! You have to always translate an "expert's" advice so that it fits your unique needs. My way of working with images was used for example. I know that my use of keywords simply doesn't work for photographers who have a staff who must find images for them or shoot a lot of stock images. They need to be able to locate very specific images related to a subject or topic. In this case, having an extensive set of keywords really helps. It takes time to do all that keywording, but in the long run, it actually cuts time. It certainly helps prevent a lot of headaches from the wrong images being selected.

But you do need to understand that this is a very personal thing. Some photographers have hundreds of keywords and spend a lot of time giving very detailed keyword data for their photos. There is no question that this makes searches highly efficient.

For me, special keywords for unique subjects do help me find them. But often my work requires me to make a selection of an image from a variety of photos — I need the variety that keywords often won't give me. So doing a lot with keywords, which can take a lot of time, is not efficient for me. I love Collections because I can visually search through a group of related images and find what I need very quickly. I don't need the keywords in that case because the visual impression itself is so important.

I really find it hard to see the images in the Grid mode for editing purposes. What would you suggest to help?

First, I would recommend you use as large a monitor as you can afford. Monitors are pretty affordable today and are well worth the cost because they are really your vision into your files. I would recommend a 19-inch LCD as the minimum size. This allows you to display your whole interface larger.

Next, you can go to the Loupe view and simply go from photo to photo there by using the arrow keys. You can set your image ratings in Loupe as well as Grid. This gives you a large image, but you can only see one at a time. You then need to keep the Filmstrip displayed so you can see how images show up in the order shot. I think that seeing images in order of the shoot is important so you can better make comparisons. Use the Compare View as needed to see two large photos displayed at once.

Chapter 6

IMAGE PROCESSING IN THE DEVELOP MODULE

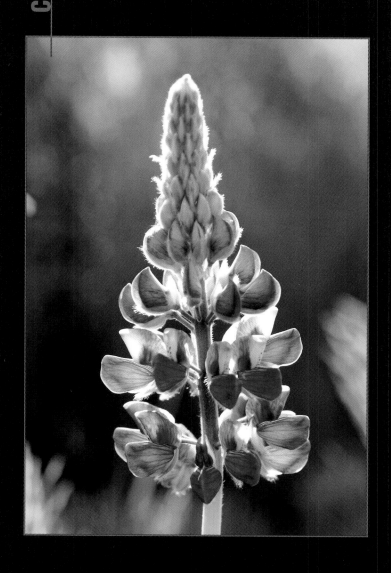

If you have used Adobe Camera Raw (the RAW conversion program that is a companion to Photoshop), you have a good start for understanding the Develop module of Photoshop Lightroom. Develop is clearly inspired by Camera Raw, but it goes much farther than Camera Raw in dealing with image processing (though the latest version of Camera Raw 4.0 that comes with Photoshop CS3 adds in many of the controls that were first added to Develop).

The most significant difference between Lightroom and Camera Raw is that while Camera Raw is associated with Photoshop, it is a separate program without much integration. They act independently, and you can never go back and forth between them. Lightroom, on the other hand, has total integration of RAW conversion and processing capabilities with every other part of its program. As shown in figure 6-1, even though you are in Develop at one moment, you can click on any module to leave it and work on the color of a photo, instantly go to print it or add a

keyword in the metadata, and then go back to work on the color again. This gives you a lot of flexibility as well as making your workflow more fluid.

In this chapter, I take you through the key controls of Develop, following a workflow that I know works for photographers.

AN OVERVIEW OF DEVELOP

If you look closely at the controls on the right side of Develop as shown in figure 6-2, you see quite a few entries that look just like Camera Raw.

At the top is the same histogram. In Basic the same White Balance settings appear: Exposure, Brightness, Contrast, and Saturation. Tone Curve has some similar elements, and Detail, Lens Corrections (not shown), and Camera Calibration (not shown) are essentially the same as Camera Raw too. There are some very new controls, which you learn more about shortly, but what you really will find is the original

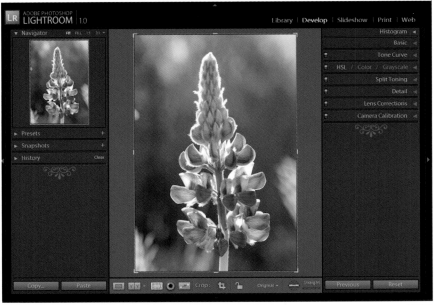

6-1

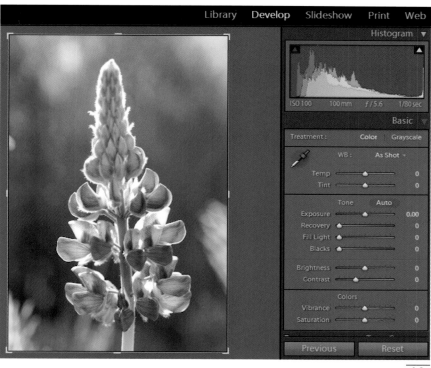

6-2

Camera Raw with big enhancements. The tools are organized better, and organized in ways that are more appropriate to the photographer — the additions provide really great photographic tools as well. This evidently influenced the Adobe programmers working on Photoshop CS3 as they incorporated many of the new features first seen in LIghtroom's Develop module into Camera Raw 4.

The right side of Develop is essentially the digital darkroom for Lightroom. The order of the control groups from top to bottom is actually a good order to follow for a standard photographic workflow. Still, you can skip around in these controls quite easily as needed.

At the bottom of the right side are two buttons. Previous takes you back to the most recent adjustments made on the image. Reset does what it says, resetting the Develop module back to defaults for the active image.

The left side of the Develop module shown in figure 6-3 holds the image preview showing you what the whole image looks like, even when you have magnified the main image, and includes a box to show you where the magnified portion of the image is in relationship to the whole photo (this operates very much the same as Navigator in Library).

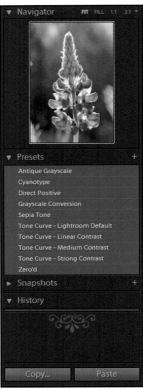

History is a unique way of remembering what you are doing. Rather than tracking every change you make, as you make it (as Photoshop does in the History palette), History only remembers the "condition" of a photo at a given point in the process (it is like a History State in Photoshop), which you can always go back to (even if Lightroom is closed). I discuss History at the end of this chapter and cover the presets of this module in Chapter 7.

Two buttons appear at the bottom of the left side, Copy and Paste. These allow you to copy settings from any adjusted image and apply them (paste) to another photo by selecting another image on the Filmstrip.

Below the image in the central work area is a new toolbar (also turned on and off like in Library by using T) as shown in figure 6-5. From left, this includes buttons for the full view of the image (Loupe view), a comparison view (showing before and after), Crop Overlay, Red-Eye Removal, and a Spot Removal tool; if Crop Overlay is selected then you see: Crop tool, a Lock option to prevent changes to the image, cropping options, a Straighten tool, and a Clear button to clear adjustments from the toolbar. All of these controls are not always visible. Clicking on specific tools, as noted with the Crop Overlay tool, changes what is seen.

There is also something altogether different: three rather unique lists. Presets is simply a list of preset adjustments that affect your image in definite and defined ways. You can quickly and easily see what each preset will do by running your cursor over the names of the presets as shown in figure 6-4 (don't click the mouse or it will be applied).

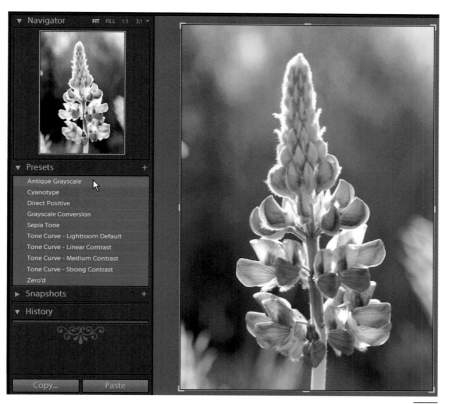

6-4

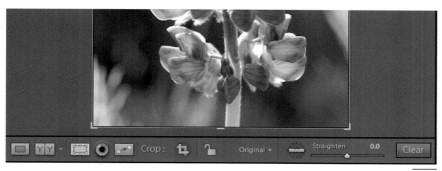

6-5

Using Crop and Straighten

One of the first things I like to do with an image is to crop and straighten it. I do this to remove distractions — technically, I cannot remove anything in Lightroom as the adjustments are non-destructive, however, doing this does feature only the important parts of the image. I don't want to have to continue to look at a crooked photo as I go along, nor do I want to be adjusting parts of a photo that are unimportant or just annoying. All that takes you away from your actual work.

You do the actual cropping of an image by clicking the Crop Overlay button (the term is a bit awkward) located under the middle work area. This is a simple function to use, but it is different from crop tools you may be used to. After you click the Crop Overlay button, immediately a bounding box shows up around the photo (you can also get that overlay to show up by pressing R without clicking Crop Overlay). You can click and drag any side, from any point, or the corners to crop the image. You can also move the cursor into the frame and click and

drag a cropped area directly. The cropped out area shows up as a dimmed part of the photo as shown in figure 6-6. As you move the edges, you see that a faint grid overlays the image. This is based on the classic "rule of thirds" for composition and can help you better define where the crop should be.

You can see the remaining area of the image by clicking Loupe view at the left of the toolbar. This cropped version now appears in all modules of Lightroom as well as the Filmstrip. A little square symbol also shows on the image in the Filmstrip to show a crop has been made. The only way to go back to the original is to click the Crop Overlay button, and then click Clear.

You can also move your cursor outside of the box to rotate the cropped area when the Crop Overlay is active. When you do this, the cursor changes to a curved cursor with arrows at both ends. A grid shows up over the image so you can better line up parts of the image as you rotate it as shown in figure 6-7. This can be a quick and easy way to fix a crooked photo.

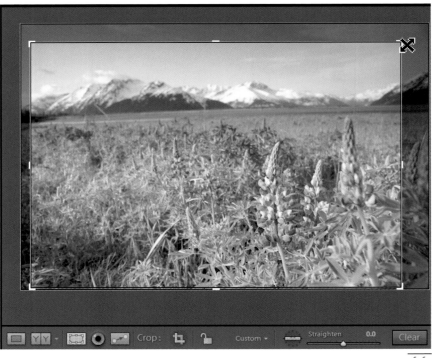

6-6

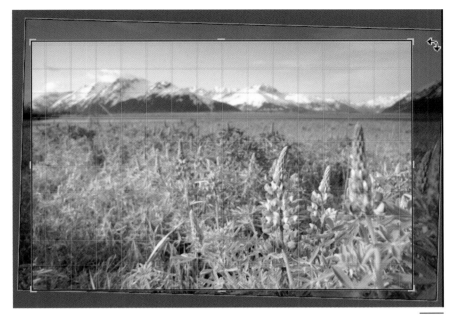

6-7

Once you rotate an image, you see a number for the angle of change appear over the Straighten slider. You can move that slider to straighten more (the grid reappears), but a more accurate way of straightening a photo is to use the Straightening tool. Click the tool that looks like a carpenter's level and your cursor changes to that icon along with cross-hairs, as shown in figure 6-8, that show exactly where you will click on the image. Now you click and drag a line across something that should be horizontal or vertical as shown in figure 6-9 and Lightroom automatically rotates the image to match.

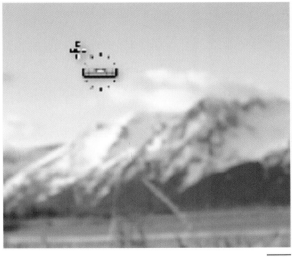

6-8

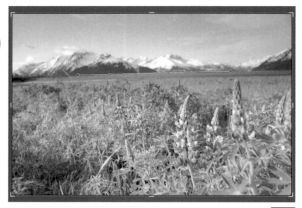

6-9

If you want a specific crop setting, you can accomplish that quite easily by clicking Original in the toolbar (Original shows up when you first click the Crop Overlay button; Custom shows up when you make a cropping adjustment) to get the Crop Settings menu. There are a set of preset dimensions you can use or you can set your own at Enter Custom. When you choose a specific size, your cropping only fits the proportion you chose. You can constrain the image's aspect ratio at any time to make the crop box keep its proportions if you hold down the Shift key as you change the crop area when clicking and dragging the Crop Overlay box.

If things get messed up and you just want to go back to the image without cropping or straightening, click the Clear button on the Toolbar. Do not use the Reset button at the bottom of the right side. The inside button only resets any cropping and straightening you have done. The bottom-right button resets everything that you have done in the Develop module.

PRO TIP

If you forget any of this, that's no problem because unlike Photoshop, Lightroom doesn't actually make the crop at this point. You can change it at any time. Lightroom only remembers the instructions for the crop and makes it permanent only when the photo is exported from the program.

Rule of Thirds

When using the Crop Overlay tool, you see a faint grid showing the Rule of Thirds. The Rule of Thirds is more of a guideline than an actual rule. It is based on dividing the image area into thirds, both horizontally and vertically. The rule says that compositions are stronger when key horizontal or vertical lines are at the third markers (this would refer to the horizon, for example) and that key subject matter is at the intersections of these lines.

This is a good guideline to keep in mind if it helps a photographer structure a photo compositionally so that subjects aren't always stuck in the middle. It can help you crop an image to make it visually more interesting. It is a problem, though, if the photographer tries to force a real-world scene that isn't neatly viewed in thirds into this grid.

THE IMPORTANCE OF BLACK AND WHITE

This isn't a section about how to work with monochrome images. If you are familiar with my books and articles, you know how important I think properly setting black and white points is to the photographer. With a good, solid black in the image and a carefully chosen white, a number of key things happen to your photograph as illustrated by figure 6-10:

> Good contrast starts with something in the image that is pure black and something that is pure white (unless you are shooting a fog, which will not need either).

> Good color comes from having a solid black and a key white in the image.

> Midtones are set best when played against carefully chosen black and white.

> A good print starts with the proper black and white.

Lightroom, just like Photoshop and Camera Raw, gives you some excellent tools for setting black and white points. I often refer to this as "setting blacks and whites." I know this is not grammatically correct as there is only one black and one white, but I believe this is a good way to think about black and white in a photo. If you think about setting the blacks, that is, all areas that should be black in a photo, for example, you think differently about the photograph than if you think about setting a black point. In fact, Lightroom uses this very term.

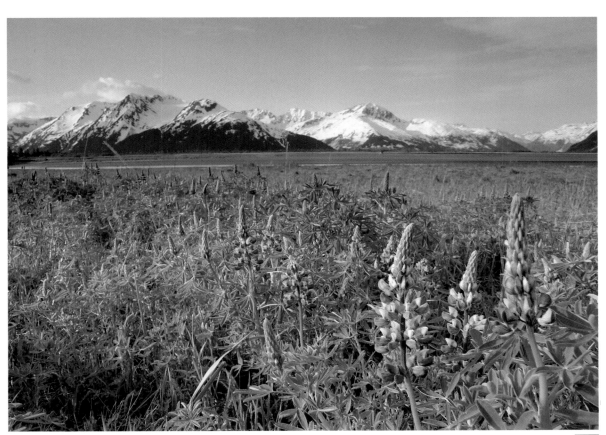

6-10

Getting a good black is not an either/or choice. It is a choice based on craft (how you work a photo), subject and composition influences (both affect what should be black), and creativity (your personal approach to an image). If you think about setting the blacks, your mind is more fluid and, I believe, more likely to see the whole idea of black differently. I have found from my workshops that photographers seem to respond better to the idea of "setting the blacks" versus setting a black point.

PRO TIP

For much of your work in the Develop module, you may find it best to hide the left panel of Presets. This gives you a larger image space for your central work area, plus it removes distractions from the processing. You get a cleaner image of the photo you are working on.

SETTING BLACKS AND WHITES

Once you have selected the proper image in Library, or from the filmstrip at the bottom, click on the Basic group of controls in Develop to open them as shown in figure 6-11. This shows you color (including white balance) first. I recommend doing that second, as color and the impact of color on you and the viewer is strongly affected by the blacks and whites in the photo unless your image looks way out of color because of a wrong white balance setting. Then you need to correct that off-color first.

Start with Exposure and Blacks in the Tone group (in the Basic section). Use Exposure to affect the whites (and highlights) and Blacks to adjust the blacks.

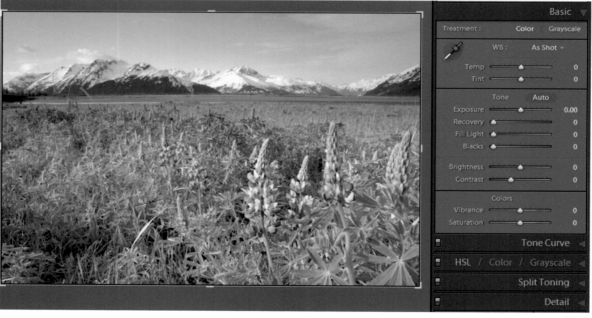

6-11

I really prefer to set my blacks first as it affects so much else in the photo, and then do whites. Plus, setting blacks is more flexible and subjective than setting most whites. Here's how to do blacks, then whites:

1. **Hold down the Alt/Option key and click and drag the Blacks slider right or left as needed.**
   The white screen that appears (shown in figure 6-12) is a threshold screen showing where blacks are beginning to appear (colors are simply where color channels have reached their maximum darkness). Read this by watching where the blacks appear and comparing that to the actual image (release Alt/Option). Don't worry if the image looks dark at this point.

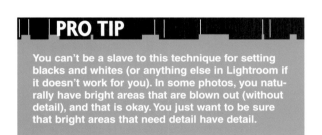

PRO TIP

You can't be a slave to this technique for setting blacks and whites (or anything else in Lightroom if it doesn't work for you). In some photos, you naturally have bright areas that are blown out (without detail), and that is okay. You just want to be sure that bright areas that need detail have detail.

2. **Tweak the blacks by going back and forth from the threshold display to color (alternately pressing and releasing Alt/Option) and seeing what is happening to the image.** How much to bring the blacks in is totally dependent on what you expect from the photo and your style. There is no absolute.

3. **Now work the whites.** Hold down the Alt/Option key and click and drag the Exposure slider to the left or right to bring in the white. The black screen that appears first is the threshold screen (as shown in figure 6-13) showing where whites are beginning to appear (colors are simply where color channels have reached their brightest). I find that white adjustment is more sensitive than blacks. In most photos, I suggest moving the slider until the screen is mostly black and the whites (or colors) just barely begin to appear. Still, this is subjective, and you have to decide what the photo needs. Lightroom is also quite good at bringing detail out of bright areas, so if you have extreme brightness that first registers as white, you might be able to use Recovery to get the whites right (which is covered later in this chapter).

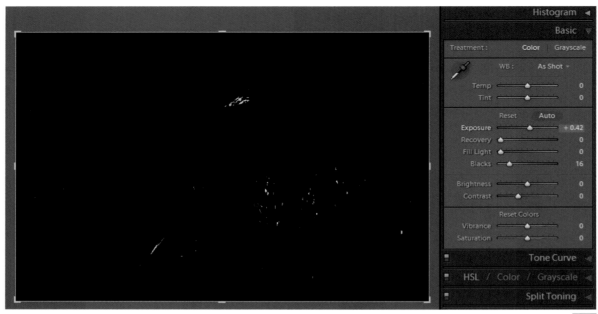

6-13

It really pays to remember that you are not perma-
nently adjusting pixels here. You are just defining
a set of instructions for Lightroom about adjustments to the photograph. That means when you
have made other adjustments that make your
blacks look wrong, for example, you can go back
and readjust the blacks at any time.

ADJUSTING MIDTONES

Once you have your blacks and whites set, you
need to adjust midtones. Midtones include everything between black and white. They are often
grouped into sections according to brightness, from
shadow to middle tones to highlight tones. Midtone
adjustment affects the overall tone, and therefore, the
colors of the image, plus the contrast. Setting blacks
and whites does affect contrast and color, too, which
is why you need to do that first.

Midtones are set four ways: Recovery, Fill Light,
Brightness and Contrast (they work well together),
and the Tone Curve. Brightness and Contrast are better than Brightness/Contrast in Photoshop, but still
not my preference for midtones. They are a little too
rough in effect for my taste, but I do use them for
simple, quick adjustments to an image that doesn't
need a lot of midtone change at this point.

Brightness affects the brightness of an image through
its midtones. Avoid making extreme changes with this
control. If you need strong adjustment, do it through
the Tone Curve. If you are trying to affect the brightest
and darkest tones (not blacks and whites), then use
Recovery and Fill Light. Contrast affects the overall
contrast of the photo by changing the contrast of midtones. Again, if you need strong adjustment, do it
through the Tone Curve.

RECOVERY AND FILL LIGHT

Recovery and Fill Light are two extremely useful controls of Develop. They affect the highlight and shadow tones respectively, and can really make a difference in gaining detail in those areas. They are quite easy to use. Increasing the Recovery values works to pull out added detail from the brightest areas of the image without affecting anything else and without making pure whites gray. I recommend enlarging the photo by going to Loupe view and clicking on the image in an area where you want to find more highlight detail as shown in figure 6-14.

Increasing Fill Light values pulls out detail from the darkest areas of the image, also without affecting anything else or making pure blacks gray. This can be a very useful way of opening up dark areas in an image as shown in figure 6-15.

A caution, however: increasing Fill Light too much makes an image look unnatural and instantly tells your viewer that you "did something" to the photo. Try boosting Fill Light to 100 and you can see what I mean. Lower numbers can make an image look just as odd, but the actual amount is dependent on the photo. Also, as you work Recovery and Fill Light, you may want to recheck your blacks to be sure they are still where you want them to be.

PRO TIP

Most controls in Lightroom are "scrubbable," especially in Develop. What this means is that if you put your cursor over the numbers box for a control, it turns into an adjustment cursor (you see it change to a double-arrow with a hand), and then you can click and drag the control directly without typing in numbers or clicking exactly on the slider.

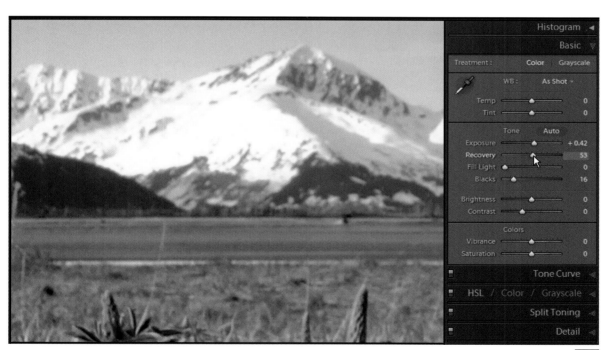

6-14

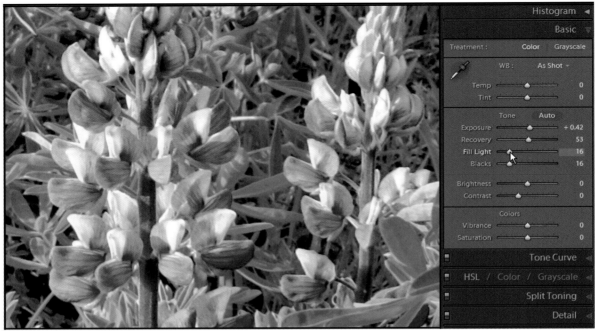

6-15

TONE CURVE WORK

Lightroom brings a totally new approach to using curves in the Tone Curve section of the right panel that is unlike anything you have seen before in Photoshop or Camera Raw. Some of this has been added to Photoshop CS3. It looks more complex than the traditional Curves of Photoshop as shown in figure 6-16, but I believe these changes have made this control far easier to use for photographers. The curve graph also includes an overlay of the image luminance histogram for photographers who like to use it.

The truly easiest way to use the Tone Curve is to skip over to Presets on the left panel as shown in figure 6-17, go to the Tone Curve choices, and quickly pick something most appropriate for your image and tastes. Presets are predefined adjustments and can be used as a starting point for working midtones. In Presets, you see four choices for Tone Curve:

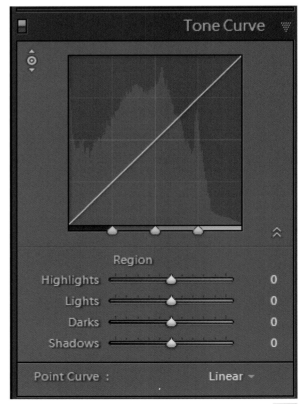

6-16

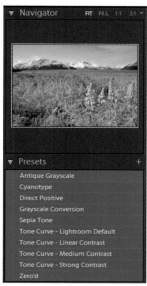

6-17

Once you've picked a preset for the Tone Curve, one way to work it is to refine it with the sliders. Sliders include Highlights, Lights, Darks, and Shadows. One thing that is really cool about these sliders is how their area of adjustment shows up on the Tone Curve. As soon as your cursor moves over one of these controls, a shaded area showing where it works appears on the Tone Curve graph as shown in figure 6-18. That makes this so much easier to understand, as you can see immediately where the control is going to change the curve. Here are some tips on using these four sliders:

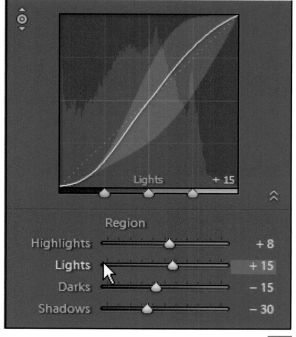

6-18

> **Lightroom Default.** This has a very slight adjustment to the curve, dropping the darkest tones slightly. This gives a nice increase to the contrast of many photos and can be a good place to start.

> **Linear Contrast.** This is the standard, straight-line curve of Photoshop. It gives a flatter look to the image than the default does, and may be what you need for your image. I find that it is often a little too flat as final adjustment, but it comes in handy for more contrasty images and when skin tones of portraits are looking harsh. I will use it to get the curve back to a straight line when working the curve more intensely as described in the next section.

> **Medium Contrast.** This drops the dark tones farther than Lightroom Default and raises the bright tones slightly, with little change through the middle. I find it works well as a starting point for many nature scenes.

> **Strong Contrast.** This increases the effect of Medium Contrast, dropping the dark tones a little more and brightening the light tones a bit. Its increase in contrast is great for low-contrast scenes.

> **Choose a slider to work with based on the photo.** If the highlights seem to be the biggest issue, start with them. If the light midtones mainly need brightening, work the Lights first. If the dark midtones really are the challenge, go to that slider. If the shadows could be darker or lighter to better affect the look of the image, go with them. However, you can't go wrong with any of them, as you can always readjust as you go.

> **Go directly to the curve if you are familiar with traditional Curves.** As you move your cursor along the curve, you see the same shaded areas for adjustment showing up, plus you see the terms — Highlights, Lights, Darks, and Shadows — appear at the bottom of the graph. You can click and drag the curve at any point.

> **Use the quarter-tone sliders.** Another way of looking at midtones is to see them as quarter tones (tones can be divided in many ways — the Tone Curve uses four sections, hence the term *quarter tone*). These are marked with sliders at the bottom of the Tone Curve and can be clicked and dragged as seen in figure 6-19. Each one then mainly affects the curve in the area above them.

ADJUSTING THE TONE CURVE BY DRAGGING IN THE PHOTO

My favorite part of the Tone Curve in Develop, and this is really a very cool new way of dealing with image curves, is to move the cursor directly over the photo and click and drag to change the curve shape from there. That's right! You can change the curve by going into the photo to the areas that need the adjustment. This has never been possible before and makes this control much more photographic rather than technical.

The adjustment is really easy to use. Click on the small bulls-eye at the top left of the Tone Curve area to access this control. In figure 6-20, you see the cursor has changed its form, and the Tone Curve now has an area highlighted appropriate to the part of the photo that the cursor is on. Now when you click and drag the cursor on the actual image in the exact part of the tones and colors you want to adjust, the Tone Curve changes with it, moving up as you move the cursor toward the top of the photo, down as you move the cursor down in the photo, as shown in figure 6-21. Finally, if you make an adjustment in one area, and then move the cursor to another tonality in the photo, the Tone Curve immediately updates and allows you to adjust there as well, shown in figure 6-22.

I believe this part of Tone Curve is a revolutionary way of dealing with midtones and is well worth spending some time trying it out. It truly is highly photographic because you are going directly into the photo to deal with the midtones as you move your cursor around rather than adjusting a curve that is separate (and visually very different) from the image itself.

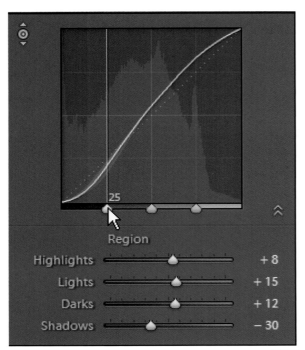

6-19

Region

Highlights		+ 8
Lights		+ 15
Darks		+ 12
Shadows		− 30

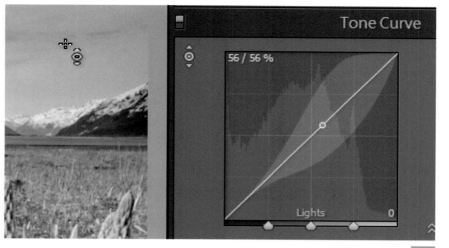

6-20

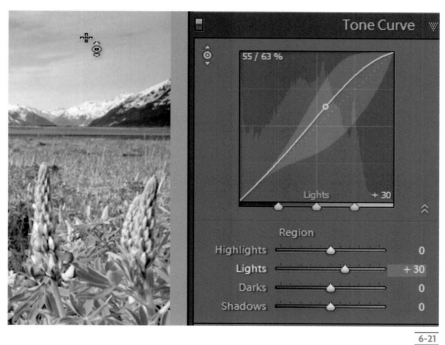

6-21

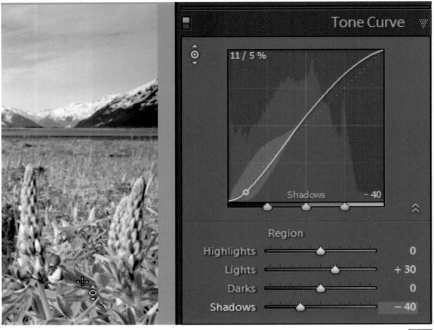

6-22

COLOR SETTINGS

It is easy to look at Lightroom, Photoshop, or Camera Raw and consider color to be a separate function from tonal adjustments simply because there are separate color controls. However, it is really important to understand that color is tightly associated with tonalities in a photo. If your blacks and whites are not set properly, then colors do not have the right snap and vibrancy. If midtones are not adjusted first, colors never look quite right.

This has been a real problem in nature photography, especially as photographers make the transition to digital. Many photographers wanted the look of Velvia slide film and would try to do this by using saturation alone. That is not the best approach and often gives garish rather than saturated color. A different misinterpretation of digital came from photojournalists who thought that cameras captured color accurately so they thought they were being pure by not adjusting color. That also is not the best approach because it often gave inaccurate colors based on an arbitrary interpretation of a scene by the camera.

I believe good color starts with blacks and whites, period. Once they are set and midtones adjusted for the image, then you can work color. Lightroom offers you multiple ways to adjust color in your photo. Each is valuable in its own way. First I discuss what your choices are, and then I go into specifics on how you can best use them. Lightroom has these color controls on the right side of the Develop module:

> **NOTE**
>
> These color controls are not grouped in one location but are found in the Basic, HSL/Color/Grayscale, Split Toning, and Camera Calibration groups.

> **White Balance Selector.** This is an eyedropper in the Basic section that lets you quickly color-correct images as shown in figure 6-23.

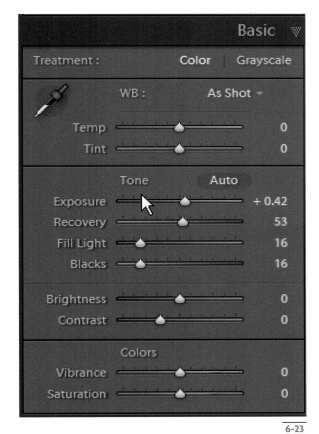

6-23

> **Color in the Basic Group.** This includes White Balance (WB), Temp, Tint, Vibrance, and Saturation as shown in figure 6-23. Temp and Tint are really subsets of White Balance. You can also change a photo to black and white here by using the Grayscale button.

> **HSL Color Tuning.** This is a wonderful color section that offers a huge amount of control, but it may be too much for many photographers. I discuss it in Chapter 7.

> **Split Toning.** A lot of people thought this was only for black and white images when Lightroom first came out as a beta, but it offers some interesting controls for color photos, too. I discuss it in Chapter 7.

> **Camera Calibration.** This is a misleading name for a control that comes directly from Camera Raw that can help refine the colors of an image. I discuss it in Chapter 7.

WHITE BALANCE COLOR ADJUSTMENTS

White Balance is a terrific tool for the digital photographer. It is one of the truly digital innovations that makes photography better. It wasn't that long ago that any photographer had some serious challenges making colors look just right in conditions that weren't optimum for the film. Slide film, especially, had a very low tolerance for out-of-whack lighting colors. The term was *color balance* for film, but White Balance does the same thing. *White balance* simply refers to making white and neutral tones neutral.

With White Balance controls, both in the camera and in the computer, problem colors under normal lighting are largely a thing of the past. Any photographer who has shot under fluorescent lighting, for example, will remember how hard it is to get good color. Now you can easily get natural color in situations that would have required a great deal of work in the past with color filtration over the lens, color temperature meters, film tests, and so on.

There are two basic ways to deal with the color balance of an image in Lightroom:

> **Quick-and-easy.** Use the White Balance Selector tool in the Basic group.

> **Ultimate control.** Use the White Balance controls in the same group.

QUICK-AND-EASY COLOR CORRECTION

The White Balance Selector tool acts like similar tools in Camera Raw and Photoshop. You simply click something in the photo and the program adjusts the image so that whatever you clicked becomes a neutral tone and everything else in the image adjusts accordingly. Here's how to use it:

1. **Select the White Balance Selector tool by clicking the icon or pressing W.** The White Balance Selector tool is that giant eyedropper icon in the Basic group. Well, maybe not giant, but it really is large and not in proportion with the rest of the settings. Check the toolbar and uncheck Auto Dismiss as shown in figure 6-24. Be sure Show Loupe is checked.

2. **Move the cursor over the image.** You see a block of colors appear next to it (this is from Show Loupe and can be changed with the Scale slider) as shown in figure 6-24. This shows you the color pixels that the White Balance Selector is looking at so you can look for something that should be a neutral white, gray, or black without color cast. The center pixel is the actual one that the control uses for adjustment.

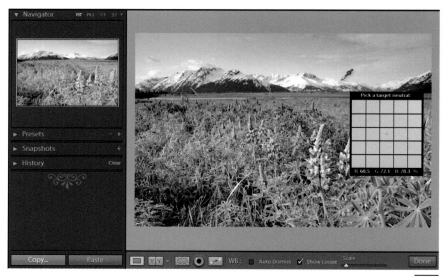

6-24

3. **Watch the Navigator for overall color changes.**
As you move the cursor over the image, the potential change is reflected in the Navigator preview as shown in figure 6-24. The change does not occur on the image until you actually click the mouse.

4. **Find what might work best and click that tone.**
The whole image shifts in color as shown in figure 6-25. If it looks good (or close), click Done. You can now tweak that color slightly in the Basic group.

5. **If the image color does not appear to be corrected properly or even looks really bad, just try clicking a different spot.** Sometimes you have to click multiple locations for this to work its best.

Keep going if a click or two doesn't give you the results you want. Do remember where you click because you might get a good, though not perfect, result that you want to go back to.

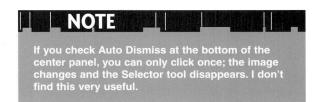

NOTE

If you check Auto Dismiss at the bottom of the center panel, you can only click once; the image changes and the Selector tool disappears. I don't find this very useful.

Very often the White Balance Selector tool gives you excellent results all by itself. Other times you have to do more adjusting with the white balance adjustments of Basic.

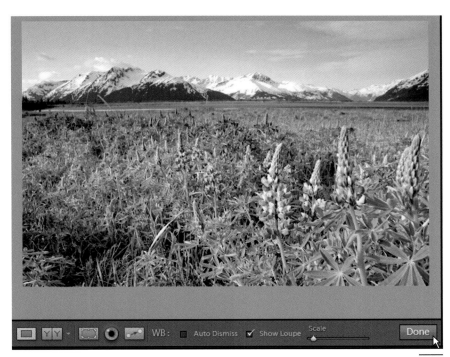

6-25

WHITE BALANCE CONTROLS IN BASIC

The White Balance section of Basic starts with actual white balance settings based on how your camera shot the scene. You could have shot this with the camera on Auto or a preset such as Sun or Cloudy. The first choice that appears to the right of White Balance is always As Shot. Even if you used Auto, the camera still makes a choice as to how to deal with the color of the light.

Here's how to use the White Balance controls (shown in figure 6-26):

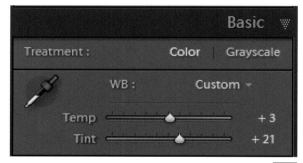

6-26

1. **If the color balance of your photo looks pretty good, leave the White Balance choices alone.** Going through them can quickly increase your work time when you don't need them.

2. **If you are not sure about the overall color of the image, try the White Balance Selector first.** If you click the triangle to the right of Custom, you see Auto as a choice. You can always try it to see if it helps, but I rarely use it because it can be rather arbitrary.

3. **If the photo seems a little too cold (cool) or warm, use Temp to change that.** The photo gets bluer when you move the slider to the left and more amber when you move it to the right. This can also be a creative control to make a photo warmer or colder (cooler) than it was actually shot.

4. **Tint affects a different continuum of color, from green at the left of the slider to magenta to the right.** Unless you have some idea for wacky creative color, normally, you will use this in small amounts. A very common use of this slider is to add magenta to get rid of a greenish cast to the photo.

Whose Color Is That, Anyway?

There is a common misconception that any RAW converter simply takes the information about color coming from the sensor and builds color the same as any other converter. That doesn't happen. Color from a RAW file must be interpreted from the RGB data coming from that sensor. Every RAW converter does this a little differently. Lightroom, like all other Adobe products, has a distinct Adobe flavor to the colors.

This is neither good nor bad, just a difference. It also means that you may want to do certain tweaks to the color balance of an image based on how your personal preferences for color contrast with the way that Lightroom processes color. You might make these adjustments in the White Balance section of Basic or in the other color groups of adjustments below Basic.

VIBRANCE AND SATURATION ADJUSTMENTS

Adobe purchased the very nicely done RawShooter software technology during its development of Lightroom. RawShooter always had a better saturation adjustment than Photoshop in its Vibrance control. Lightroom developers have now included both Vibrance and Saturation under the Colors section in Basic as shown in figure 6-27.

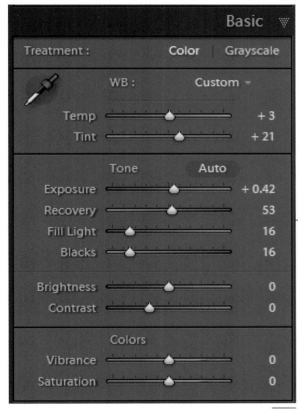

6-27

Equate the Saturation slider with caution. There is a tendency among photographers, especially nature photographers, to boost this saturation control way too much. This is a pretty heavy-handed way of dealing with color. Too much use of this slider can easily

result in gaudy, unattractive colors at worst, and out of place colors at best.

The gaudy bit often comes from photographers adding a little saturation, then a little more, and a little more, until the whole thing gets out of hand. Another way it happens is when an image has one color that recorded poorly, so to compensate, the photographer boosts the Saturation control for that color, making the others look bad. If they don't look bad, then they often look out of place: a color that is not central to the subject (or the composition) gets boosted too much, drawing the eye of the viewer away from what is really important in the image.

Vibrance is a better tool for overall saturation control. Colors look richer and detail does not block up as much when using it. Still, use both sparingly. Keep the Vibrance control in the 0 to 35 range when increasing saturation, and unless you are after some special effect, keep the actual Saturation slider in the 0 to 15 range.

USING SYNC, COPY, AND PASTE

This is a good time to talk about the buttons at the bottom of the left panel: Copy and Paste. They provide really handy ways to adjust multiple photos at once. Frequently, you will have a set of images of a similar subject in the same conditions. If you adjust one photo correctly, you then can adjust them all. This allows you to, in essence, batch-process groups of photos. All of the adjustments in the right-side groups of Develop can be synced to any other images you want. Most of the time, you are largely syncing the core exposure, contrast, and color settings I discuss in this chapter.

Clicking Copy results in a dialog box with the choices shown in figure 6-28. This is where you tell Lightroom what settings to copy to another image. The settings are rather straightforward and reflect the changes made in the Develop module.

Copy Settings

☑ White Balance   ☑ Treatment (Color)   ☐ Spot Removal

☑ Basic Tone   ☑ Color   ☐ Crop
  ☑ Exposure   ☑ Saturation   ☐ Straighten Angle
  ☑ Highlight Recovery   ☑ Vibrance   ☐ Aspect Ratio
  ☑ Fill Light   ☑ Color Adjustments
  ☑ Black Clipping
  ☑ Brightness   ☑ Split Toning
  ☑ Contrast
    ☑ Lens Corrections
☑ Tone Curve   ☑ Chromatic Aberration
  ☑ Lens Vignetting
☑ Sharpening
  ☑ Calibration
☑ Noise Reduction
  ☑ Luminance
  ☑ Color

[Check All] [Check None]   [Copy] [Cancel]

6-28

Here's how to use Copy:

1. **Make your adjustments to a key photo as needed.**

2. **Click Copy and the Copy dialog box appears for you to choose the adjustments you can copy.**

3. **Select as many adjustments as you want by clicking whatever needs to be copied.** You can click Check All to have all included or Check None to clear the list so you can check a few selected adjustments.

4. **Click Copy and the adjustments are saved to memory.**

5. **Ctrl/⌘+click an unadjusted image in the Filmstrip that you want to have the same adjustments applied to, and then click Paste.**

You can also do the same thing to a group of images, but then you must use the Sync command. Sync only appears as an option at the bottom of the right panel once multiple photos are selected. Here's how to sync images:

1. **Make your adjustments to a key photo as needed.**

2. **Select the other photos by Ctrl/⌘+clicking them in the filmstrip at the bottom of the Lightroom interface.** The Sync button now appears at the bottom of the right panel.

3. **Click Sync and the new dialog box appears for you to choose the adjustments you can sync.**

4. **Sync as many adjustments as you want.** The dialog box is the same as the one that appears with Copy. Again, you check whatever adjustments you want to copy or sync among the images.

5. **Click Synchronize and the images will have the same adjustments applied to them.**

WORKING THE DETAIL GROUP

Skip down to the Detail group in Develop as shown in figure 6-29 and you find some important controls — controls that you have to think a bit about before using. Sharpening is something that all digital images need, but the question is: When do you sharpen? Luminance and Color both affect noise reduction in an image.

You have probably heard the admonition not to sharpen an image until you are done working on it. This is because when you are working directly with pixels, some adjustments can affect the quality of sharpening if you do the sharpening too early in the process. In Lightroom, no adjustments affect any pixels until you export the photo from the program; therefore, theoretically, you could sharpen at any time. In fact, as a default, Lightroom applies sharpening instructions to all photos.

Sharpen uses a more advanced algorithm than Unsharp Mask in Photoshop and has absolutely nothing in common with the Sharpen filter in Photoshop. It is a subjective tool as shown by the image in figure 6-30. What one photographer considers too little, another thinks is just right, and both photographers will be correct for their particular subjects and uses of the image. Smaller image files often need less sharpening applied than higher megapixel files.

Be careful not to sharpen too much. One problem that is consistent among pros and amateurs is that if a

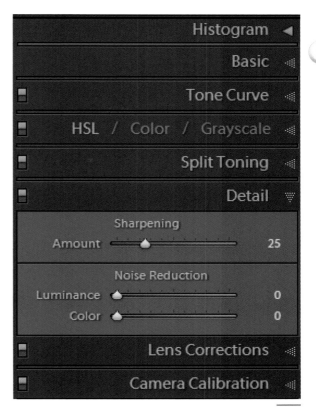

6-29

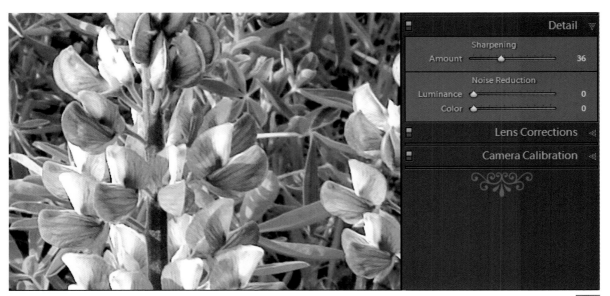

6-30

photo is not quite as sharp as it should be, it has a large amount of sharpening applied, which is usually oversharpening. While it is true that certain subjects, such as a tack-sharp architectural photo or an expansive rocky landscape can handle more sharpening, others, such as people or soft-focus flowers, can't.

You have to decide what is appropriate for your image, but be careful about oversharpening that leads to a harsh quality to fine tonalities. Sharpen in Lightroom cannot be overused to the degree that Unsharp Mask can, but it still can be overdone.

Be especially wary about how you use noise reduction sliders. While both can reduce the appearance of noise in an image, they both remove some of the fine detail in your photo as well. If you have serious noise problems in your photo, I recommend exporting to Photoshop, and then using a specially designed noise reduction plug-in such as Imagenomic Noiseware or Kodak Digital GEM.

However, the Detail group of controls does help when your image just has a small amount of noise. Luminance works on general luminance noise (this looks like sand on your image), while Color works strongly on color or chroma noise (this looks like color speckles on your image). Luminance has only a minor effect on color noise and Color has little effect on luminance noise. Look for noise in under-exposed photos, images shot with high ISO settings, and dark areas of a picture.

I recommend you keep Luminance to less than 30 or you can significantly reduce the appearance of sharpness of small details. You may discover, however, that keeping some noise makes your photo look sharper (this is an old retouching technique — add grain or noise to a slightly out-of-focus image and it looks sharper because the grain or noise is sharp).

I recommend keeping Color even lower: 10 or less, except when you have some strong color noise obscuring other detail. I usually keep it at 0. This control changes tiny color details to match their surroundings — exactly right for noise, but exactly wrong for the real color details in a subject.

USING LENS CORRECTIONS

Lens Corrections is a group of adjustments that you might use often or never. It all depends on the lens itself, the lens/camera combination, how big you want your photo to be used, and the subject. Some lens designs are superb for any use and never need correction. All lenses interact with the sensor in ways that change as you change megapixels. You may find that a certain lens works fine on one camera, but when you use that same lens on a higher megapixel camera, you start to see lens aberrations that weren't visible before. In addition, if your photo is used small, you may never see any lens issues; yet if that same picture is blown up to a big display print, you can see obvious defects along the edges of the composition.

Lens aberrations that need correction typically show up along the edges of the frame. Click your photo to enlarge it, and then move it around until you get to an edge as seen in figure 6-31. An easy way to do that is to go to the small preview image at the upper left and click inside the box showing where the magnified view comes from, and then drag it to an edge. Look for an edge with strong contrasting lines — this is where lens aberrations show up. You might see some color fringing along these edges (which could use correction) or none at all. The image in figure 6-31 is from a full-frame fisheye lens for a small-format digital camera and shows this color fringing at the far corners of the frame when high-contrast subjects are photographed.

If you see colors along the edges (or you just want to see if there are some there) go to Chromatic Aberration in Lens Corrections. For red or cyan fringing, use the Red/Cyan slider; for blue or yellow, the Blue/Yellow slider, as shown in figure 6-32. The algorithms used for this correction are sophisticated and shift pixels when the image is exported to fix the problem. If moving the sliders around has no effect, then you have no aberration problems that Lightroom can affect.

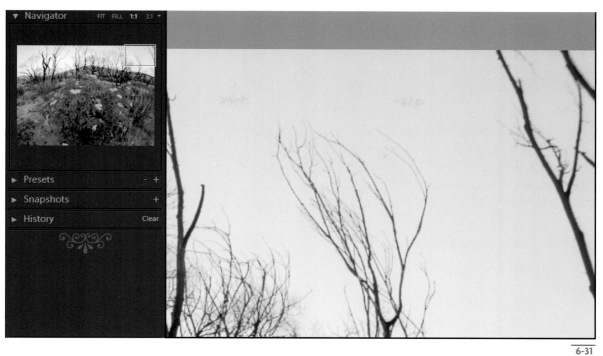

6-31

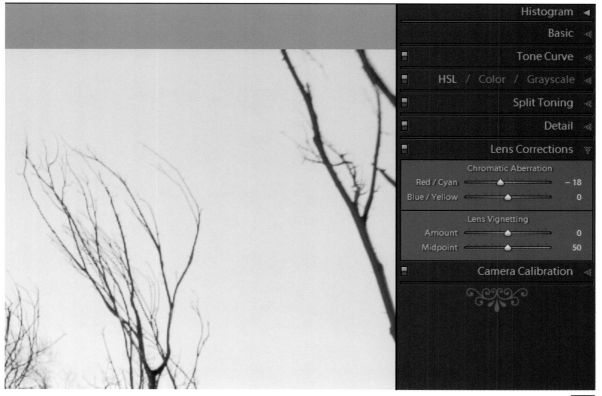

6-32

125

Lens Vignetting deals with an issue sometimes seen in extreme-range zooms as well as full-frame sensors. What happens is that the edges of the photo darken from the way light is transmitted from the lens and received by the sensor.

Be sure your image is seen in its entirety in the central work area. Amount lightens the edges to the right and darkens them to the left. You can use this to correct image edge darkening or to add it for creative effect. Midpoint alters where the center of the change occurs over the whole image.

HISTORY AND SNAPSHOTS

To view History and Snapshots, you need to be sure your left panel is visible. History in the left panel as shown in figure 6-33 is like the History palette in Photoshop. It remembers all the adjustments you do as you do them. You can go back to a specific adjustment, although remember, in Lightroom, you don't necessarily need to. All adjustments are non-destructive, so you can always go back and change anything without harming the quality of the image. Adjustments are instructions only until you export a photo.

History can be helpful in returning to a certain point in your image work or to go back and see what a specific adjustment was. One thing that is quite different about Lightroom's History compared to the one in Photoshop is that Lightroom remembers the history of an image's adjustments so that any time you go back to a photo that has been adjusted, you can quickly check and see what was done. Clearing History removes the record of the adjustments but the adjustments themselves are not affected.

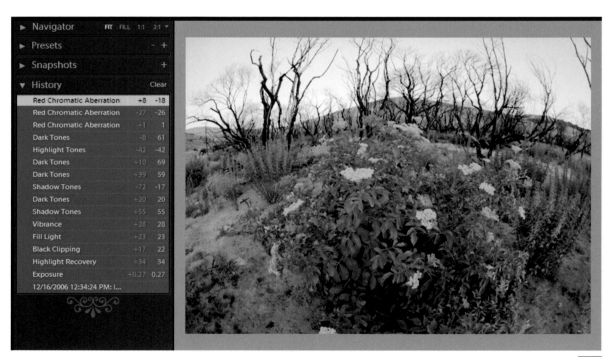

6-33

Snapshots as shown in figure 6-34 is a lot like the photo states in the History palette of Photoshop. It records or saves the state or condition of an image at certain points in your adjustments. You can record these Snapshots of any image as seen in the central work area. This can be when you have reached a certain stage in the process that you want to remember or you can go back to the History, click on a certain point there, and record that adjustment as a Snapshot.

Snapshots is not just about remembering your adjustments. You can also use this as a very powerful tool to try out different adjustments on a photo and compare them (Virtual Copies are another way of remembering different adjustments). Here are some tips for doing that:

> Once you've made an important adjustment, save it by adding it to Snapshots by clicking + and giving it a name in the dialog box that appears.

> Try an alternative adjustment to the original image. Make your new changes, and then save that to Snapshots.

> You don't need to go in order. This is an important and freeing concept when using History. Click any point in History that you want to use as a basis for a new Snapshot.

> Make multiple interpretations of an image, saving each one by adding it to Snapshots. This is like having versions that can be used for a client, for your own experiments, and so on.

X-REF

For more information on using Virtual Copies, see Chapter 11.

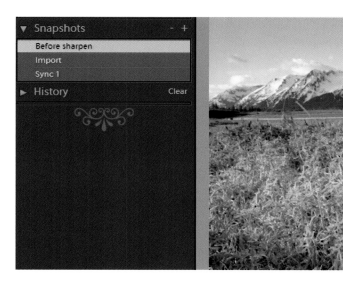

6-34

■ **I remember from earlier in the book that you can turn the panels of Lightroom on and off. What would you recommend for those choices in the Develop module?**

That is absolutely right, but it is not a simple question to answer. This is a highly personal choice. Some photographers like seeing certain parts of the interface open, even if they aren't using it, just because it reminds them of things to do. Other photographers turn off whatever they can, thinking that what they are not using is just distracting.

For a lot of the work in Develop, you can certainly hide the bottom Filmstrip by clicking the bottom arrow. You don't really need to know what other photos are waiting for you (and maybe that is even a source of stress!). It is important to have the Filmstrip available if you want to sync images, but you can quickly go back to the Filmstrip by putting your cursor at the bottom of the screen or by clicking the arrow there to bring it back.

In much of Develop, you don't need the preview at the left or the presets. The presets are helpful for Tone Curve use and the preview helps when you have the image magnified. This is less clear when it comes to the value of keeping it open or hidden and really depends on the photographer. Hiding it does allow the center image to show more when it's magnified.

You seem to lump highlights, midtones, and shadows all together as midtones as you control midtones with the Tone Curve. Why?

Traditionally in photography, black and white are considered differently than all the gray tones in an image (or equivalent in colors). You are adjusting black, white, and gray tones separately, so photographers will typically call all the gray tones midtones. The gray tones are between black and white; hence the name midtones.

Highlights in Lightroom are the lighter tones above middle gray, yet they include a little more than pure highlights and actually affect all tones above the middle grays to some degree. Shadows are the darker tones below middle gray, and they also affect brighter tones to some degree. This makes Highlights and Shadows midtone adjustments, no matter what Adobe calls them. Some photographers break up midtones into quarter tones, using such terms as *shadow quarter tones, mid-range quarter tones,* and *highlight quarter tones,* but still all of these are affected by midtone adjustments.

You don't seem to always follow the exact order of controls on the right side of Develop. I would think the order in Lightroom had a specific purpose.

It does. The controls are grouped by type of control from a Lightroom perspective. However, I am a firm believer in working an image based on its needs and teaching that philosophy rather than purely following the program. When working an image in the Develop module, I think photographers are best served by doing adjustments based on the very photographic approach:

> Set blacks

> Check whites

> Adjust midtones

> Correct color

> Enhance color

These are how a photographer looks at an image, but they do not follow how Lightroom organizes the tools.

Chapter 7

ADDED PROCESSING IN THE DEVELOP MODULE

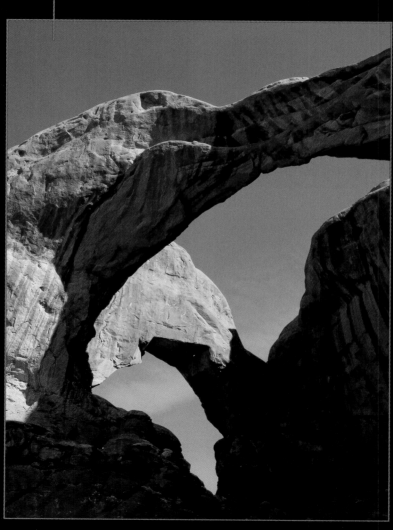

You can do a great deal of work on images using only the core processing features of Lightroom that are discussed in Chapter 6. If you want to keep work in Lightroom simple, you can stop there and skip this chapter.

However, this chapter covers some added, distinctive features that can really help you get the most from your images. While Camera Calibration is imported from Camera Raw, the rest is new and unique to Lightroom. In addition, in this chapter, you also learn about the excellent black and white conversion capabilities of Lightroom that offer very high-quality black and white images.

HSL/COLOR/GRAYSCALE

This section probably has the most variety of inter-related controls in Lightroom, let alone the Develop module. HSL/Color/Grayscale is shown in figure 7-1 and is definitely very powerful in its capabilities to affect colors. This is a key area to understand if you really want to affect color in an image. For nature photographers and others who love the saturated colors of Velvia and the old Kodachrome, this is the place to go. And for any photographers who need to correct specific colors that weren't captured properly by a digital camera (and that is pretty common), this is the place to make corrections.

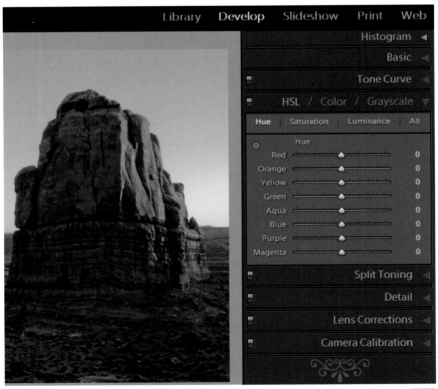

7-1

> **HSL.** At first, HSL looks very complex because it can change the hue, saturation, and luminance (HSL) of eight different colors: red, orange, yellow, green, aqua, blue, purple, and magenta. When you click HSL in the Category bar, it becomes the active item. You see tabs for Hue, Saturation, Luminance, and All. Tabs for the first three each have sliders to control the eight colors. If you click the All tab, you see 24 different sliders because this view groups all the controls together.

> **Color.** If you click Color instead of HSL in the Category bar, you get a new way of looking at the same Hue, Saturation, and Luminance controls, but now all three are seen at once, as shown in figure 7-2. This option groups the controls by color rather than type of control. I can't say that one method is better than the other — it really does depend on the needs of the individual photographer as well as how he or she likes to work with color. I prefer the HSL grouping that keeps hue, saturation, and luminance separate because it lets me do saturation changes on different colors all at one time. That is a stronger need for me than changing the hue.

7-2

> **Grayscale.** The third part of this right-panel group in the Develop module is Grayscale. This changes an image to black and white and offers some quite powerful controls for better black and white conversions. I cover this later in the chapter.

Don't be intimidated by all of these controls. What HSL does is pretty simple — it changes specific ranges of color by the color itself (hue), the intensity of that color (saturation), and its brightness (luminance). What makes the controls complex are all the choices. This control is like Camera Calibration (explained later in the chapter), but with more capabilities.

That said, if you know Photoshop, you can simplify how the HSL part of this group of controls works in a hurry. The Hue/Saturation control of Photoshop is a common way to adjust color. If you use it for specific colors rather than overall adjustment (in other words, use the drop-down menu of colors from Master and not adjust in Master), you have a great deal of control over the individual colors in a photo.

That is exactly what HSL offers. Photoshop's Hue/Saturation has the same choices, but you don't see them all available at once like you do here. Having them all out in the open makes it easy to go from color to color, but it does mean you have to find your color amongst all these choices!

There is no step-by-step approach to using the HSL controls because the colors that need adjustment in your photo influence which specific sliders you use and how. Here are some ideas, though, that can help you master HSL:

> **Start by using your photo and subject as a guide.** What colors need tweaking in your photograph? What colors are not registering correctly? Are any inaccurate? Do any need intensifying to make them look better? Are any colors too intense and take away attention from other colors?

> **Work one color at a time.** Look at your photo. So often photographers using Photoshop see a weak color and try to make it look better by increasing saturation of the whole image — not the best approach. This tool forces you to work each color separately, which is how it should be. Figure 7-3 shows saturation being adjusted only on the red rocks of Arches National Park at sunrise (which

happen to be orange rather than red because of the yellow of the rising sun) and the blue sky. Such individual adjustment gives you so much more control, plus it complements how digital cameras really work, which is that they don't deal with colors equally in a way that would match what we see with our eyes.

> **Use the photo for direct color control.** Just as in the Tone Curve, HSL can use your cursor to recognize and adjust color directly on the image. This is a very cool feature and makes the color adjustment very responsive to how you look at your photo. Click the button slightly above and to the left of the word "Red" to access this. Then click on the color in the photo that you want to adjust, and drag the cursor up or down to make the adjustment more or less, respectively. In figure 7-4, you can see the blue sky of this scene being adjusted. This will adjust hue, saturation, or luminance, depending on which part of HSL you are in.

> **Fix inaccurate colors.** Certain colors cause problems for digital sensors. Consistently, certain blues and violets record inaccurately. This can be important for nature or documentary photographers who want to get a color right, and can be critical for advertising photographers who need to match a client's color needs.

PRO TIP

I find altering the hue of these colors very helpful in nature photography. It is very common, for example, for flowers to record as a color that is not accurate. This adjustment lets you correct that. Also, I find that a number of digital cameras tend to record greens too yellow. This adjustment also lets you correct that.

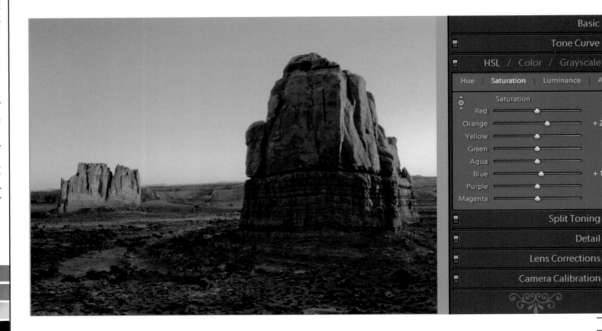

7-3

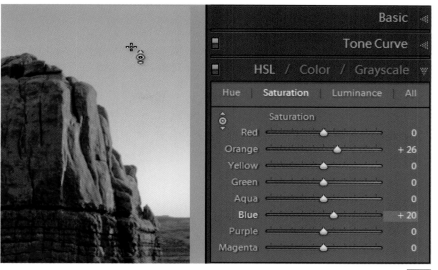

7-4

> **Use the order Hue, Saturation, Luminance for individual color correction.** Use Hue for your color if the color is off in its actual color (for example, a pure green looks blue-green) and needs correction. Once the "color of the color" or hue is right, go to Saturation to affect its intensity. Increase or decrease its intensity so that the color is optimized or enhanced for your composition and subject. Use Luminance to make the color brighter or darker.

> **Fix color imbalances.** It is very common in a photograph to have some colors record inappropriately compared to others. This is not the same as inaccurate colors — the colors can be accurate as to hue, for example, but record too saturated or too bright compared to another color. Reds are a good example of this — they are often out of balance from other colors. You can change this in HSL quite nicely.

> **Use the Before and After views.** It is very easy to over-enhance the saturation of a color by adjusting a little at a time while your eye adjusts to each change. If you have a reference (the Before), you are less likely to do that. Lightroom offers a great way of seeing before and after by clicking the Before and After view mode button in the toolbar, as shown in figure 7-5. This button is the second from the left, under the central image. This view mode actually gives you multiple ways of seeing a before and after; figure 7-5 is just one of them. You can cycle through them by clicking the view button and see which ones you like best.

A note on the Before and After views: I tend not to use this a lot for early adjustments because I am looking for some different things from how the whole image looked before and after I started adjusting. I like to use it with color adjustments, such as the example here, because color can be such a critical thing. Slight changes in hue or saturation can significantly alter the look of a photo, yet slight changes can be hard to see without a reference. The Before and After views give exactly that reference.

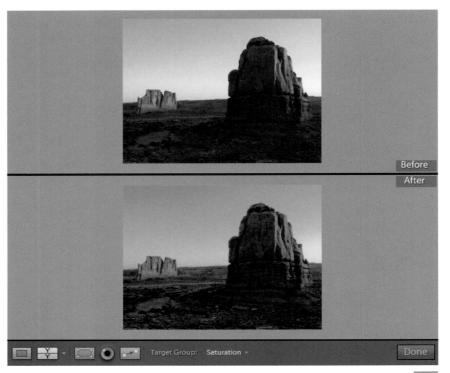

7-5

PRO TIP

To identify more precisely what color or colors need adjustment, find that color in the photo. How do you do that? One way is to use the Saturation tab. Click on a color that you think might be correct and move the slider all the way to the left, removing its color. You then see gray in the photo. If that shows the right parts of the photo, you know you have the correct color. You can also click and drag in the photo, clicking on a color, and then dragging it to zero saturation. See if that shows the correct parts of the image; then you also know the correct color by looking at which one in the list changed. Undo either of these saturation removal changes by pressing Ctrl/⌘+Z or resetting the number to 0.

SPLIT TONING FOR COLOR

Split Toning is a very effective new tool for Lightroom. I don't use it for every photograph, but for the ones that respond well to this control, it's great. A lot of photographers use this for black and white photos, to give them some very effective color toning effects, and many quit there. I like it for its color effects.

Split toning lets you affect the color of highlights and shadows separately, as shown in figure 7-6. You can go wild and wacky with these adjustments, making your subject look totally different in color, or you can use them to enhance and optimize the existing colors. I mostly do the latter because that is most appropriate to my work, and it can really add a finishing touch to an image. But the choice is yours.

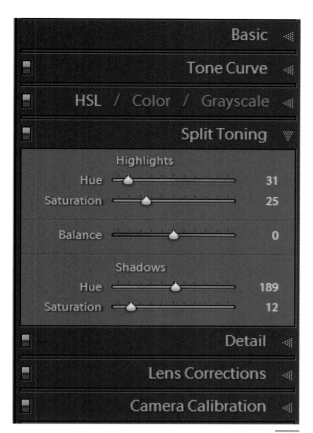

7-6

Here's what happens in this control. You work both the hue and saturation of the overall color of highlights and shadows separately. No effect occurs, however, until Saturation is moved above 0.

Here's how I like to work with Split Toning:

> **Start with Highlights.** Unless I know I really want mainly to affect dark tones, I start with Highlights because the effect is easier to see.

> **Move Saturation to around 40 or 50.** You're not going to use one of these numbers unless you want a special effect. However, the hue changes are easiest to see when this control is set to at least 40, as seen in figure 7-7. You have to have some number other than 0 in order to choose Hue.

> **Adjust Hue.** Change the color of your highlights as appropriate to your subject. For example, outdoor scenes often look quite nice with added warmth to the highlights, so you can add more yellow to amber there.

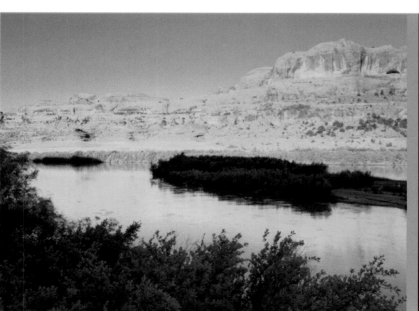

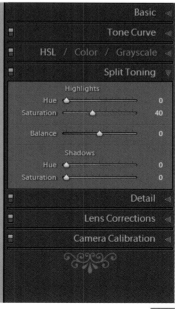

7-7

> **Move Saturation down to an appropriate level.** How much you move it down depends on your scene. I like to move the slider back to 0, and then start reintroducing the highlight color change until the photo looks good, as shown in figure 7-8.

> **Go to the Shadows sliders and move Saturation to around 40 or 50.** Again, you're not going to use one of these numbers unless you want a special effect; you're just making the hue changes easier to see and choose, as seen in figure 7-9 where the slider is set to 45.

> **Adjust Hue.** Change the color of your shadows as appropriate to your subject. For example, outdoor scenes often look quite nice with added cool tones to the shadows, which gives depth to the colors of a scene, so you can add more blue there.

> **Move Saturation down to an appropriate level.** How much you move it down depends on your scene. I like to move the slider back to 0, and then start reintroducing the shadow color change until the photo looks good. I often find that unless I have a problem with shadow colors, they usually look better with Saturation at a lower number than the Highlights Saturation. Additionally I often find I need to readjust the Highlights Saturation to balance the change in Shadows, as shown in figure 7-10.

> **Turn on the Before and After views.** I feel you can't properly adjust this control without these views, also shown in figure 7-10.

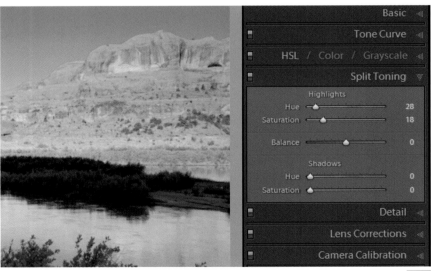

7-8

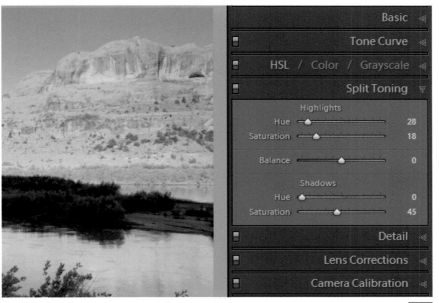

7-9

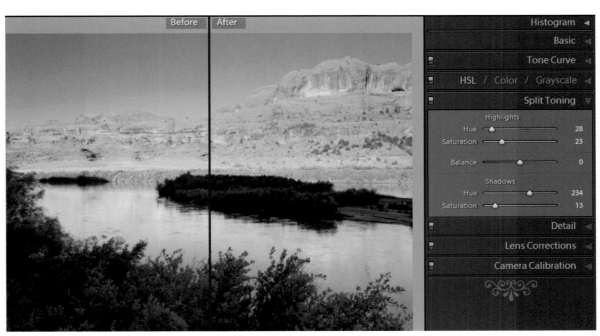

7-10

CAMERA CALIBRATION

Camera Calibration is another useful color-adjustment part of the Develop module (and even Camera Raw), but with the addition of the HSL group, I find I use Camera Calibration less. While it supposedly is for tweaking how a camera sees colors (hence the name), most photographers use it for other purposes, so the name seems misleading at first.

The camera sensor itself and the camera's A/D converter affect how that camera responds to color. Even camera models from the same manufacturer can have different responses to colors because the sensors are different. Camera Calibration was developed to enable you to affect this color response at a different level from simply changing white balance or saturation. You can adjust the hue and saturation of the primary computer colors of red, green, and blue to, in a sense, "calibrate" a camera for a better color response, as shown in figure 7-11. However, this is much more a computer thing than how photographers normally see pictures.

So, most photographers don't use this control for that purpose. They use it to tweak and affect colors based on a specific subject and scene. And indeed, this gives the photographer another way of working color in an image. Very often if a photograph needs more color saturation, this is a better place to do it than using Saturation in Basic. You can adjust red, green, and blue separately, which frequently gives better colors because you can respond to individual color needs rather than making an overall color adjustment that may help some colors, but might hurt others. However, I think that HSL is more intuitive for the photographer (plus it has that really great click-and-drag-on-the-image color adjustment).

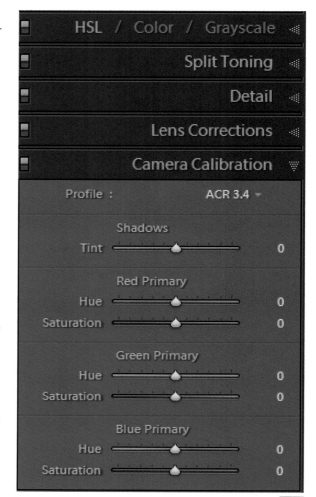

7-11

This potential was strongly illustrated when I recently helped judge the Wildlife Photographer of the Year, a prestigious international competition that attracts some of the top nature photographers in the world. Nature photographers have long liked lively colors like those that came from Velvia. This was evident in the competition from a reoccurring problem — photographers increased the overall saturation to boost the color intensity, but this overall change often over-adjusted one color, making it look out of place and unnatural, even though the other colors looked okay.

That could have been solved using the Saturation control in Camera Calibration. There is no one set of steps to use this, so I can't give you a step-by-step on its use. However, if you understand how it works and what to look for as you work with it, you can quickly benefit from this Lightroom feature. Here's what you need to know:

> **Shadows.** You probably won't use this much. It basically affects the tint of dark tones of your image toward green (left) or magenta (right). If you really want to affect shadows, Split Toning, which I describe earlier in the chapter, offers more control.

> **Primary color hue.** You can fine-tune the hue of each of the primary colors: red, green, and blue (these are primary colors of light, which is what your camera is working with). This can be extremely valuable for cleaning up a color that just won't record right in the camera. You can't make any of these primary colors into another primary color, but you can adjust the range of each one's color characteristics. Hue for red alters red from a magenta red to a yellowish red. Greens go from yellow-green to blue-green. Blues go from blue-green to a magenta.

> **Work more than one hue.** As you adjust a hue, you may find that it affects another color that you do not want changed. Try a different color and adjust it. In fact, often you can use these hue adjustments to fix colors that have become contaminated from other colors from any number of sources.

> **Primary color saturation.** In this case, you can fine-tune color saturation by primary color. This is extremely useful, and frequently, a better way to adjust the color saturation of the image. In the case of the Wildlife Photographer of the Year competition, photographers could have largely solved the problems we found from too much

overall saturation by using these sliders. You may even find that while you need to increase one primary's saturation, you need to decrease another.

> **Use the Before and After displays.** When making color changes like these, you really need to see what is happening to the colors. Sure, you can see the change as it occurs in the center work image, but if you don't have something for comparison, it is easy to over-adjust colors because your eyes compensate for some of the change as you look at the monitor.

PRO TIP

Be cautious about over-adjusting color saturation. Intense color has become very popular in everything from ads to snapshots. If you are doing purely documentary work, then obviously you need to be careful about making colors accurate and not overdone in saturation. Otherwise, increasing saturation is not a problem in and of itself — only when it is done blindly, just to "boost colors" without also watching to see how these colors really look in the image. It is, unfortunately, only a short step from vivid to garish.

CONVERTING COLOR TO BLACK AND WHITE

Black and white photography has seen a real surge in interest. When color began to dominate photography back in the 1970s, black and white was seen by many as old and antiquated. Photographers quit doing it, darkrooms were closed up, and black and white as a creative option was seen as an oddity and not something most photographers did.

In recent years, black and white has seen new popularity. Some people are even opening up old darkrooms. Black and white film is still being used.

You don't have to shoot black and white in film or digital (in cameras that allow this). You can get very high-quality black and white images from color when you use Lightroom. Some photographers imply that somehow this is "cheating" and you lose the discipline of the craft of shooting black and white from the start. I would say that converting color to black and white still requires a disciplined approach in order to do it well, as shown in figure 7-12 and figure 7-13, plus it offers some excellent and versatile options in getting black and white tonalities that you can't get if you shoot black and white from the start.

There is no question that some photographers have made a real art from photographing in black and white from the start. If this suits you, then go for it. All of the tonal controls in Develop (blacks, whites, and midtone adjustments) discussed in this chapter and Chapter 6 apply to processing a pure black and white image. Plus, you can use split-toning to give very nice color effects to shadows and highlights in a black and white photo.

For many photographers, though, shooting color and then converting to black and white presents a strongly creative workflow that offers added control options. When colors in the world are changed to black and white tones in the camera (whether you shoot film or digital), you are locked into those tones. When you shoot in color and translate colors to black and white tones in Lightroom, you have many more options on how they make that translation.

For example, if you shoot a red flower in black and white, you can, through the use of filters, change the tone from light to dark, but then you are stuck with that tone. If you shoot a red flower in color and then bring it into Lightroom for conversion to black and white, you can change it to a range of tones as needed. You are not limited to the tone as shot.

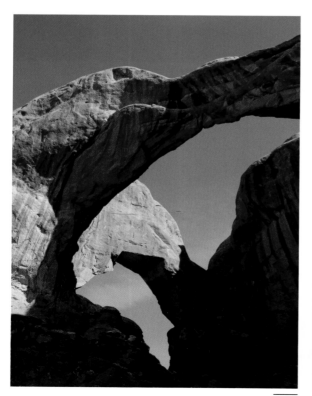

7-12

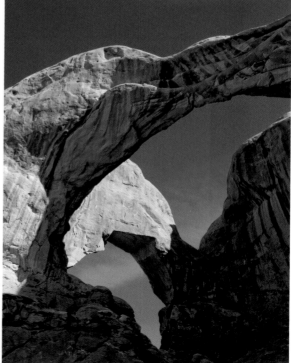

7-13

Using Grayscale in HSL/Color/Grayscale

Lightroom's primary way of changing color to black and white is Grayscale in the HSL/Color/Grayscale group on the right side of the Develop module. You can also convert to grayscale (black and white) in Basic, but I don't recommend this "auto black and white" option. It uses a similar set of changes to what you might get from the Grayscale mode in Photoshop and none of the controls you will find in the Grayscale section of the HSL/Color/Grayscale group.

While the automated Basic Grayscale works, I would not use it for anything except basic black and white. Simply accepting the "auto" translation may give you black and white, but I find it rarely gives the optimum black and white tones for a particular subject and scene's colors. How colors translate to tones of gray has a huge effect on the effectiveness of a black and white photo. Compare figure 7-14 with figure 7-13. This new translation is okay as that simple, auto black and white conversion, but is not nearly as effective.

Remember that ultimately, black and white is about color and how that color changes. If you remember that, the Grayscale Mix shown in figure 7-15 is fairly easy to use. (However, ease of use and mastery of use are different things — practice helps you master this control.) It is set up with sliders to affect how a particular color translates into gray. Moving any slider to the right makes that color a lighter gray in the photo. Moving a slider to the left makes that color a darker gray.

Black and white photography needs contrast, which comes from adjusting these sliders, or everything blends together with the same shades of gray. Yet if you get a group of photographers together who then convert the same scene to black and white, you usually find a set of very different interpretations. Some prefer high contrast; others like more subtle gradations and changes in tone. Black and white should be about interpretation — another reason why Auto

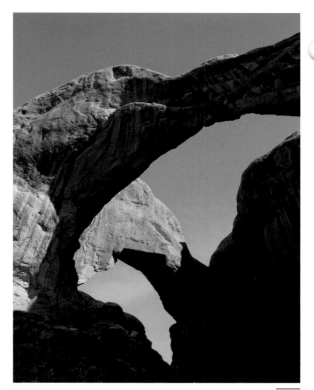

7-14

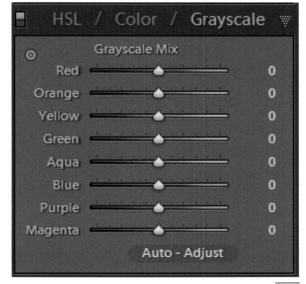

7-15

should be a limited choice for anyone serious about black and white images, although Auto is what comes on first by default. Just don't stay there!

Here are some ideas for you to consider when working with Grayscale in the Develop module:

> **Use the photo for direct color control.** Just as in the Tone Curve and HSL, Grayscale Mix can use your cursor to recognize and adjust color directly on the image. This is an absolutely brilliant feature for black and white conversion. Click the button slightly above and to the left of the word "Red" to access this. Then click on the tone in the photo that you want to make lighter or darker. As you drag the cursor up or down to make the adjustment, Lightroom actually recognizes the appropriate color (or colors) and changes how it translates into grayscale tones! I find that remarkable. In figure 7-16, you can see the red rock of this scene being adjusted. This is one of the best ways of translating color into black and white tones that I know.

> **Use combinations of sliders.** Almost always, I make one color lighter and a different color darker, as shown in figure 7-17. When using several sliders, you also should control exactly which color is affected. By that I mean that often colors in a scene are not always precise matches to specific slider colors. You may find when moving one slider close in hue to that color that the adjustment doesn't work as well as you'd like. So you add a similar color and change it, making it lighter to add to the color range, or darker to limit the range of color affected.

> **Don't be afraid to make big moves with these sliders, even maxing them out.** I like to make big moves because I like contrast in black and white. Some photographers like more subtle effects and never max out these sliders. My point is not that you have to max them out, but that you can do it as needed with no ill effects on the photograph.

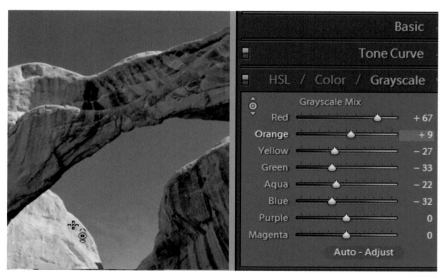

7-16

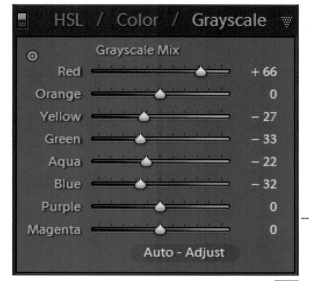

7-17

To get the most out of an image in black and white, you have to still pay attention to the blacks, whites, and midtones, as I discuss in Chapter 6. Simply converting an image to black and white without checking blacks and whites, and setting midtones gives you less than the best results, and you can end up making unneeded adjustments in the Grayscale controls.

GIVING BLACK AND WHITE SOME COLOR

A long tradition in classic black and white photography is color toning. It was done to give the image some color other than just neutral tones, and in many cases, the toning was done to increase the life of the print. Color toning gives black and white photos a different dimension. Some photographers prefer a purely neutral black and white image, but others find color toning gives their photos an added richness.

Color toning is very easy to do in Lightroom. Once you have a black and white conversion, go to Split Toning, as seen in figure 7-18. Highlights now affect mainly the lighter tones in your photo, while Shadows color the darker tones. The Balance control affects how both deal with the entire image, including pure white and pure black. You can use this control with black and white like this:

1. **Get your best black and white conversion first.**

2. **Move Saturation of Highlights up to about 50 percent.** This lets you see the color toning without it being too strong. You won't necessarily keep this setting, but it helps in first adjustments.

3. **Change the Highlights Hue until you like a color tone on your photo.** Warm colors give a sepia tone; bluish colors give a cool tone.

> **Watch out for colors that have similar brightness.** Red and green are the classic examples of this. If you use Auto for a photo that has strong red and green colors, you end up with a plain gray photo with none of the contrast that the colors displayed. Work those colors in the Grayscale Mix so that they separate and appear as different tones.

> **Revise black and white conversions in Basic and Tone Curve.** You won't need to change every black and white conversion, but many times the black and white version of an image needs new black and white points, plus midtone contrast.

> **Turn on the Before and After views.** I find this is often very helpful because I can see where the colors are in the Before. This way I can better decide which sliders to use to make them lighter or darker grays or where to click for direct color control by clicking and dragging.

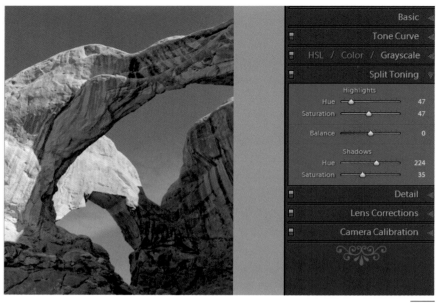

7-18

4. **Refine the Saturation of Highlights.** Move it up or down until you like the effect. If you like the overall color at this point, you don't have to go further — use it as is.

5. **Move Saturation of Shadows up to about 30 percent.** This lets you see its effect on color toning without it being too strong. You also won't necessarily keep this setting, but it helps in first adjustments.

6. **Change the Shadows Hue until you like a color tone on your photo.** Shadows and other dark areas of a black and white photo often look good with a slightly cool tone to them. However, you can also use a similar color to Highlights for a very rich effect as well.

7. **Refine the Saturation of Shadows.** Move it up or down until you like the effect. Usually, I find I like a lower saturation for the color in Shadows.

DEVELOP MODULE PRESETS

Develop adds Presets to the left side panel that are premade controls for certain adjustments and effects that you can use directly with a single click. There are ten presets that come with Lightroom, as shown in figure 7-19, plus you can add your own. Four are related specifically to black and white conversion of color photos, one is for a special image adjustment in color, four help with using the Tone Curve (as I mention in Chapter 6), and one brings all adjustments back to their defaults.

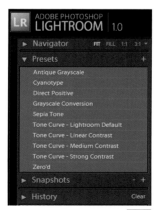

7-19

You can quickly see what any look like by holding your cursor over the preset (don't click) and watching the preview image above the presets. You can apply the presets to the image by clicking any of them. You can get back to the standard Lightroom adjustments by clicking Lightroom Defaults.

The four black and white conversions offer different ways of translating colors and tones to simply using the Grayscale Mix adjustment on the right side of Develop. They include changes to the Tone Curve that Grayscale Mix does not. These presets are

> **Antique Grayscale.** This is a straightforward black and white conversion that you then adjust with Split Toning to give an old look with a warm color, as shown in figure 7-20 (this is similar to, but different from, Sepia Tone). It looks like an old black and white photo, I suppose, with its warm and bright tonality. It uses a strong highlight hue and saturation adjustment in Split Toning that warms up the highlights considerably, while it adds some color to the shadows, too, though a slightly warmer hue with less saturation. It uses a Tone Curve similar to, but slightly lighter from, the Lightroom default.

> **Cyanotype.** Cyanotype refers to an old type of black and white printing that gave a cool-tone image, shown in figure 7-21. In this preset, the black and white conversion is a little darker and moodier than Antique Grayscale. It uses a flat Tone Curve for less contrast. Split Toning is used to give the cool-tone, bluish color in Hue, and then Saturation is used moderately. The shadows do not change in color.

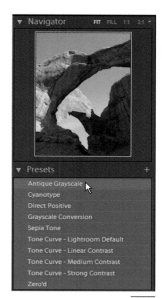

7-20

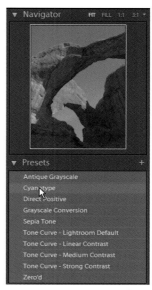

7-21

> **Grayscale Conversion.** This is a straightforward conversion to black and white, as shown in figure 7-22, that changes the auto settings of the Grayscale Mix and brightens the darker parts of the photo by moving the bottom part of the Tone Curve up.

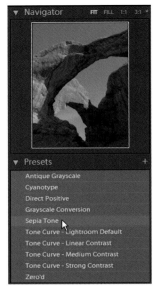

7-23

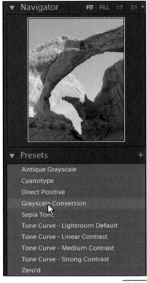

7-22

The special color image preset is

> **Direct Positive.** This gives an overall adjustment to the photo, boosting contrast and color to give a look that is similar to what you expect from slide film, as shown in figure 7-24.

> **Sepia Tone.** This is a darker black and white conversion than the Antique Grayscale or Grayscale Conversion presets, as shown in figure 7-23, that has a Tone Curve much closer to the center, a bit like Medium Contrast in the Tone Curve presets. It then adds a strong warm or sepia tone to the image (a traditional black and white toning), which is similar to Antique Grayscale but has a different look. Sepia Tone uses Split Toning to add the warm color, using the same hue for highlights and shadows, though it has less saturation than Antique Grayscale in highlights, and more in Shadows.

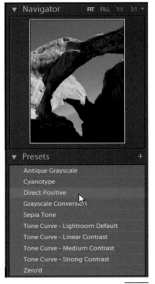

7-24

7

Added Processing in the Develop Module

I describe the four Tone Curve Presets in Chapter 6 as they relate to the use of the Tone Curve. They can be very helpful for resetting the Tone Curve for your use. To summarize, they are

> **Lightroom Default.** This really cranks up the highlights, moves up the middle tones, has no effect on the dark areas, and most of the time makes the bright areas rather bright.

> **Linear Contrast.** This is the standard, straight-line curve of Photoshop. It gives a flatter look to the image than the default, but may be what you need for your image. It can be a good place to start with an image that is a bit contrasty to begin with.

> **Medium Contrast.** This is closer to the default of the Tone Curve in Camera Raw. It drops the dark tones slightly and raises the bright tones also slightly, with little change through the middle. It can be a good starting point for many digital images, especially for most nature scenes.

> **Strong Contrast.** This increases the effect of Medium Contrast, dropping the dark tones a little more and brightening the light tones a bit. It is great for low-contrast scenes.

The last entry in presets, Zero'd, is the same as a Lightroom default and zeros out all settings made in Lightroom on a given photo. As you change an image with any adjustments or use presets, you may feel you just want to get back to the original photo as seen by Lightroom. This is the control that does it.

To get the most from the presets, consider them fast ways to get some adjustments to a photo, even as quick previews if you just run your cursor over them. I find this can generate some ideas on how I might approach a particular photo.

Then use the Preset adjustment as a starting point. If you like it, great, but you often find some additional tweaking helpful to get the most out of a photo.

Consider that these preset adjustments can never "know" what your actual photo is; they can only offer interesting changes that work for many photos and photographers. Your interpretation of them can be very important in getting results that work for your images.

MAKING YOUR OWN PRESETS

Lightroom makes it easy to create your own presets. It is a way to save adjustments that you use regularly and turn them into "presets" to use again and again. If you have certain types of photographs that need regular ways of processing, you may find that creating your own presets (or saved adjustments) for them speeds your workflow.

To create a preset, select a "standard" photo, one that works well for the adjustments you want to use in a preset. Adjust it optimally to create a consistent way to control images for this preset.

To save those adjustments and create your preset, you do this:

1. **Click + at the right of Presets (you remove Presets by clicking –).** A dialog box appears, as shown in figure 7-25, for a new preset that is very similar to the one you saw for the Sync button. It includes nearly all of the adjustments on the right side of Develop.

2. **Choose the settings that you want to use for your preset.** You can simply use them all to match your photo exactly as adjusted. Or you can select just the key adjustments that create the effect you need for your preset.

3. **Type a name for your preset in the Preset Name box, and click Create.** The new Preset now appears in your Preset list.

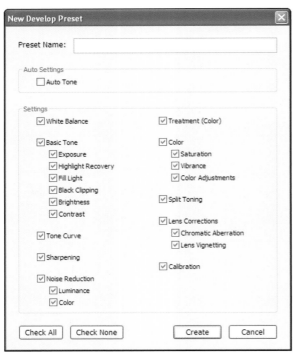

7-25

There are many ways you can make new presets, and you will get ideas for them as you gain experience working images in Lightroom. However, here are some ideas that might help you get started:

> **Create black-and-white conversion presets.** You can set these up to make certain colors lighter or darker. For example, you can get a "red filter" preset by using Grayscale Mix and setting the red and magenta sliders all the way to the right to make reds lighter, then the blue and cyan sliders all the way to the left to make them darker. Or you can create a "foliage" filter for black and white by using Grayscale and moving the green and yellow filters all the way to the right.

> **Create color enhancement presets.** Make a red enhancement preset by going to HSL Color Tuning and increasing the Red Saturation slider, and then going to Camera Calibration and moving the Red Saturation slider all the way to the right. Similarly, make green and blue enhancements by using the Green and Blue Saturation sliders in Camera Calibration.

> **Create unique desaturated looks for images.** The mostly black and white photo with a slight bit of color can be a very interesting look. Try using the HSL saturation controls to desaturate each color differently.

> **Create a high-contrast look with the Tone Curve.** Go to the Tone Curve and make a steep ascent from bottom to top by moving the lower section downward and the upper section toward the top of the graph.

Q & A

In Photoshop, you can refine your color selection for adjustment in Hue/Saturation by clicking specific colors in the image area and the colors are automatically selected. Can you do anything like this in Lightroom?

No, that type of control is not possible. But I think you have something even better with the direct click-and-drag adjustment of HSL. You may not have the precise colors noted for you, but you are directly changing specific colors on the photo.

If you really want to use Camera Calibration to calibrate a camera, how could you do that?

On an engineering level, this is not the tool to use for that. There are programs on the market that can help you calibrate a camera, though I have not found any all that useful.

On a more photographic level, you can create a preset for a specific camera that uses Camera Calibration to adjust for that camera's biases in capturing color. You can go the scientific route and get a color checker chart, photograph it, then tweak how it looks in Lightroom with Camera Calibration, and save those settings as a preset.

I tend to take a more subjective approach. I find that certain cameras have biases that directly affect the colors in subjects that I shoot. I have found some cameras, for example, make greens too yellow. I can then select a photo that has that subject and those colors, adjust it in Camera Calibration to make the colors look better, and then save that as a preset. In the green example just given, I can adjust the Hue and Saturation sliders for Green in Camera Calibration to get better greens, and then save that as a Green preset.

You don't talk much about the Color section of HSL/Color/Grayscale. I understand you don't like it, but it seems like it would be a good way of isolating adjustments to a specific color.

That's true on both counts! It can be a good way of isolating adjustments to a specific color and I don't like it. That can be seen as a good example of how photographers really do respond to controls and tools in Lightroom differently. Just because I don't like the control does not mean it is not very useful to folks who like the way it separates colors.

One big limitation is the lack of the direct photo control. There is no button to select to allow you to click-and-drag on the photo to directly change the hue, saturation, and luminance of a color. I find that click-and-drag option to be very intuitive and helpful for the photographer.

Chapter 8

PRESENTATION POSSIBILITIES IN THE SLIDESHOW MODULE

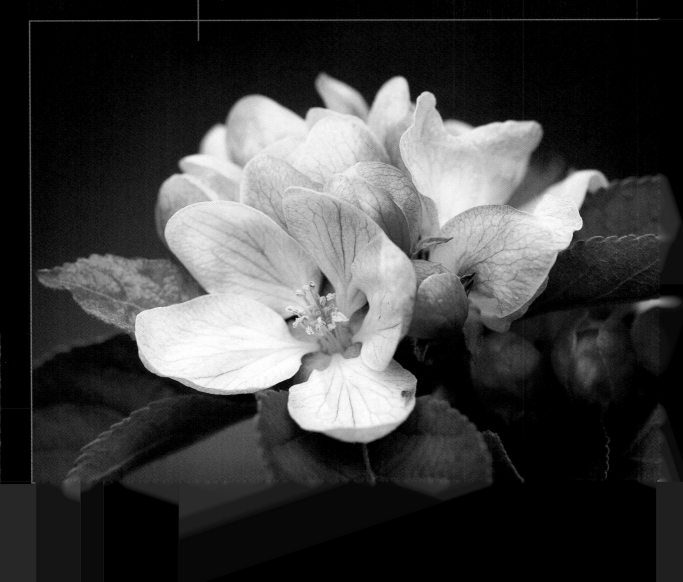

Slide shows are a strong tradition in photography. Yet, in recent years, the true slide show has greatly declined. Kodak even quit making the classic Carousel projector. Few people still set up a slide projector and screen to show off their latest trip to Europe.

Luckily, the computer can now fill this function. Anyone can project images as a "slide show" (even though there are no true slides in digital photography) that look better than ever. It used to be a major effort to do a slide show with music and dissolves as transitions between pictures — you needed special equipment, including a minimum of two slide projectors, a tape deck, and a control unit. Now you can do music, slides, transitions, all from the camera, and never have a single image jam, the music get out of sync, run out of slide tray space, or have the two slide trays lose their sync.

Lightroom's Slideshow module offers a simple, yet quite elegant, way to assemble your images for a slide show presentation. You get to it by clicking Slideshow. In this chapter, I give you the basics of using Lightroom tools to create a slide show. In Chapter 9, I focus on how you can use those tools to put together images to make a great slide show.

THE SLIDESHOW MODULE LAYOUT

Like all Lightroom modules, Slideshow uses the same organization of panels as the rest of Lightroom, as shown in figure 8-1. Here's an overview of the four main panels and their functions:

> **Center work area.** This holds the main photo, plus slide details like titles.

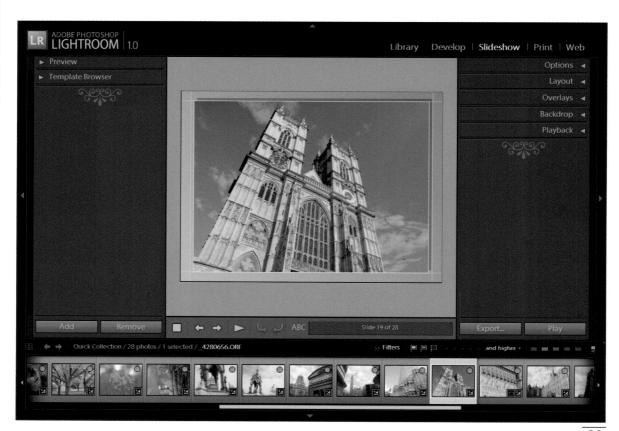

8-1

> **Right panel.** As in all other modules, this is the adjustment side of the module. It is where you change backgrounds and other display features for individual slides, plus control the timing of the images and use of music.

> **Bottom Filmstrip panel.** This is a key element of Slideshow. It is where you arrange your photos in the order needed for the slide show. While you probably hide it in other modules, this is one module where you need to keep it always available.

> **Left panel.** This is where you find more "presets," though, in this case, they are called templates, plus a preview photo.

In addition to the panels, there is once again a toolbar under the central photo that can be used to work on images, as shown in figure 8-2. It includes these tools:

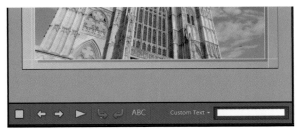

8-2

> **Playback controls.** These are at the left side of the toolbar. Play, at the right, plays your slide show from the image you have selected from the Library grid or the Filmstrip. The others affect how you move around within your slide show. The square at the left takes you to the beginning of your show images. Next are two arrows: the left one steps you backward through the photos, while the arrow to the right steps you forward through the images. This can be very helpful for seeing how one photo goes against another.

> **ABC button.** In the middle of the toolbar is a button labeled ABC that you click to add text or titles to your photos in your slide show. When you click it, the Custom Text box appears (which also gives options for automated text based on metadata). Otherwise, this box simply shows the numbers of your images in the slide show.

SLIDESHOW WORKFLOW

As with the workflow in any part of the digital process, every photographer will discover what works best when he or she uses the Slideshow module. However, there are some things about working with a slide show that affect how you might use this module.

Slide shows are about a group of images being shown consecutively. How they are edited and organized makes a big difference in your final show. Lightroom gives you a lot of choices for making your show look aesthetically interesting, but these choices can be a distraction if the organization of the show is not right. I am suggesting a workflow that works well for retaining the primary function of the show: that it is a group of images shown together in a particular sequence that creates an effect greater than any individual photo. I go into more detail about setting up specific visual elements for a slide show later in the chapter.

Here's a workflow that will get you started in creating an effective slide show:

1. **Set up a "basic" slide background to start your edit and organization process.** Do this by clicking Default in the Template Browser. Next, click on the Identity Plate (if one is on the center photo) and delete it. Then click the file name and delete it. Now click + on the Add button at the bottom of the (left) panel. A new Template dialog box appears. Type Basic and it appears in the Template Browser. Now any time you click this, you get a simple, basic background for your slides. You only need to do this once and it is part of your Template Browser.

2. **Select a group of images in Library for your slide show, put them into Quick Collection, and then go to Slideshow.** You can also start sorting your images in the Grid view of Library. While this works very well, this also complicates things for giving an overview of the process, so I do not go into detail about it until later in the chapter. Following the simple process in this section gives you a slide show very quickly.

3. **Set your "view" to a simple image of the photos in the center work area.** Use the custom basic setup in the Template Browser I describe in step 1, as shown in figure 8-3.

4. **Make your images, your "slides," small enough in the Filmstrip that at least ten or more show up in that work panel.** You can make the Filmstrip larger or smaller by clicking and dragging on the dividing line below the toolbar, as shown in figure 8-4 (your cursor changes to the double arrow when you are in the right position). Your thumbnails are small now, but you are not looking for details at this point. Make the thumbnails large enough that you are comfortable with what can be seen.

5. **Move slides around on the Filmstrip by clicking and dragging.** Give the slides an order that you think will work for a slide show. This is just like sorting slides on a linear lightbox.

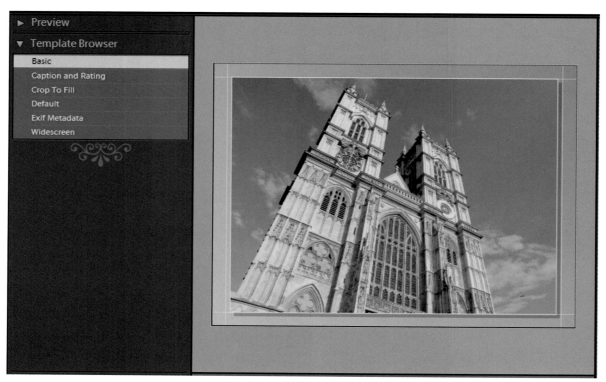

8-3

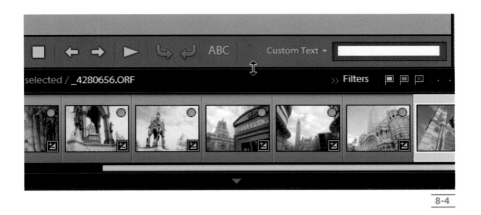

8-4

6. **Go through images one at a time by clicking the right-facing arrow in the Playback area.** See if you like the arrangement of the photos.

7. **Revise the image arrangement as needed.**

8. **Adjust the images' brightness, color, or contrast so they better fit the grouping of photos.** You often discover an image looks too bright or too dark when it is contrasted to another one that comes before or after it. One great thing about Lightroom is the ability to go back to Develop whenever you want and make a correction like this so an image (or images) better fits the sequence.

9. **Work out a look for your image presentation.** Start with the Template Browser — move your cursor over the choices to see what they might look like in the preview area above the browser, as shown in figure 8-5.

10. **Refine the look for your image presentation.** Use the adjustment controls on the right side of Slideshow to do that.

11. **Click Play to see how the photos actually look playing for a specific time and with a transition.**

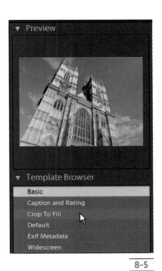

8-5

12. **Refine the timing of your presentation.** Use Playback in the right panel to change the length of time each slide is on and transition timings.

13. **Add music (select Soundtrack in Playback).** Refine the timing of your presentation to match the music by changing slide duration, or adding and removing slides, or both.

155

Selecting and Grouping Photos for a Slide Show

To produce a slide show, you need a set of images to work with. Lightroom offers you a number of ways of doing this starting with the Library module. Allowing you to move among modules as you need their capabilities is another strength of Lightroom's modular design.

Here are several ways you can group images for a slide show:

> **Multiple selection.** You can open a Folder or Collection in Library and use the standard computer selection tools to select a group of photos. Click on an image to start the process, and then Shift+click another photo and everything between is included. Or you can select as many individual photos as you want by going through the images and Ctrl/⌘+clicking desired pictures.

> **Rate photos.** You can go into a Folder or Collection and use Lightroom's rating function to select a group of images. If you keep one rating specifically for slide shows (such as 2), you can use all other rating numbers for ranking and sorting photos for other purposes. You can sort to the rating and then select them all (Ctrl/⌘+A) or move them to Quick Collection. You can only work one Folder or Collection at a time for Slideroom.

> **Quick Collection.** For me, Quick Collection is the best way to start selecting images for a slide show. You can easily and simply select images to go instantly into the Quick Collection by clicking the small circle that appears over the top-right corner of an image in Grid or Filmstrip when you run your cursor over it, as shown in figure 8-6.

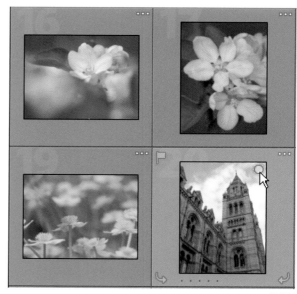

8-6

You can remove an image from Quick Collection by clicking again on the same circle. A big advantage of this technique is that you can add and subtract photos continuously from Quick Collection from diverse Folders or Collections. You then click Quick Collection in the Library category of the left panel of Library, as shown in figure 8-7, and go to Slideshow to use the photos. The disadvantage of Quick Collection is that it can only handle one group of images.

> **New Collection.** Another great way to group photos for a slide show is to create a Collection specifically for your show. You click + in Collections and give your new collection a name based on your slide show topic, as shown in figure 8-8; then you have a unique collection for

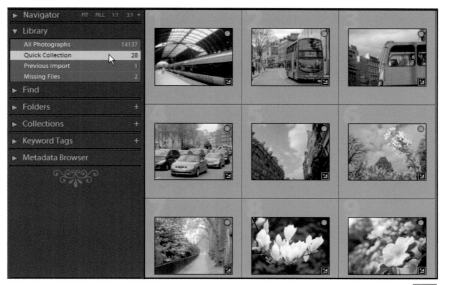

8-7

the slide show. I think the easiest way to get images into this new collection is to use Quick Collection to gather the slides, then select them all and drag them onto your new Collection, as shown in figure 8-9. A nice thing about this approach is that you can always keep your group of photos together. You can add to it later as you have new Folders and therefore need a new slide show. And you can remove old photos you no longer want. If you no longer need this collection, it is easy to delete, too (click the – sign). You can also group all slide show collections into one Slideshow Collection. Create the Slideshow Collection first. Then as you need new and specific slide show groups, click Slideshow first, and then +. When the dialog box appears, select Create as child of Slideshow.

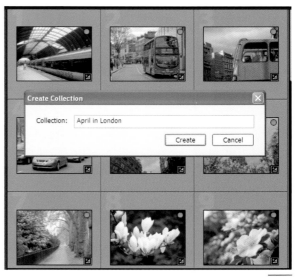

8-8

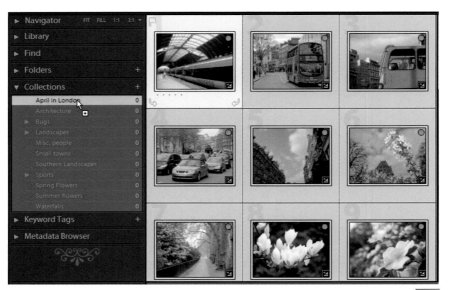

8-9

ORGANIZING AND EDITING YOUR IMAGES

After selecting a group of photos, start organizing and reediting your photos for the show. This can be done in the Library Grid mode or on the Filmstrip. Either way, you are going to be changing the order of your images. This, for me, is a very important reason for having them in their own unique Collection. I don't like arbitrarily rearranging images in a Collection (though you can always use the sorting capabilities of Lightroom).

You must start organizing in the Library Grid view before going to Slideshow. To get as much space as possible in the central work area for this job, try hiding all of the panels, as shown in figure 8-10.

This work area is excellent for doing a slide show. You need to see how the photos look together in order, and you need to see the organization of the show. As nice as Lightroom's display tools are for creating a look for each image, a slide show is about a group of images, about a story from beginning to end, about how one image relates to another, and so forth. Having a "slide table," or a large work area, allows you to see many, or even most, of your photos at once while keeping them sized larger. In addition, that large work area makes it a lot easier to drag images around to change their order.

You do, indeed, play with the slide show organization by dragging and dropping your photos into new places. And you remove photos from the collection by pressing the Backspace/Delete key (Ctrl/⌘+Z brings it

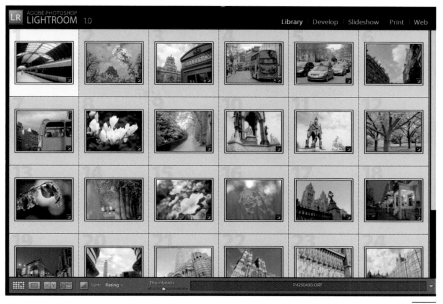

8-10

back through the Undo command). This does not remove the photo from Lightroom, just from the Collection and your work area.

Here's how I like to work with this virtual slide table:

1. **Look at all the photos and get an idea of what topics or types of images should come first, which should come second, and which should be last.** In Chapter 9, I give more details on how you might do this.

2. **Start moving photos around to fit that order.** Click and drag an image to a new, better location for the slide show, as shown in figure 8-11 if you compare it to figure 8-10. Click directly on the image itself to drag it, not on the "mount"; also, you can select several images at once and drag them together to a new location. Delete photos that don't fit.

3. **Go to a single image in Slideshow at any place in your slide set and use the Forward arrow to go through the photos.** Does the order make sense? Do images seem to go together?

4. **Go back to the Grid (use the little grid icon at the far left of Filmstrip) and rearrange images as needed.** This takes you back into the Library module. As your show is refined, you can probably stick with Slideshow and rearrange your images in the Filmstrip rather than going back and forth to the Library Grid view.

5. **Be sure you have interesting beginning and ending slides in your group.**

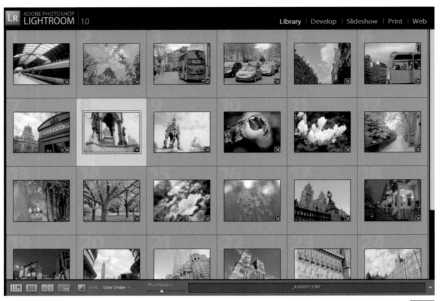

GIVING YOUR SHOW A UNIQUE LOOK

At this point, it is worth refining how your photos display in the slide show — give your show a graphic look. Turn the right and left panels back on, as shown in figure 8-12, so you can access the tools needed for this graphic look.

In this module, it helps to start with the Template Browser to get an idea of possible choices you have. With practice, you will probably not need to do this. You may even set up your own, custom templates based on your slide show needs, but that comes later.

Lightroom allows you to control how large the photo is within the display area, the background behind it, drop shadows and borders for the images, and what text is included. You can really create a very elegant-looking slide show with these tools.

The Template Browser includes five default choices (six now, if you have added the Basic template), as shown in figure 8-13. As you move your cursor over each template choice, the Navigator changes, but nothing is changed on your center image until you actually click the choice. Each one offers you ideas, as well as a complete change to the look of your show:

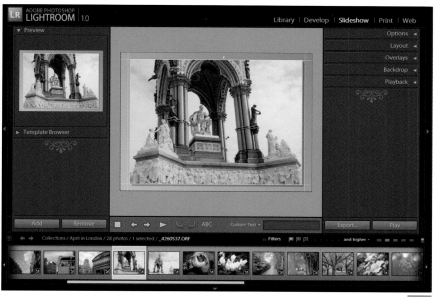

8-12

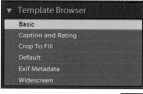

8-13

> **Caption and Rating.** This template reduces the size of the photo to allow a gray background and image effects (this template has a drop shadow and a thin white border), plus it includes the photo's Lightroom rating and any caption information associated with the image, as shown in figure 8-14. When you first look at this (or any other template), you may see a grid of white lines. They are guides only and can be turned off in Layout by deselecting Show Guides.

> **Crop To Fill.** This option enable you to fills the screen with your photo, as shown in figure 8-15, cropping the image if necessary so it fits without any gaps. This is a way that you can show nothing but the photo. You can click and drag the photo to make it look its best for the crop. For horizontal photos, this may be fine and may even tighten up your composition. However, this really destroys verticals. You shot a vertical for a specific reason, so it seems to me a mistake to now turn it into a horizontal by cropping it to fit the horizontal screen. Crop To Fill can be useful if all of your photos are standard-sized horizontals, but if you include verticals, I suggest another choice.

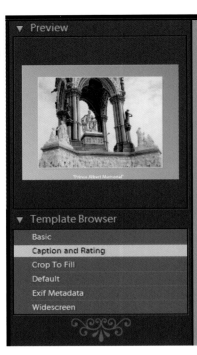
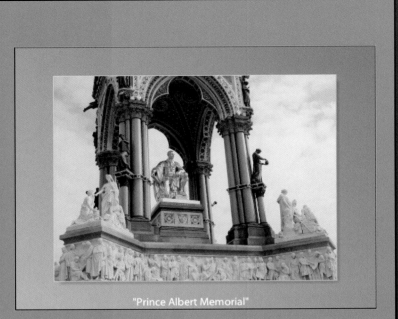

8-14

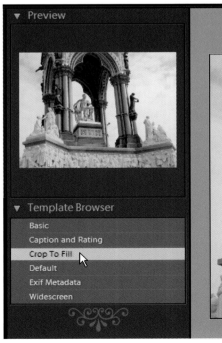
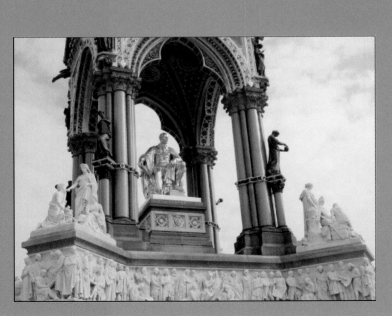

8-15

> **Default.** Here you get a slightly bigger image than Caption and Rating, plus the file name is displayed below the photo and your Identity Plate (if you created one under Edit ⇨ Identity Plate Setup, which I explain fully in Chapter 2) at the top left. You can change either or both as desired. Default uses the same gray background, white border, and drop shadow as Caption and Rating, as shown in figure 8-16.

> **Exif Metadata.** This template changes a lot of things. First, the image is now displayed as the same size as Default, but with a black background and white border, as shown in figure 8-17. Second, the image includes a lot of information. At the top left is an identity plate if you are using one, and at top right, the date the photo was shot.

Centered below the photo is information about the photographer as it was used in the metadata, including Creator (name), Creator City, and Creator State. At the right is camera Exif data including f-stop, ISO speed rating, and focal length used. (You can change this.)

> **Widescreen.** The name of this option is a little misleading. It seems to imply that your photo will be full width, which would mean verticals are cropped. Actually, what you get is "full frame" — you see the whole image and it fills the screen to its full height or width without cropping either, and then a black background fills the gaps. No borders or drop shadow are used, as shown in figure 8-18.

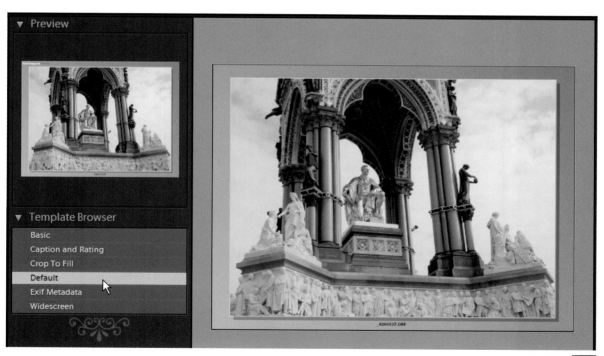

8-16

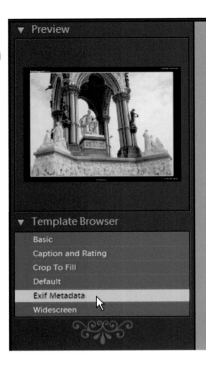
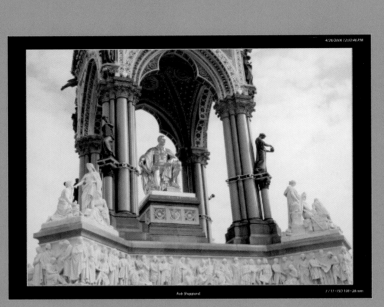

8-17

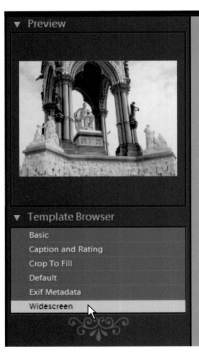
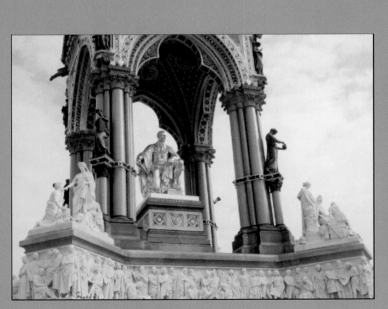

8-18

Making Your Images Pop, Adding Backgrounds, and More

To set off your photos for the best look, you can use Lightroom to control everything around the photo, as well as the photo size and time on-screen. These controls are in the right panel of Slideshow, as shown in figure 8-19, and include the following:

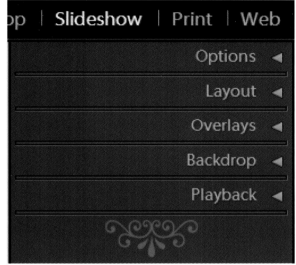

8-19

> **Options.** Here you control how the photo fills the screen, what border the photos will have, and the type and amount of shadow behind the photo (drop shadow).

> **Layout.** This section lets you adjust the margins or spaces around the photo in the display area on-screen. It also has a place to turn on and off Guides.

> **Overlays.** In this area, you control whether you include your Identity Plate and how strongly it shows, if the image rating (from Library) shows and how big it shows, and how text overlays are applied.

> **Backdrop.** This important section lets you change how your background appears, including color, gradients, and even a background photo.

> **Playback.** Here you can change how long the slides are on the screen, the timing of transitions, and the use of music.

There is no simple workflow to using these tools. You can start at the top of the right panel and move down, and that works in many cases. However, in some slide shows, the background may be the critical issue, so you start with Backdrop. In other shows, the timing of the images might be the most important thing for you, so Playback is the place to start. Or perhaps you really want a specific look for your display so that Options, Layout, and Backdrop all need to be open and in use at once — for example, you really can't set a drop shadow properly until you select the right background.

It is important to realize that all adjustments in Slideshow affect all photos. You cannot change individual photo settings in Slideshow.

I think the best workflow is this:

1. **Start with a template that you like (and perhaps one you make based on your main needs for slide shows).**

2. **Choose if you want to show the Identity Plate or not because that visually affects the next choices.**

3. **Choose and adjust the background (because it affects shadows and borders).**

4. **Adjust the margins so the photo looks its best on the background and with any Identity Plate.**

5. **Change the border and shadow so the photo looks good against the background.**

6. **Set the timing of the slides to fit your needs and add music as appropriate.**

CHANGING THE BACKGROUND OF THE IMAGE DISPLAY

The background around your photo strongly affects how a photo looks (it is called Backdrop in Lightroom). While you can do all sorts of interesting background effects for a simple printed image, you need to be careful what you choose here because the background is going to be the same for all photos. You need something that complements your other images and doesn't detract from them.

In Backdrop, you have several options, as shown in figure 8-20. Here's how to work them:

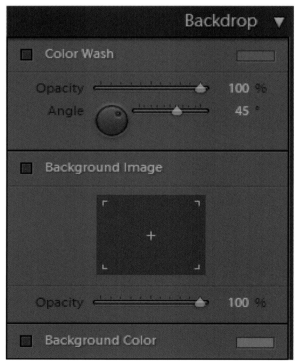

8-20

> **Background Color.** Normally you select this option first even though it is at the bottom of the Backdrop controls. At the right is a color options box. Click it to get a Colors dialog box for choosing background color. This little box has a number of choices that offer you different ways of choosing color based on your operating system's approach to color. I don't recommend getting deeply caught up in this. Slide shows, as I mentioned earlier, should be based on the group of images that make up the content of the show. Choose simple colors that don't distract from your photos.

> **Color Wash.** I recommend you try this. This setting provides a nice gradient to the background instead of a flat color based on the Background Color, as shown in figure 8-21. You choose a second color to blend with the first background color by clicking the color box to the right of Color Wash. You then change its strength with the Opacity slider and its direction with Angle. You can click the little circle "dial" and drag it to change the angle (the dark small circle visually shows where the gradation is starting from) or use the slider. I recommend choosing light and dark neutral colors, with a darker color at the top and lighter at the bottom, as shown here.

> **Background Image.** Here you can add a specific photo as a background for your slide show. You have to drag it in from the Filmstrip, so you need to include it in your grouping or add it to your group of images later so it appears there. It comes in at 100 percent, which is pretty strong and will likely overpower your slide show. Use the Opacity slider to bring that intensity down so it truly is a background photo, as shown in figure 8-22.

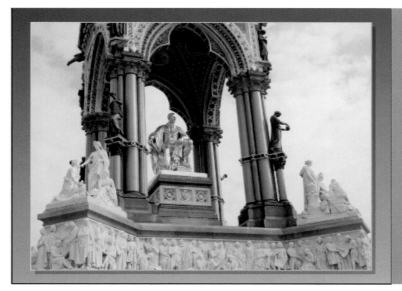

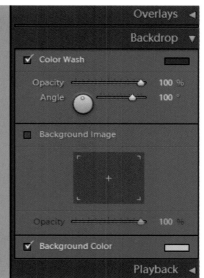

8-21

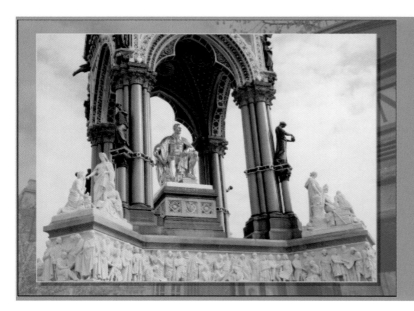

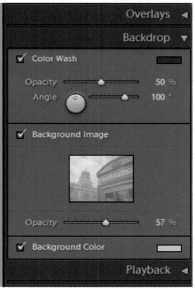

8-22

Options and Layout tools let you design how the image displays in the slide show. They offer different controls, as shown in figure 8-23, but both affect how the image looks in relation to the background and the display space. These are less dramatic than a background choice, but they really add a finishing touch to your photos.

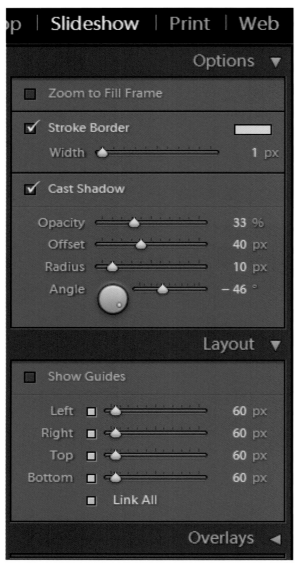

8-23

Options affects the size of the photo, the border, and the drop shadow. Here's how to use the settings there:

> **Zoom to Fill Frame.** This makes your photo fill the image display area, cropping it as needed. You can click the photo and drag it around so the cropped area is more aesthetic or it gives you a better view of the subject. I don't care much for this personally, especially if I have vertical photos. This essentially gives you the effect of the Crop To Fill template.

> **Stroke Border.** This puts a border around your image. You can make it black, white, gray, or any color you want. Clicking the color box at the right displays the Colors dialog box. This border can be a very important part of your photo, helping to set it apart from the background. A dark photo against a dark background might look nice, but the two will blend without a light border. I find that light gray to white borders and black borders both look quite good, the choice depending on the background. In figure 8-24, I set Width wider than the default so it would show up better. The actual width you choose is a very subjective decision based on your personal taste and the photos used.

> **Cast Shadow.** This creates a nice drop shadow for your image, also seen in figure 8-24, giving the display some dimension and depth. There are four controls that go with it that affect how strong the shadow effect is, and you should vary them depending on the background. Opacity is the strength of the shadow itself — more opacity makes the shadow darker; less makes it lighter. Be wary of making this too dark (though that depends on the darkness of the background) or the shadow becomes too strong and may compete with the photo.

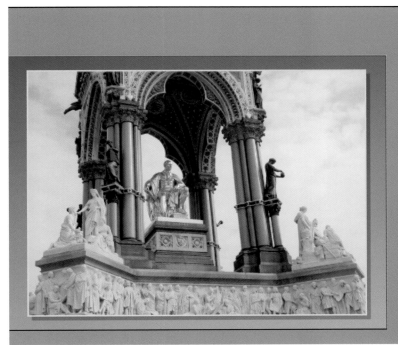
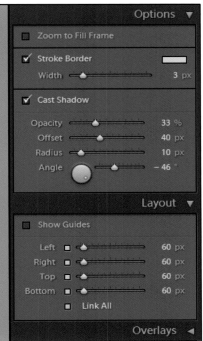

8-24

Offset affects the positioning of the shadow relative to the photo and changes the appearance of depth between the photo and the background. As you change Offset, you will want to change Radius, too. Radius adjusts the softness of the shadow edge — as Offset increases, usually you'll want to increase Radius as well. Also, you can change Radius at any time for a gentler effect. Angle is where the shadow appears. Most of the time, you will want the shadow to appear to the bottom and right of the photo or the bottom and left. That mimics how the sun creates shadows. For an odd, even sinister effect, you can put the shadow above and to the left or right of the photo. Click and drag the slider or the dial for Angle changes.

Slide Layout tools change the position of the photo within the display area. Here's how to deal with these controls:

> **Show Guides.** Click this option on or off to reveal or hide the guides in the work area, as shown in figure 8-25. Sometimes the guides distract you from seeing what the overall display looks like, and they are worth turning off. You click the guides in the center work area and drag them in or out to change the size of the photo, as shown in figure 8-26.

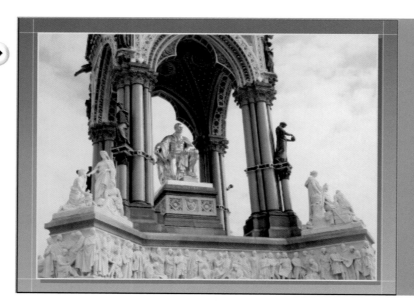

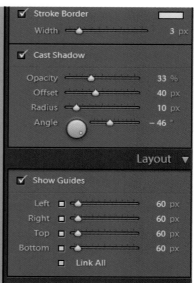

8-25

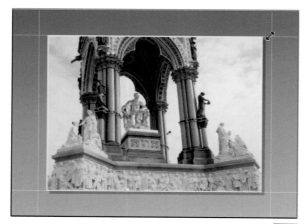

8-26

> **Margins.** Below Show Guides are margin controls (though they aren't labeled as such) that change the space around the photo — Left, Right, Top, and Bottom, as shown in figure 8-25. Click and drag the sliders to make any adjustments (they are also connected to the guides and change if you click and drag them as well). Note the check boxes at the left side of the sliders: When checked, they turn a light gray to denote that

they are active. When Link All is active, all of the sliders are also active and move in unison — change one and the others change, too. Deselect any one of them, and that one moves independent of the rest.

This can be extremely useful in positioning your images. If you want classic display proportions where the sides and top are the same, but the bottom is different, deselect Bottom and change it separately. Or maybe you have a graphic that you want on the left side of the images (maybe a logo applied through the Identity Plate); then you can deselect the left side and move it independently to gain the needed space.

TIMING AND MUSIC

Slide shows always have to be timed in some way in order to progress from slide to slide. Lightshow enables you to time your slides in the Playback controls shown in figure 8-27. You can change how long the slides are up, how long the transition is between images, and if you use music with them.

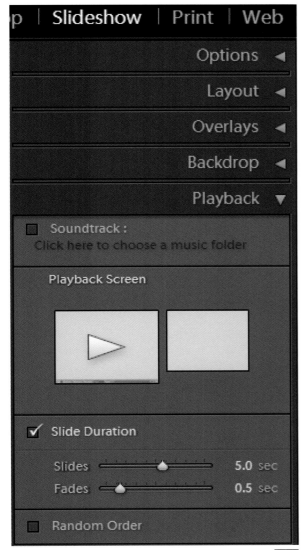

8-27

 shows the Slideshow | Print | Web panel with Options, Layout, Overlays, Backdrop, and Playback sections. The Playback section shows Soundtrack: "Click here to choose a music folder", Playback Screen with two preview screens, Slide Duration checked with Slides 5.0 sec and Fades 0.5 sec, and Random Order.

the screen? How long should the fades — the time it takes for a slide to dissolve between the images — last? This gets tricky. You want slides on long enough for an audience to appreciate and enjoy the image, but not on so long that they get tired of it. Four seconds is a good minimum to consider — faster than that is hard for most audiences to deal with unless you want a kinetic effect that is more important than the images themselves. Ten seconds is a good maximum to consider — longer than that will seem tedious to most audiences unless there is something in the photos that they really need to study. The fades between slides need to be related to both the time the slide is on-screen and the type of show. I tend to prefer shorter fades or dissolves (dissolve is a more traditional term for blending one image to another through a slide change) of 0.5–1.0 seconds.

A very short transition makes a show lively and active, but it can also make it harsh. A long transition gives a show a poetic feeling, with a gentle pace, but it can also seem tedious. If you use music, the pace and tempo of that music strongly influences your choice of transition time.

> **Soundtrack.** You can attach music to the show with this choice, as shown in figure 8-28. When you click the Click here to choose a music folder text, you access your hard drive (or other storage media) and you can go to a folder where you keep music.

X-REF

In Chapter 9, I give you some ideas on how you can use music to the best effect in Lightroom.

The timing you do in Playback affects all images. You can't alter them for a specific slide or group of slides. That said, here's how you can use them:

> **Slide Duration.** This is an important choice that is oddly placed near the bottom of this set of controls. How long do you want a slide to appear on

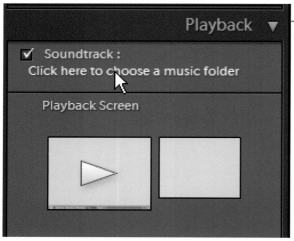

8-28

> **Playback Screen.** This option is designed for computers that are set up with more than one screen or display. Simply select the screen that you want to use for playback.

> **Random Order.** It is unlikely a photographer would select this option for most slide shows. This setting at the bottom of Playback takes your carefully ordered images and mixes them up. It can be useful for slide shows that are used as backgrounds for an event (that is, they just play without people focusing on them) or for slide shows during breaks in a seminar or other long programs where, again, people don't focus specifically on the images.

WORKING WITH TEXT

In Slideshow, you work with text by using the ABC button below the work area, as shown in figure 8-29. When you have text on or by the images, you can click ABC and two new buttons become active to the left of it: Rotate Left and Rotate Right arrows. Also, clicking text or ABC gives you an active area to the right (seen as Custom Settings in figure 8-29) that allows you to control text. You can also click on any text and use the Delete key to remove it. All of these are overall text effects; that is, you do it once and it affects all photos. You cannot change text on any individual photos in the Slideshow module (though you can do it by using captions in the metadata). If you want an overall title to your program, you must create such an image in Photoshop; Lightroom is not designed for doing that.

I suggest being conservative in your use of text. Your photos should be the stars of your show, not clever text or special messages. But often, you will want to include some text to give your show and its images context or ownership. Here's how you can work text for your slide show:

> **ABC button (add text).** Click this button to add text to the photo, as shown in figure 8-30. You get an active text box to the right of ABC called Custom Text. You can type whatever you want in that box. Nothing appears in the photo until you press Enter or Return. Click and drag the text to the position you want.

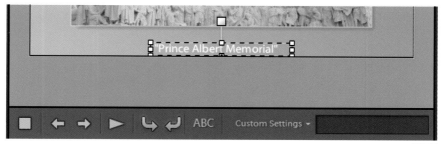

8-29

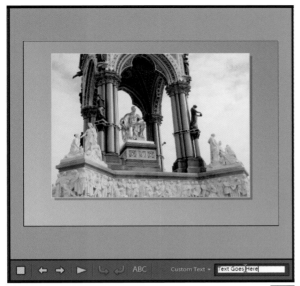

8-30

> **Edit text.** Click on the text you want to change and it becomes active, as shown in figure 8-31. You size the image by clicking and dragging the control boxes around the outside of the active

text. Rotate it by clicking the arrows to the left of the ABC button.

You can change the font and type variations such as bold or italic in the Text Overlays category of controls on the right panel of Slideshow. Just click the font name or face type for a drop-down menu like the one shown in figure 8-32 for font choice.

> **Defined text choices.** If you click on the words to the right of ABC (it will likely say Custom Text), a drop-down menu of text options based on file names and metadata appears, as shown in figure 8-33. This is mostly a rather specialized use of text, but professional photographers who are using a slide show to present images from a shoot might need some of this specific data. The Edit choice gives even more options for automating text, as shown in figure 8-34 (the Text Template Editor dialog box appears). If you want separate captions for each image, you can choose Insert Caption, then go to Metadata in Library and put in specific captions there.

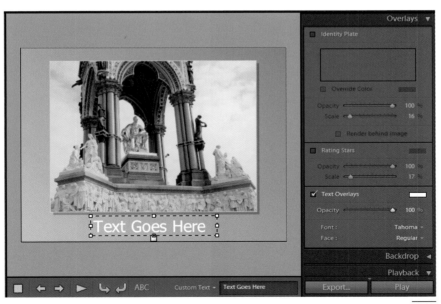

8-31

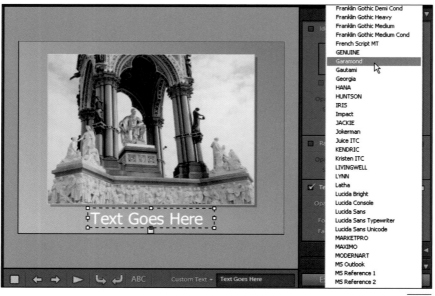

8-32

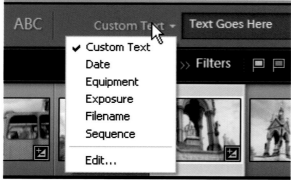

8-33

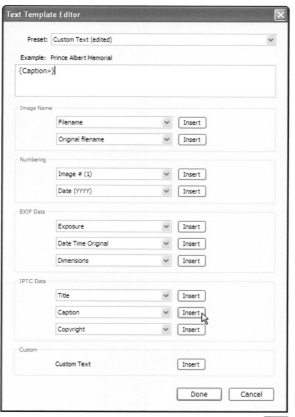

8-34

WHAT OVERLAY OPTIONS DO YOU NEED?

Many slide shows look their best simply displayed, without a lot of extras, such as text and your Identity Plate. However, many pros want some identification for their work, especially if they produce a slide show for promotional purposes. You do this in Overlays. Start by selecting or deselecting Identity Plate, as shown in figure 8-35.

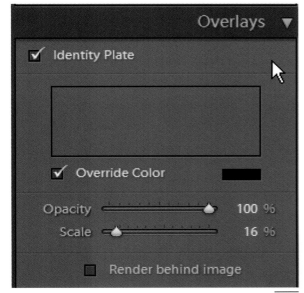

8-35

You need to select how the Identity Plate displays (though you may change this later as you change your background). Click and drag the Scale slider to make the graphic larger or smaller; click and drag the Opacity slider to make it stronger or fainter. You change the position of the graphic by clicking on it in the work area and dragging it into place. You can also make the photo overlap this graphic by selecting Render behind image and moving the Identity Plate behind the photo.

Next, you can choose to display ratings by selecting Rating Stars. You can adjust the color of the rating by clicking the box to the right of Show Ratings, which

gives you a Color Choice dialog box. And you can change the density of the rating with Opacity and the size of the rating graphic with Scale.

At the bottom is Text Overlays, which was covered earlier in this chapter.

MAKING YOUR OWN TEMPLATES

At the beginning of the chapter, I very briefly discussed making a unique Basic template to help you set up images for a slide show more easily. Now that you know how to work the adjustment controls in Slideshow, you can set up a template to show off your slides any special way. Here's how:

1. **Create a unique image display that you want to save.** This can include text, background, photo location, drop shadow, and more — basically anything on the right side except Playback.

2. **Click Add in the Template Browser, as shown in figure 8-36.** This creates a new entry in the Template Browser, also seen in figure 8-36.

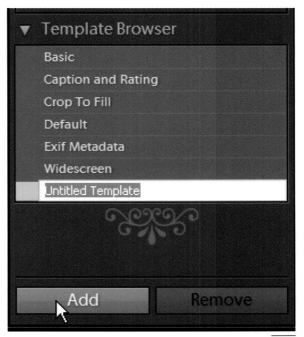

8-36

3. Type a name for your template.

4. Press Enter/Return to accept the new template.

If you make a mistake, it is really easy to correct. Delete the new template (select it and click Remove), make the changes needed to your slide show, and then create a new template and name it.

PLAYING AND EXPORTING

When you complete your show, you can try it out. Clicking the Play button at the bottom of the central work area plays it in the work area — all the panels are still visible. Clicking Play under the right panel plays the show over the whole screen — nothing

is visible except the slide show, as shown in figure 8-37. In the case of the Play button, the show starts from the active slide selected in the Filmstrip. If you want the show to start from the beginning, click the first button in the playback controls to return to the start of the images, and then click the Play button. The full-screen Play starts the show from the beginning.

To use your slide show anywhere other than within Lightroom (including sending the show to others or playing it on the Web), you need to export it. Click Export at the bottom of the right panel. The Export Slideshow to PDF dialog box appears, as shown in figure 8-38.

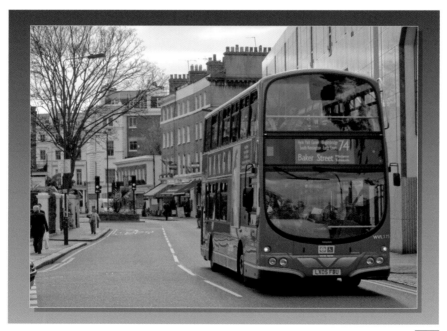

8-37

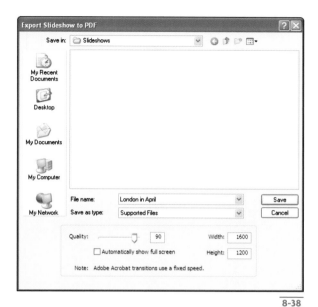

8-38

You need to make a number of choices in that box:

> **Save in: Destination Folder.** This is pretty standard computer stuff. Simply tell Lightroom where to put the finished slide show file (choose a destination folder).

> **File name.** This is also standard computer workflow. Give your file a name.

> **Quality.** In Export, you have one file format choice: PDF. PDF slide shows are playable by most computers — they simply need Adobe Reader. Quality and Size settings affect how big the final file size will be, as well as the image quality of the photos in the slide show.

If you have a need to create as small a show as possible for transmission over the Web, for example, then you can use a lower Quality setting and a small size, such as 640 × 640. If you are going to show your images directly on a computer monitor or project them with a digital projector, I recommend keeping the Quality high (80 or above) and the size at 1200 × 1200 or more. You can also make the size specific to a display device resolution. Full Screen or not simply tells Adobe Reader how to display the image when opened. At this time, it is not possible to export music with images from Lightroom. You can only play music with a slide show if it is played from Lightroom.

■ **I understand why you want to see as many photos as possible in the work area, but frankly, when they get small enough to do that, I can't really see them. What do you suggest?**

That is really a good point. As an aging baby boomer, I can understand the need for better visibility of small items. There are several things you can try:

> **Look at the thumbnail photos as subjects, not full images.** You don't really need to see all the details in order to sort and edit most of them.

> **Be sure to use a large monitor.** Lightroom works best with a large monitor. I suggest a 19-inch monitor as the minimum size when using this program and larger is better.

> **Make the images as small as you can accept them.** Then scroll through them as you organize and edit. This makes the drag-and-drop organizing harder, but you can still do it.

> **Have a pair of computer glasses made.** I have a pair of glasses that are designed for optimum vision at computer screen distance, and they really help. They even include bifocals for closer distance vision. Things at a distance might not be as sharp, but these glasses really make a difference for working at the computer.

I like to use title slides in my slideshows. I do presentations of my work for environmental causes, and I want to emphasize certain points with words counter-posed against the slides. How can I do that?

To be honest, I am not sure that Lightroom is the place for doing a lot of that. PowerPoint or Keynote offer a great deal of power for using images and words. However, they are also more complex and don't have the inter-module power that Lightroom offers.

Doing a few title slides in Photoshop is not that hard to do. You can even create a title using an existing slide and have it automatically show up with the rest of your images in Lightroom. You will learn more about working between Photoshop and Lightroom in Chapter 13, but here's a quick overview regarding title slides:

1. **Export image directly to Photoshop.** Right-click on a photo in the Filmstrip. Select Edit in Adobe Photoshop from the contextural menu. In the Edit Photo dialog box, choose Stack with original and Edit a Copy with Lightroom Adjustments in the same menu, then click Edit. This takes you to Photoshop, plus it creates a copy of your original image that is filed in the same location as your original.

2. **Add text in Photoshop.** Using the Text tool will create a new layer. Keep the layer so you can go back and edit it later if needed.

3. **Save your photo with its name from Lightroom using Save (do not use Save As).** Now your text will show up immediately on the copy image back in Lightroom and can be used as needed. You don't need to do any exporting or importing in or out of programs.

4. **Edit text as needed.** This image can then be edited and text changed later (because it is still a layer) by exporting directly back to Photoshop, but this time in the Edit Photo dialog box, choose Edit Original. You do not want a copy at this point, nor do you want Lightroom duplicating the file.

Chapter 9

MAKING A BETTER SHOW IN SLIDESHOW

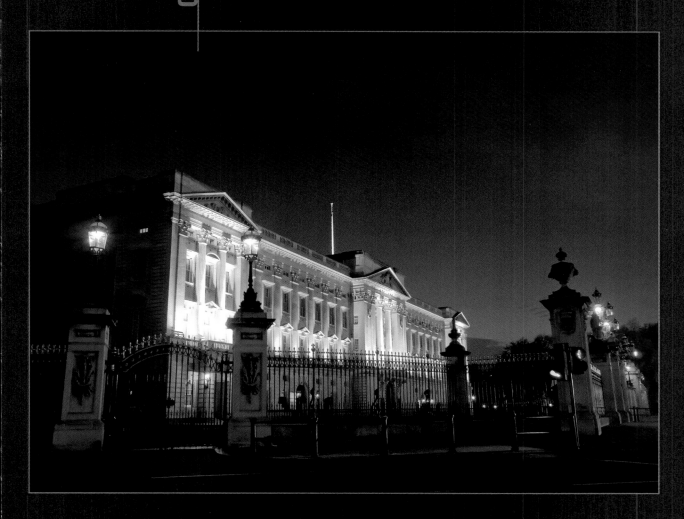

Knowing the basics of Slideshow and how to use the controls is important when you want to create a slide show of your images. In the last chapter, you saw the flexibility and adjustments that are possible. There are many books and classes on dealing with adjusting a photo that apply to Lightroom; after all, the adjustments really are based on Camera Raw and Photoshop. This is not true for slide shows in the computer.

A slide show is a totally different animal than an individual photo or a print. Therefore, you have to treat it completely differently. You must see photos plural and not be stopped by a photo singular. That is a very important distinction. Sometimes a photographer puts together a slide show that is basically a series of single images. While these photos may offer something, such as size or the capability to show images in different locations, they usually don't work as well as an entity in and of itself.

In this chapter, you earn more about working with slides to make an effective slide show. You learn to use Slideshow controls to make a group of images work as a group, to create something greater than just a simple showing of individual images, and to create a real show.

STARTING THE ORGANIZING PROCESS

The Grid view of Library is a great place to organize your images into a show, as you saw in Chapter 8. I want to put that organization into a different perspective: I am going to use some terms to describe the views that are not "official" Lightroom terms, but terms that I think are more descriptive of the process. You can use the work area two ways to organize your photos:

> **Use the "Overview view."** This is the Grid view, as shown in figure 9-1. It gives you an instant overview of images — in the specific view seen in this figure, I reduced the size of the thumbnails by using the Thumbnails slider at the bottom so all of the images in this short show appear. You can see which photos are together and which are not; where images are within the whole show; and you can move the images from one area to another to find new relationships among them. The beginning, middle, and end of the show is quickly visible; and Grid view enables you to instantly look at the photos in front of and behind a selected photo in order, and then change the order by just clicking and dragging photos.

PRO TIP

Remember to make your work area as large as possible by hiding the other panels to the left, right, and bottom of the interface. You can bring any of them back when you need them by clicking the arrows on each respective side.

> **Use the "Single Image Playback view."** This is the work area of Slideshow, as shown in figure 9-2. When you use it with the forward and backward controls below the work area, you can move from photo to photo as if you are actually viewing a slide show. This lets you see what happens when one photo changes to another. It also gives you the chance to actually view how a group of photos works together, seen one at a time.

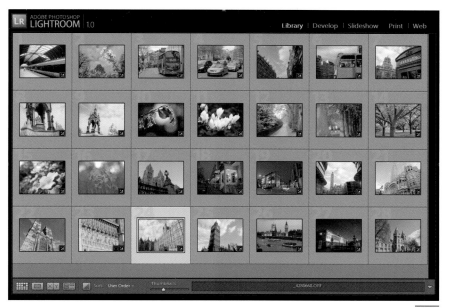

9-1

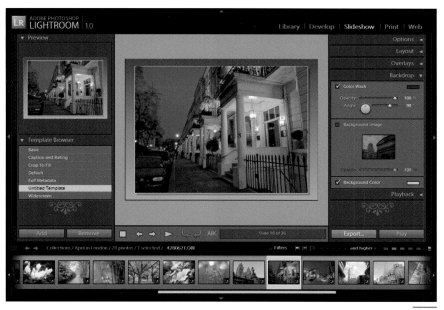

9-2

> **Integrate your use of "Single Image" and
> Filmstrip views.** This is very important. When
> photos seem to work together in a grouping in the
> Grid or Filmstrip views, you need to also see how
> they play against one another, one at a time, in the
> "Single Image" view. As you watch photos in
> the "Single Image" view, you will see awkward
> changes, so you need to go back to the Filmstrip,
> as also shown in figure 9-2, and rearrange pho-
> tos. With practice, you will find this works very
> quickly and easily.

WAYS TO ORGANIZE A SLIDE SHOW

There are many ways to organize a slide show, and
you will develop unique groups and arrangements
of your images that will provide a distinctive stamp to
your shows. I know, however, that many photographers are so used to working single images that they
struggle a bit with producing a great slide show that
brings images together into one entity.

I say this again, because it is key to doing a good slide
show: Think of what the images form as a group and do
not look at them as individuals. I recognize that some
photographers will use Lightshow simply as a way of
presenting a PDF file of photos for a client, and the
"group" is simply selects from a shoot. Still, it is worth
remembering, even then, that images interact with each
other. How you position them in relation to each other
and how they sequence together affects the viewer's
impression of both the overall group of photos and the
individual shots. Putting some thought into organization
and flow for even the simplest show can create a show
that has more impact and effect on your audience.

First and foremost, a slide show should have a beginning, such as figure 9-3, which shows an entry into
London using the train, and an end, such as figure 9-4,
a night shot of Buckingham Palace. Think carefully
about which photo you want your audience to see first
and which it will see last. I can tell you that many slide
shows are weakened because the last slide didn't finish
the show on a strong note, or worse, didn't seem to
finish the show at all. Sometimes, that finish is simply
your credits, and I will discuss creating text slides later
in the chapter. Still, the last slide before those credits
needs to provide some sort of closure for the viewer.

Another thing to keep in mind is that the overall show
should have a flow. While it is important that the
beginning and end images lead the viewer through the
start and finish of the program, there must be some
sort of transition between images as the program
moves through them. This does not have to be spelled
out for the viewer, but the viewer needs to sense
there is a reason for the images used and the order
they appear.

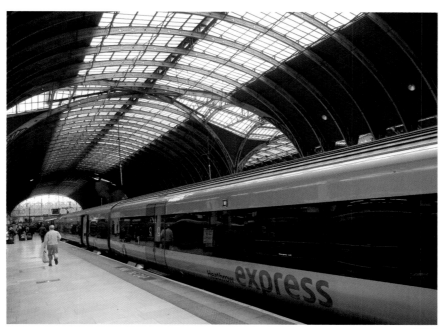

9-3

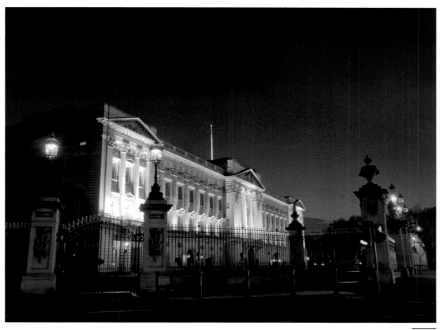

9-4

Short sequences within the overall slide show can be helpful in building the whole show. A show will keep an audience's interest if there are changes within it, including short sequences that build up to mini-highlights or peaks of things like graphics, thoughts, or emotions, and then go to another sequence. You can apply all of the ideas in this section to both the whole show and short sequences within that show.

With those guidelines in mind, here are some ideas that may help you get started (unfortunately, these are hard to show in a book, but you can find many great examples of slide shows on the Web if you check the Web sites of newspapers — most major papers show off photos in slide shows):

> **Story.** Story is a classic technique for organizing anything that takes time for the viewer to see and understand it all, whether that is a novel, a movie, or a slide show. Story, at its most basic level, is something that has a beginning, middle, and end. That means you look for slides that create a beginning to your show, find other slides that make a strong ending, and then fill in the rest with images that make sense as a transition from beginning to end. Story is not about what you studied in English class in high school; it is about organization in such a way that a "story" is created with your images, a sequence that keeps the audience interested as it builds from beginning to end. It gives the audience something to follow, something to anticipate. You can also create little mini-stories within the overall story that can be especially helpful when you work with a long show.

> **Color.** Color can be a way of organizing photos, including working images against each other to give them more impact. Color can be used to group photos, as shown in figure 9-5, to make transitions among them, and to create a sequence or "story" about color. It is rarely used as a basis for an overall story (that is, you start with one color and end with another), though it can be. Changing colors for the story usually is a technique used for small sequences. Colors can also be kept consistent through certain parts of a show to add impact to that particular color or to keep the audience's attention on the subject rather than color changes. You can also use color to jar the viewer by changing dramatically from one color to another as sequences change within a show, as shown in figure 9-6 (though this example uses subject matter and shapes to offer some consistency for the viewer). Be careful of this, however, because it can be so jarring that you lose your viewers for a moment as they try to track what is going on.

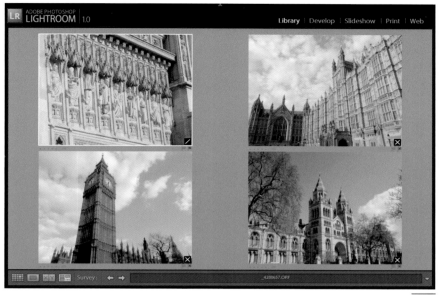

9-5

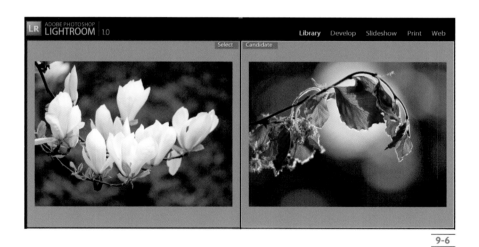

9-6

> **Tone.** Tone is another visual technique to bring images together. You can group photos by their overall tonalities (bright or dark, for example), as shown in figure 9-7, by their tonal atmosphere (a crisp light versus a soft light, for example), and so on. You can also use tonal changes (contrasting tones) to build a sequence or to create a visual exclamation point for the audience (like color, however, you have to use such contrasts carefully or you risk losing your audience). Color and tone are two major graphic elements that can link and build sequences in a slide show. You can use them to deal with images that are otherwise quite different in subject matter.

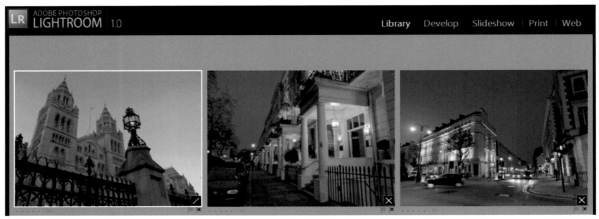

PRO TIP

You might have noticed that the figures of images here are shown using the Survey view of the Library mode. This is a good view to use when you want to compare just a few images with each other rather than seeing the whole slide show.

> **Subject matter.** The subject is, of course, the traditional way of organizing slide shows for teaching or informing an audience. I deliberately did not put it first because I think too often it is the only thing considered for a slide show. But even if the subject is the key to a particular show, you still need to organize it beyond lumping a bunch of photos together simply because they apply to the same subject. This is where attention to color and tone can be extremely useful. The wrong colors and tones running into each other can jar viewers enough that they lose track for a moment of what you are telling them about the subject. Story can also help keep viewers on track by giving them something to follow and anticipate.

> **Chronological.** This is another traditional approach to a slide show, and when it is done right, it can be very effective. Chronology, just by

definition, offers the story elements of a beginning, middle, and end. But be careful not to be a slave to the timing of shots because that can put photos together that visually compete or fight when they are shown. When working a chronological show, it is very helpful to watch for how colors and tones interact and to be especially careful that you guide the viewer and not annoy him or her because of jarring contrasts.

> **Context.** Almost always, a slide show, or at least elements within it, will have a context. Context is the setting for the images — environmental, psychological, geographical, sociological, historical, and so on. This can change through a show. If context is important to your message or the audience's appreciation of the photos, then you need to select photos and order them in such a way that context is preserved. This can be especially important for short sequences. Audiences get annoyed when they are happily viewing a context, say historical, make a transition to a new context for the images, say geographical, and then get a random historical image tossed at them.

> **Framing.** As you change the framing of a subject from wide shot to medium shot to close-up, you change the way a viewer looks at your photo, as

shown in figure 9-8. This has a lot to do with composition, but it is also has to do with the distance to the subject, lens choice, and so on. You can organize photos by how they are framed. You can put a group together that is all framed the same, such as a group of close-ups, or you can group images based on how they change from close-up to wide shot. Making deliberate choices about how one image goes with another because of framing can pay off in smoother, more effective slide shows. If you don't pay attention to this, you may find viewers have trouble visually grasping a change from a wide shot to a close-up, for example.

> **Builds.** Building a sequence of images is totally unique to a slide show. You can take a series of photos from a distant wide shot to a close-up to help a viewer focus on details. You can build a sequence from a close-up to a wide shot to bring a viewer to a new view. You can show sequences of action, building to a climax. You can group images that come together to build a visual journey through an area. You can build a lighting effect, showing a subject gradually changing as

the light changes on it. Builds, however, typically need to be shot for that effect when you take the photos in the first place. This is something to keep in mind as you photograph — can you take a few additional images to create some sort of build for a sequence?

> **Punctuation.** Punctuation in a slide show is just like punctuation in writing. It is something that allows the viewer to pause, that separates parts of a show, that helps a viewer better understand the show, and that gives special attention to a specific image or sequence. Pauses, like commas, can come from simple, peaceful images or even black slides (which I explain later in this chapter). Exclamation points come from big changes, such as a jarring change in color or tone, and can wake an audience up (again, a warning — be careful how much you do this or you risk losing your audience). Question marks come from specific images that make a viewer think and wonder what is happening in the photo. A period comes from an image that is definitely an ending to a sequence.

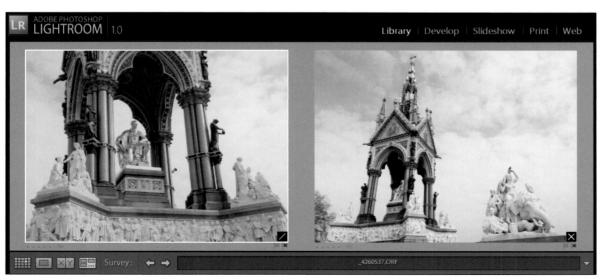

9-8

You can use these ideas individually for organizing a slide show or combined in all sorts of ways to get the most out of your images. Any technique you use should be used to create a slide show that as a whole is much greater than the sum of its parts.

It is very important to realize that a slide show is not about putting photos in front of an audience. If you do that, your show becomes photographer-centric and can lose your audience. Good communication, which is what an effective slide show is about, is not simply about what is "told" (or shown) to an audience. It is also much about what the audience actually "hears" (or sees) in that effort. Therefore, a good slide show is about creating something that affects and communicates *with* an audience, not at an audience.

PRO TIP

As you go through your images, you may notice that some look different than expected when you play them against specific photos before and after. They may look brighter, darker, have a different color balance, and so on. Lightroom makes it very easy to compensate for this. Just go back to Develop with any images that give you a problem and adjust them for the slide show. You might want to save your original adjustments by creating a Snapshot in the Develop module, or you could use a Virtual copy by right-clicking the photo and choosing Create Virtual Copy, then making the adjustments on it.

TIMING A SLIDE SHOW

Once you have the basic organization for a show, give it some sort of timing as to how long each slide is on-screen and how long the transitions are between each image. This affects how the photos look together and gives a distinct mood or impression of the photos for your audience. As you change timing, you may find you need to readjust some of your photos. Two photos that looked good when you saw them quickly together might not work right if there is a long dissolve (or blending) of the images as they transition from one to the other.

You change the timing of your slide show in Playback. You can change the duration of slides (how long each one stays on-screen) from 0–20 seconds, as shown in figure 9-9. Twenty seconds is a very long time when you consider this is how long each image stays on the screen. That might be something to use for a slide show that is just a background to an event, however. Transitions between photos also range from 0–20 seconds — I am not sure what you would do with a slide show that had 20 seconds for each slide and 20 seconds of transition to change between them.

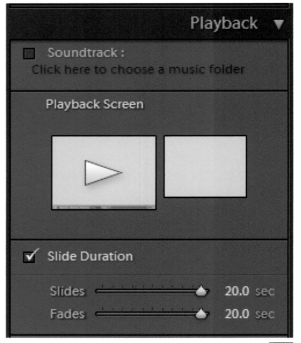

9-9

How long or short the slides stay on-screen and the length of transitions is very subjective. You need to preview your show and see how the timing feels, based on what you are trying to accomplish with the slide show. In addition, timing may be limited by your computer. Lightroom has to find and load each image from the hard drive as it plays a slide show. If your hard drive is slow, your RAM amount too small, or your processor speed too slow, you may find the show does not play properly at short duration times.

Here are some things affecting your timing choices that you might want to consider:

> **Setting for the show.** Where is the slide show going to be shown? What sort of place is it? Who will see it? Each of these affects how long images need to stay on-screen. For a show with a group of art directors, you may want to go through images pretty quickly, as they are generally used to seeing photos quickly and will get tired of images that appear too long on-screen.

> **Use for the show.** How is the show being used? For example, you might be using a show for a marketing introduction, which would likely need an energetic, lively pace; or you might use a show for a community organization that will want to see images on-screen longer so the audience can look them over, finding things they recognize.

> **Images in the show.** The photos actually seen in the show can dictate the timing of the show. A slide

show of detailed landscapes, such as in figure 9-10, needs some time for the audience to really look at each image. A show of sports action, such as in figure 9-11, might look best when the photos change quickly, giving an impression of lively action.

> **Music used.** A fast-paced music track looks silly with slowly changing photos, while a majestic orchestral fanfare will not work well with fast-changing photos. You need to play your music against the photos and see if the music and slide tempos complement or fight each other.

Timing, and all of these ways of thinking about timing, affects your choice of how long a slide is on-screen as well as how long the transition is between two slides. Usually, you will combine short times for an image to appear on-screen with short transition times. Conversely, you will typically combine long times on-screen with longer transition times. There are no absolute rules about this, however. Try different settings with your images, click Preview, and see how they affect the show.

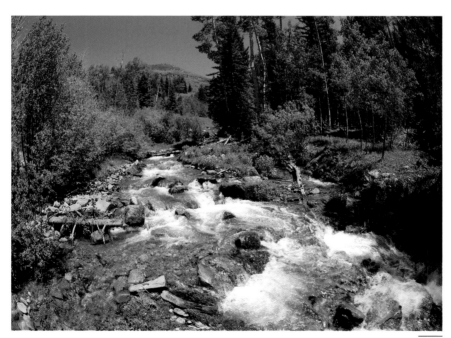

9-10

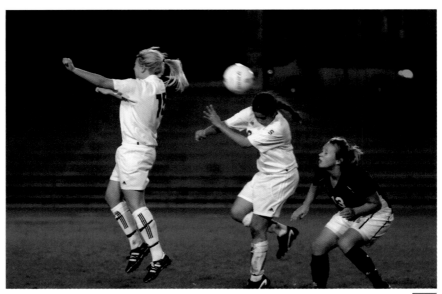

9-11

WORKING WITH MUSIC

Music can be an important way to enhance a slide show (though obviously I can't show you examples of this in a book). Lightroom has very limited capabilities with music — it can only be used when a slide show is played directly from the Slideshow module. However, that doesn't mean you should take it lightly. Just the fact you can add music at all increases the possibilities for your show.

In order to choose the best music for a slide show, it is worth considering how it might affect your images. Here are some things to consider:

> Music can set the right mood for your images.

> Music can affect and determine a pace that makes sense for the content and use of the show.

> Music gives your photos an emotional quality. With music, you can make a show happy, sad, moody, joyful, majestic, and so forth.

> Music can change the appearance of your images. It affects how an audience looks at, and, therefore, perceives, the photos in the show.

> Music changes the mood of the audience.

> Music can affect how long a show seems. You can actually take the same show with the same transitions and timing, play it with two different pieces of music, and the show seems to take different times to finish.

Because music has such a powerful effect on a slide show, it needs to fit the images and setting of the show. Picking some popular music just because you like it and attaching it to your images might actually change the show in a negative way if that popular music fights the images and their organization.

That brings up an important point. You cannot simply use any music with your slide show for any use of that show. Music is copyrighted material. If you use music from some album for a personal, private showing of images that you do not, in any way, charge for, you can generally use any music without getting permission. However, should you use that music for any show that is shown publicly, especially when money is involved in some way (a fee is charged for admission, a charge is made for the class, and so on), you are breaking the law. It is illegal to use copyrighted music for such purposes.

There are other sources of music. You could work with a friend who has a band (and we all know musicians in our circle of acquaintances that would love to have their music featured for a credit), buy royalty-free music, download music that has no rights restrictions, and so on.

PRO TIP

You can also create your own music quite nicely with some computer programs that build music sequences for you (and at a specific length). One that is easy to use and has a lot of flexibility is Sonicfire from SmartSound Software. This program lets you pick types of music and then builds a unique soundtrack to a specific length that you can use with slide shows. Being able to get a specific length is extremely useful for serious slide show creators.

WHEN YOU NEED BLACK

Slide shows need black. They work best if they start from black and end with black. Lightroom does that for you automatically, but you have no control over it. You may need a longer opening (to allow some music to play first, for example) or you may want to make a transition between sections of your

show or when the music changes. Going to black for a moment is a good way of telling your audience the subject is changing, as shown in figure 9-12 (though you have to be careful that you don't have dramatic music ending right as you go to black or the audience will think the show is done).

To add a black moment to your show, you need a black image. It is a good idea to have a collection set up specifically to hold black images. You can simply shoot some black, way-underexposed images the next time you are shooting by leaving the lens cap on, setting the camera to manual, and shooting at very small f-stops (such as f/16) with a very fast shutter (such as 1/1000 second). Shoot a bunch of these, and then put them into a collection for use as needed.

You can also create some pure black images in Photoshop and save them as JPEG files. (This keeps them small and inconsequential on your hard drive — JPEG has no effect on a solid color of black.) You then import them into Lightroom and keep them in a collection (or you could just leave them in the Folder that they come in as).

Note that I suggest multiple black images. That is because you have to use a new one every time you need a black slide.

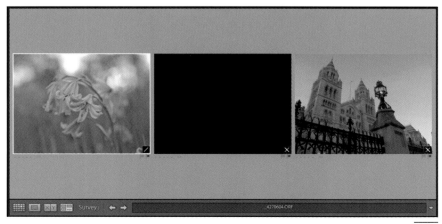

9-12

TITLE SLIDES

Lightroom gives you no way of doing title slides. Yet, title slides can be very important to a show. To create a title slide, you must go outside of Lightroom for this. You can use any text program that lets you save TIFF or JPEG files. You can create titles in Photoshop by making a blank image about 1600 × 1200 with a background that complements the slide show background and then adding text. This is shown after importing this image back into Lightroom in figure 9-13. You can also use a program such as PowerPoint or Keynote to make title slides and export them as JPEG files. Import these into Lightroom. At this point, you might create a Lightroom collection for slide show graphics, such as text and black slides.

Title slides can be an important addition to a slide show. They can help begin your show, giving it an actual title, as shown in figure 9-13, along with any other important information (such as identifying the photographer). They are very useful as endings for a show, giving important credits or photographer contact information, and they can be quite helpful for setting apart sections of a show.

WORKING THE BACKGROUND OF YOUR SLIDE DISPLAY

While I have put this section last in this chapter, you can alter the background — the image settings, layout, overlays, background settings, and so forth — at any time. I think it is best to do it after you have your basic organization and tone set to the slide show, as that affects the kind of "setting" each slide resides in as it plays on-screen.

Background includes more than just the backdrop of the photo display area. You learned the basics of Options, Layout, Overlays, and Backdrop in Chapter 8. Now, I give you some ideas on how you might integrate these tools into the production of an effective slide show.

CREATING A BACKDROP FOR YOUR SLIDES

I am going to skip down to Backdrop, which controls the background graphic or image behind your slides. I think it is good to start here because the colors, tones, or images you use in your backdrop affect the additional elements, such as Stroke and Shadow in Options, and image placement, in Layout, you use in the show.

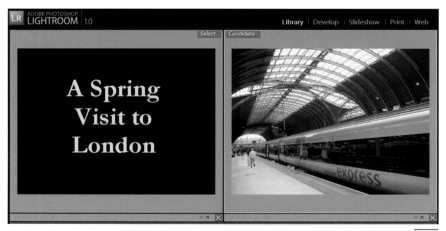

9-13

The color of your backdrop greatly affects how the images appear to the audience. Neutral tones keep colors constant, while strong colors can change the appearance of colors in the image. When two colors come together, they interact visually, causing us to see them as changed colors — this is called *simultaneous contrast*. Compare figures 9-14 and 9-15 and you will see what I mean. The only difference in the photos is the color around them, yet the actual images look different.

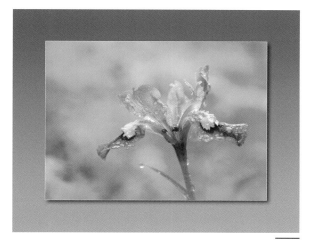

9-14

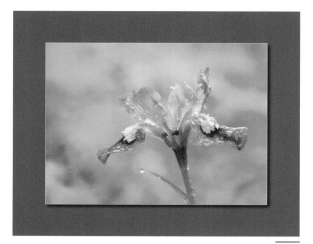

9-15

Backdrop colors are sort of like a mat used around a photo when it is framed. They set off and complement the image. A very important difference, however, is that a mat typically appears with one photo. Your slide backdrop must work with all photos. This is why you need to be very careful about using colors, especially strong ones, for a background. That can adversely affect the images displayed. They can make your photos look less colorful or create unpleasing color interactions.

Here are some ideas you can use when choosing a backdrop color:

> **White.** White can look very elegant, especially when it is used with black and white images, as shown in figure 9-16. White, though, is obviously very bright, so it can quickly take the viewer's attention from the photo, especially as the area of white gets larger. The use of a black stroke border can help. Also, a shadow can add too much contrast that may take away from the images. White can make dark colors look even darker, even to the point of giving them less apparent saturation.

> **Black.** Black is a dramatic, rich background. It can make colors lively and bold, as shown in figure 9-17. It also reveals weaknesses in contrast in your photos, making any weak blacks look gray and dull. Try a white stroke border with it; a shadow won't show up.

> **Grays.** Grays are always a good, neutral color for a background. You've seen them throughout this and the last chapters. You can use them from light to dark, gaining some of the characteristics of white or black while minimizing the problems. A light gray, for example, can still look quite elegant, yet it will have fewer problems with darker colors compared to pure white. A dark gray offers many benefits, such as lively, dramatic colors with less harshness than black.

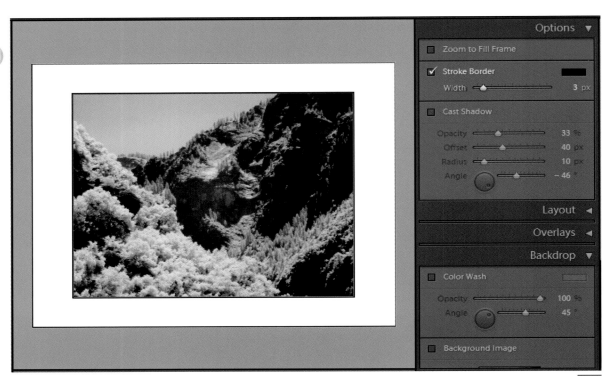

9-16

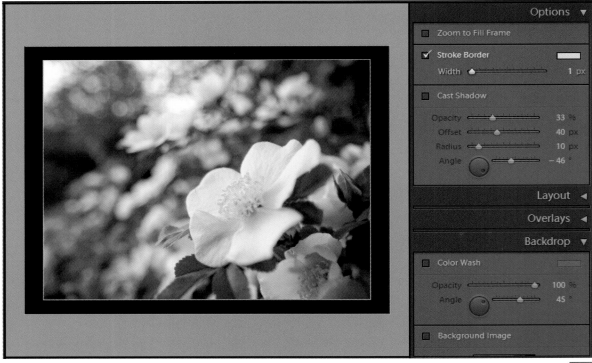

9-17

> **Colors.** Colors in the backdrop can be very important if you use client colors, for example. You can also use color to set a tone for the slide show, though it is generally best to use colors that are not very intense. Dark, less saturated colors can give a rich look to the slide show without causing too many visual issues. Often it helps to use colors as part of something else, such as part of a Color Wash, as shown in figure 9-18.

I like Color Wash a lot. It is a classic technique, with an almost retro slide effect. A dark gray on top and light gray on the bottom of the backdrop give you a highly directional setting for your photos. You might want to experiment a bit with Angle to see what works best with your photos.

Other colors that work well together in a wash include dark blue and medium blue, dark violet and medium violet (both turned way down in saturation), light gray and white, and black with almost any dark color. Avoid strong reds (they always compete with your photo) or bright yellows (they attract the viewer's eye and create some strong color effects).

USING OPTIONS EFFECTIVELY

The main controls you will be using in Options are Stroke Border and Cast Shadows. Zoom to Fill Frame is too limiting, in my opinion, for serious photographic slide shows because it crops arbitrarily, plus it makes verticals into horizontals.

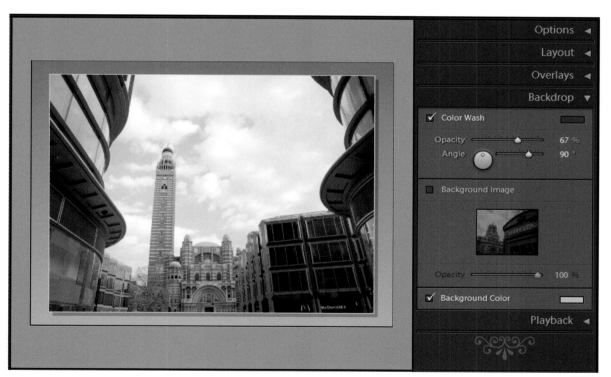

9-18

The choice of border and shadow settings is highly affected by both the color of the backdrop and the tonalities of the photos. Stroke tends to have the strongest visual effect on the photo because it puts a border all around the image. Most photographers find that either a white or black border gives a nice look for the photo. I find that in most slide shows such a border gives the images a more finished and polished look.

The choice of black or white is very personal and highly dependent on the photos and the background. If most of your photos are light in tone, the backdrop is light, a black border often looks nice (if black looks too strong, try a dark gray). If your photos are mostly dark in tone, the background is dark, a white border can be a good addition to your photo. You have to try them (and it is simply a few keystrokes to change) and see what looks best for your needs.

On some photos, such as an image with bright sky against a light backdrop or a night photo with dark sky against a dark backdrop, a border becomes a necessity. Without it, your viewers will have a hard time seeing the photo. Compare figure 9-19 and figure 9-20 to see what I mean.

Be wary of colors. A colored border can create some very undesirable interactions with the photos. That doesn't mean you can't use colors for Stroke Border, just use them carefully and deliberately. One place they would be appropriate is with a themed slide show, such as the Fourth of July, where some strong colors are the norm.

Shadow size and density is a very personal decision. Photographers vary considerably in how strong they want this effect. The backdrop color and tone also affect how you set up a shadow. A dark background needs a darker, and often a sharper-edged, shadow.

A light background with a soft, gentle shadow might make a photo look best. When you use a photo in the background, you often find that the shadow needs to be considerably darker and larger in order to work well.

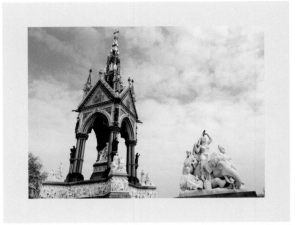

9-19

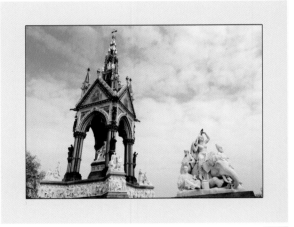

9-20

SETTING UP LAYOUT CONTROLS

The last step that I typically use for a slide show is to set how big the image is against the backdrop and where it is positioned in the frame. The default of Slideshow is to make the margins all equal and to move in and out together, as shown in figure 9-21. This keeps the actual space around the photo consistent, but not necessarily equal. If your photo is not cropped to match the working area, it cannot give equal space all around it. The best example of this is a vertical. If it fits between the margins top and bottom, there is no way it can have the same margins at the sides because you are working with a horizontal

method of presentation, your computer screen or digital projector.

How big the margins need to be depends on how large the resulting slide show will be seen, text needs, the backdrop, and your personal tastes. With the margins sliders all checked (Link All), you can move the sliders all together to make your photo larger or smaller in the display space. You might also try unchecking the bottom and move it up — this offers a traditional art presentation where the photo sits slightly high in the display area, as shown in figure 9-22 (this can be a very nice look).

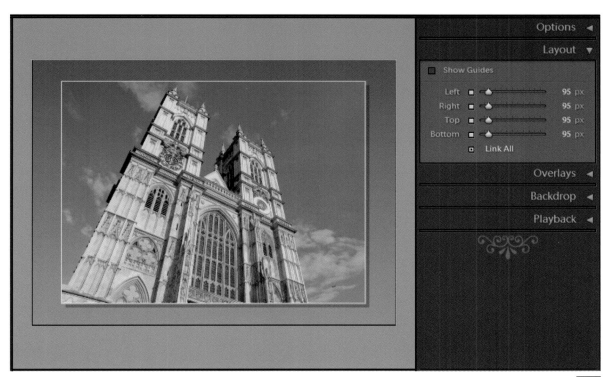

9-21

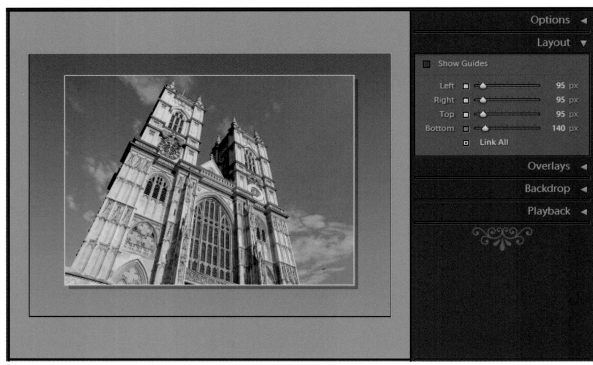

9-22

Having smaller photos in a large space is also an artistic way of presenting images (though it can look rather pretentious if the photos are too small). That sort of layout needs to have a backdrop that complements the photos and space, plus they need to be displayed with good size, whether that is on a large monitor or with digital projection. Smaller photos are also needed if much text is used or there is a large Identity Plate.

Images that nearly fill the display space can also look quite nice, especially with the right border and shadow. However, be careful about moving the photo edges too close to the display edges, as the images will then look cramped.

Q & A

You did not talk much about Overlays in this chapter, yet it is obviously important as noted in Chapter 8. How would you use it effectively?

That's a tough question for me to answer, because I don't find Overlay options all that useful for slide shows. There are occasions where having an Identity Plate can be helpful to give an identity to the show (especially if the show is being used for promotional reasons), but as soon as you add such a plate, you need to adjust the layout of the slide so the two look in balance on the screen.

I have no use for Ratings. That is really a distraction, I feel, for a slide show. The viewer should be watching the show without thinking about how the images are ranked unless they truly are judging images (such as in a contest or client-based sorting usage). I do understand that some photographers find this useful for specialized presentations, but most of the time, I can't see its value.

You talk about using black or titles as a way to break up parts of a show or add punctuation. Could you also use solid colors or even special images?

Absolutely. The advantage of black is that it is neutral and it recedes to the background. It is always a safe transition. As soon as you use something stronger, you get more attention from the audience, so you have to be able to use that attention wisely.

Title slides can be effective transitions, and they can look good on many backgrounds. If you use a photo for a transition, you need something that doesn't compete with the rest of the show. This can be a good place for a gentle use of your business or client's logo. You can also use an out-of-focus image with text over it, which offers a lot of dimension, too.

To me, it seems like music is really important. I can't understand why you can't keep music with the slides when a slide show is exported from Lightroom.

I totally agree. Unfortunately, Lightroom uses the PDF format for slide shows, and at present, that format does not save music with it. Lightroom is really great for creating portfolio presentation sorts of slide shows where the photographer talks about the images, but not so much for emotional slide shows with music.

If you really want music with your slides, you probably should check out the Pro Show Gold program from Photodex Software for Windows or FotoMagico by Boinx Software for Mac. Both allow all sorts of slide show effects and precise use of music.

Chapter 10

MAKING SENSE OF THE PRINT MODU

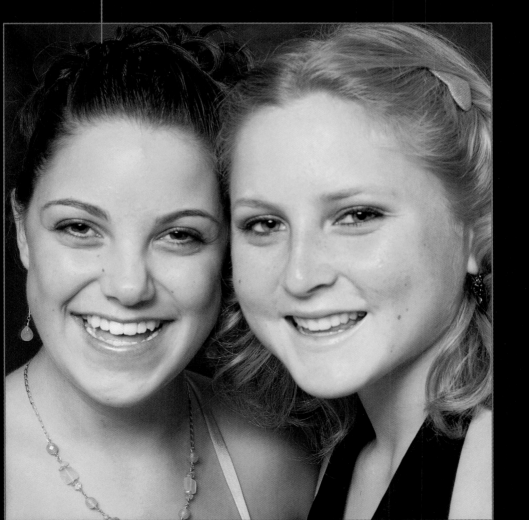

One of the great joys coming from the change from shooting film to digital is the opportunity to get really great prints that are optimized for the subject and photographer, as shown in figure 10-1. Everyone who used to try to get a good, custom print from a slide or negative knows what a challenge that could be. Sometimes it would take multiple visits to the lab when an image didn't print right and had to be reprinted. Or, you'd often just accept the print as is because it was "good enough" and any changes weren't worth the back and forth with the lab. You probably know what I am talking about.

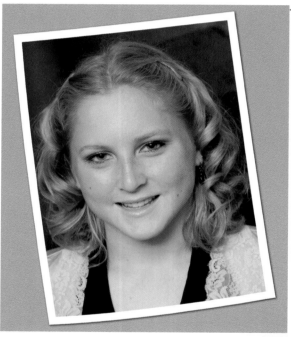

Digital photography and high-quality inkjet printers have really changed this. Yet, setting up a program like Photoshop for printing could be daunting for a lot of photographers. Digital printing offers a great potential, but not everyone had been realizing this when using standard image-processing programs. Further, the expectation that digital could solve all photo problems led to disappointment with prints when they didn't quite measure up.

Lightroom takes digital printing and makes all of the settings much more accessible. They also make more sense to the photographer. The Print Module offers some outstanding features to help you get the best prints from your photos, and it is the tight integration of this module with the rest of the program that enables you to go beyond making a good print to making great prints.

THE PRINT MODULE LAYOUT

The Print module is set up like every other module in Lightroom, as shown in figure 10-2. You should begin to see a consistency in what you can do based on what you know about other modules. Print has the same four-panel interface:

> **Center work area.** As usual, this holds the main photo. By default, it also includes rulers that show how the image is sized for printing and information about the print "job" including the number of pages, the printer, and the paper size in an Info Overlay. Also by default, this area also displays everything as a vertical sheet of printing paper. You immediately see how your photo will appear on the paper, along with non-printing guides that show things such as margins and the active image area.

> **Right panel.** As in all other modules, the right side of Print is the adjustment side of the module. It is where you change how the photo prints on a page, the information that prints with it, the image resolution, and so forth.

> **Bottom Filmstrip panel.** This standard photo display area can be quite helpful in Print to allow you to quickly choose images for multiple prints or several images on a page.

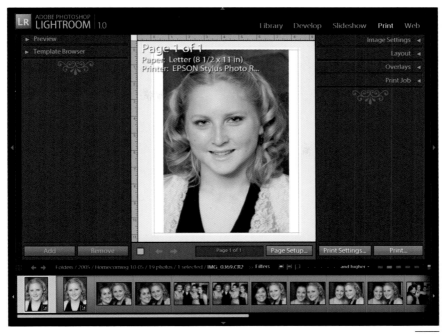

10-2

> **Left panel.** Once again, you find presets here, which are like Slideshow in that they are called templates, plus a preview area that shows what the templates look like as you move your cursor over them.

In addition to the panels, you see several features that are unique to the Print interface:

> **Workspace toolbar.** Just below the center work area is a very simple toolbar for printing shown in figure 10-3. At the left is a square that takes you to the first page of a multipage printing job. You can go page to page by clicking the back or forward buttons, just right of the square (or by just using the left and right arrows on the keyboard). You can also jump to a new printing page by clicking the box that says Page 1 of 1 in figure 10-3.

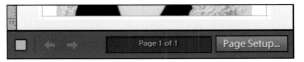

10-3

PRO TIP

I find that all of the panels are so useful for printing that I go back and forth among them. Because of that, I like to keep them all visible while I am in Print.

> **Page Setup button.** This button, located at the right side of the Print toolbar, takes you to your system's standard dialog box for choosing paper size, orientation of the photo (landscape/horizontal or portrait/vertical), and properties of the printer driver.

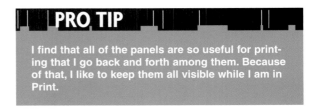

> **Print Settings button.** This is similar to Page Setup and is where you can also access your printer driver to adjust things like the paper used, borderless printing, and color management on and off.

> **Print button.** Now you can print your photo, though as a last check, this button allows access to the printer driver again.

One other thing to keep in mind about the Print module is that it creates an area called a cell for the photo to exist on a page. You will be adjusting such a cell to change how large the photo is on the printed page and its orientation.

Print makes printing easier and more intuitive for photographers. It brings out key printing adjustments and puts them into a logical framework for use.

PRINTING WORKFLOW

There are a lot of excellent choices in the Print module. You will typically find that you use certain choices again and again, while others are rarely used. And if you have contact with other photographers, you'll quickly discover that these choices are quite variable, even to the point of argument over which is truly "best." My feeling is that the best settings are those that give you the results you want, regardless of how any other photographer might use Lightroom.

However, there are some things about printing through Lightroom that affect how you might use the Print module. The workflow described next is one that I find useful to start with. It is a good, standard workflow for printing from Lightroom. With experience, you may find you want to alter this for specific printing needs.

1. **Select an image in the Filmstrip or Library for printing.** Usually, this is an image you have finished adjusting in Develop, but you can print any image at any time.

2. **Turn off the Rulers by pressing Ctrl/⌘+R and the Info Overlay with Ctrl/⌘+I if you find them distracting.** I often do turn them off in order to get a cleaner-looking interface, as shown in figure 10-4.

3. **Adjust Page Setup for the desired print size.**

4. **Choose the Maximum Size in the Template browser.**

5. **Adjust the size of the photo in Image Settings and Layout until you have what you need.**

6. **Add any Overlays that are important.**

7. **Set your resolution, color management, and print sharpening in that order and as needed in Print Job.** This order is a good habit to use if you work in Photoshop, too. While the order has no effect on Lightroom adjustments (none are applied until you actually tell the program to print or export an image), the order definitely affects Photoshop adjustments. I like to stay consistent.

8. **Set up the printer driver for the right paper and adjustments using Print Settings.**

9. **Print the photo.**

10. **Evaluate the image as a print (not just how it compares to the monitor).** Use Develop to make adjustments and print again.

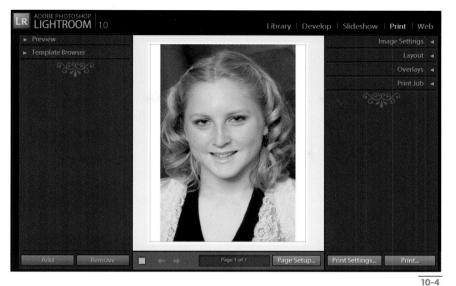

10-4

SELECTING PHOTOS FOR PRINTING

A great thing about Lightroom is how easy it is to go from any module to another. You can go through a whole range of photos in Library, select a photo (or a group of photos), and then go instantly to Print; or you can work on a photo in Develop and go right to Print with it, as shown in figures 10-5 and 10-6.

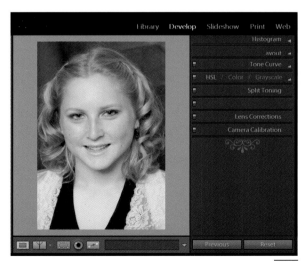

10-5

10-6

If you need to search a lot of photos in a shoot or collection for a print, then you are probably best off using Library for its Grid view and search capabilities. Many times, however, the Filmstrip will be an easy way to find photos for printing because it can be immediately accessible in Print. Filmstrip is also a convenient place to make multiple photo selections for making prints of them all.

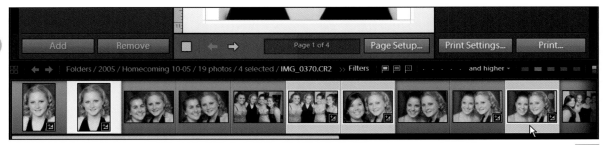

Simply click any photo in Filmstrip to instantly load it into the Print work area. Then Ctrl/⌘+click other images in the Filmstrip to add them to a group for printing. These additional images do not appear directly in the Print work area; however, you know they are included because they become highlighted in the Filmstrip, and the page numbers at the bottom of the central work area change to reflect the added images, as shown in figure 10-7.

Page Setup Choices

After you click Page Setup, a very standard dialog box (shown in figure 10-8 for Windows and figure 10-9 for Mac) appears that you will recognize from Photoshop and most other programs that you print from. This is based on your operating system and is only accessed by Lightroom. This is one area that looks significantly different in Windows and Mac computers. Neither offers any real advantages here, but you need to know how your system deals with the choices for Page Setup.

Choose your printer if it has not been selected for you automatically. This ensures that the paper size choices are limited to those that the printer can actually handle. The key settings you need to check in this dialog box are Paper Size and Orientation. Paper Size lets the computer (and Lightroom) know how big the paper is that you are using so it keeps those dimensions straight from Lightroom to printer software.

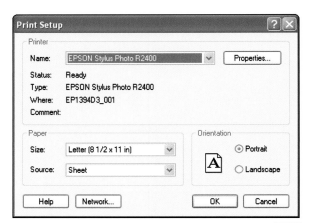

10-8

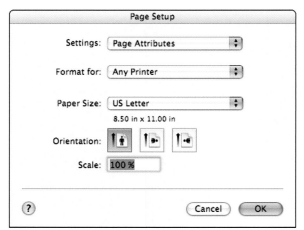

10-9

Orientation is, at its simplest, the way a photo is shown, either vertically or horizontally. However, it also affects how Lightroom places photos into certain templates and layouts of photos on a page. By default, Lightroom places your photo onto a vertical page in the display area when it is printed full size. If you use a multiphoto per-page template, you may find your photo doesn't use the space orientation you prefer. If you want something different, change it here.

Leave the scale of the image in the Mac dialog box to its default of 100%. You can control sizing better, and with more efficiency and quality, if you do it within Lightroom and not here.

PREPARING THE PAGE FOR PRINTING

Print offers you four groups of controls on the right side of the interface, as shown in figure 10-10. These enable you to set up the page with your photo for printing so that it looks right and prints optimally.

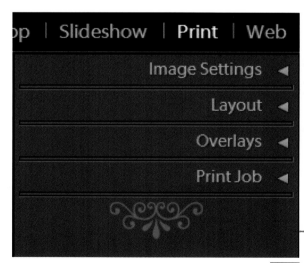

10-10

You have to start somewhere in order to use these controls. I recommend using the Maximum Size Centered template (shown in figure 10-11), which gives you an image centered on the page at the maximum size printable for most printers when borders

are included. After you work a bit in Print, you may want to create your own templates as a standard based on your most common printing sizes and use them as starting points for Print.

You can immediately print from any template and get good results. However, I think you'll find that you often want to be able to control the print more, creating a page that can be as unique as the photo, a page custom made for a client or a page for any special needs that you have. That's when you need to go to the right-side controls.

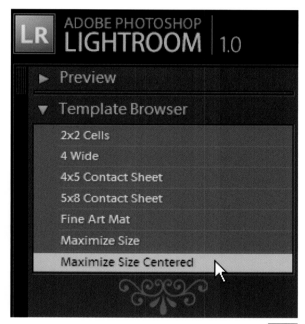

10-11

USING IMAGE SETTINGS

This group of controls, shown in figure 10-12, gives you three simple options that you either turn on or off, plus a fourth, separate option that lets you add a border to the image when printed. They are important choices that greatly affect the look of your photo as printed.

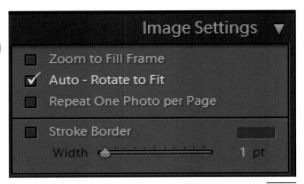

10-12

Here's how to work with them:

> **Zoom to Fill Frame.** Click this and Lightroom immediately fills the cell used for the photo, cropping the image to fit. That cell area is the portion of the printing page in between the margins. If you do not click this, the photo fills as much of that area as possible without being cropped, so there will be gaps on two sides unless the cell's proportions are exactly the same as your image.

When you select Zoom to Fill Frame and the image is cropped to match the cell proportions, you can change where the cropping occurs. Move your cursor over the photo — it turns into a hand, as shown in figure 10-13 — and you can click and drag your photo to make it better fit the crop. Some photographers love this option, as it allows the printing paper to be more fully filled with image; yet others hate it because it crops their photos and does not show the image as originally shot. Both are valid opinions; decide which works best for you and your photos.

> **Auto-Rotate to Fit.** Most of the time you will likely leave this selected. This means that the image is rotated so that it fills the cell with the long side of the photo matching the long side of the cell, and the short side of photo matching the short side of the cell. This is the "best" use of the cell in terms of space used. However, there may be times that you want to rotate an image differently so that it fits the page overall with a certain orientation,

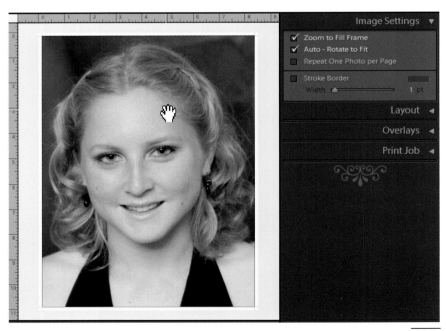

10-13

regardless of the cell orientation. An example of that would be a horizontal photo placed onto a vertical page so that the page stays vertical and the photo is still oriented in its correct horizontal position. Then you would deselect this option.

> **Repeat One Photo per Page.** This option only works when you have multiple cells on a page, such as the 2x2 Cells template. With this choice, Print fills each cell with the same photo on a single page, as shown in figure 10-14. This is a great way to print duplicate images in a hurry.

PRO TIP

You will often have the need to produce duplicates of images to give to people who work with you on a shoot (professional reasons) or for family and friends (personal reasons). You can do this very quickly with the Repeat choice. Select multiple photos, choose a template with several cells (or make your own, as explained later in the chapter), select the check box for Repeat, and you will have as many pages as you have photos, each page showing one photo multiple times.

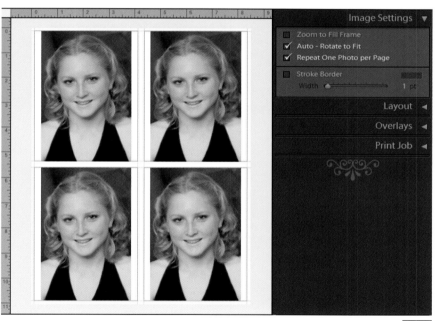

10-14

POSITIONING YOUR PHOTO WITH LAYOUT

With those basic choices from Image Settings out of the way, you can move on to how the photo will appear on the overall printed page. Layout allows you to set margins around your photo, set specific photo sizes (cell size), and decide how many photos appear on a page, as shown in figure 10-15. The flexibility of this part of the program can make for an overwhelming number of choices. Here's how I would suggest you use it (the order is not from top to bottom):

1. **Turn your guides on or off.** The Show Guides group seen at the bottom of this right panel category can help you judge the overall sizing of images, but they can be distracting when you are making a final evaluation of your photo and its position on the page. If you find them distracting, turn them all off by deselecting Show Guides, or you can turn off specific guides that you don't want to see by deselecting them one at a time.

2. **Check the Cell Size.** This is the specific size that your image will be printed. You can change it by moving the Height and Width sliders or by clicking and dragging on the numbers themselves. A detail of what the cursor looks like when you click and drag directly on a number is shown in figure 10-16. All control numbers in Lightroom act this way. Photoshop CS versions also do this, but not everyone knows that. If you have never tried this, just click and drag on a number to see how it works.

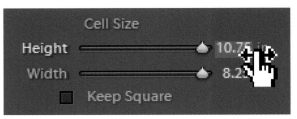

10-16

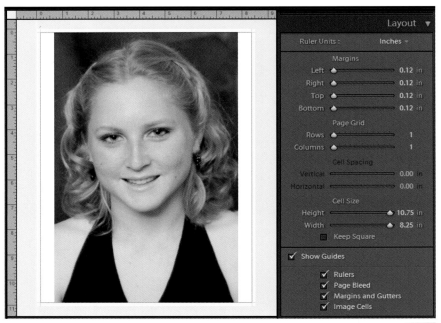

10-15

If you want a group of prints that include both horizontal and vertical photos in the same location (for a portfolio presentation, for example), you might want to select Keep Square and be sure Zoom to Fill Frame from Image Settings is deselected. That keeps all of your photos the same proportion (they can only be as wide or tall as the square) and centered in the same place. You can also use Keep Square with Zoom to Fill Frame in order to create square images on the page.

3. **Move the photo on the page.** Use the margins to move the image up or down, and right or left within the page. If your photo has room within the page, you can move it as needed and the cell size remains constant. If your photo does not have space, then the cell size changes as you change the margins. You can't miss this as the photo very obviously changes in size. If you need a certain image size on a specific size of paper, you may be limited as to where you move your margins. If not, you can move margins to create visual space as needed.

WHEN TO USE OVERLAYS

For many, many photographs, you won't use Overlays much, as shown in figure 10-17. This is really a specialized group of print adjustments that can be extremely valuable if you need them, but they can also be choices that many photographers never use. It is worth knowing what this group of adjustments does for you and how you might best put them to use, including the very valuable Border and Crop Marks options.

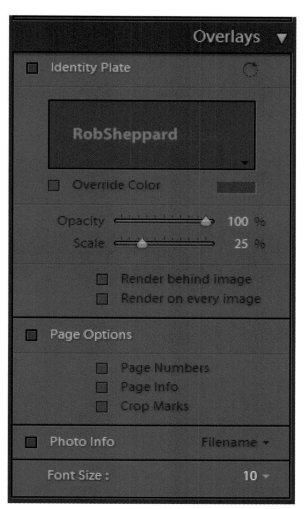

10-17

211

> **Identity Plate.** You've seen how Identity Plate can be used with the overall Lightroom interface in Chapter 2 and with slides in Chapter 8. It is something that clearly identifies your images with you, and if you are a working pro, with your business. Attaching an identity plate to photos being submitted to a publication, for example, can be very important. Adding an identity plate to all of your prints can appear pretentious, so you need to think about how it adds or detracts from your photos.

You add your identity plate by selecting Identity Plate, as shown in figure 10-18. At this point, you can choose from your standard graphic, or you can create a custom graphic by using the right drop-down menu shown in figure 10-19 and accessed by clicking the arrow at the bottom right of the Identity Plate preview. Change the Identity Plate's size and strength with Opacity and Scale (or you can just click and drag the anchor points around the Identity Plate, as shown in figure 10-18). "Render behind image" and "Render on every image" make the Identity Plate partially hidden by the image or appear on every photo, respectively.

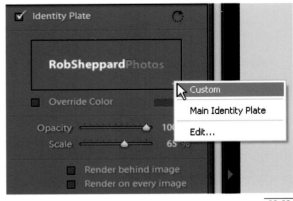

10-19

> **Page Options.** Select Page Options to include Page Numbers, Page Info, and Crop Marks on the printed page. Page Numbers and Page Info are rather specialized. Page Numbers is obvious, and you would only use it if you have a lot of images that you need to keep in certain order. Page Info gives information about how the page is set up for printing and can be used for testing prints and printers. Crop Marks can help you cut multiple photos from a page so that they come out even and correctly trimmed.

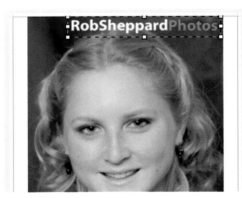
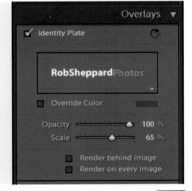

10-18

> **Photo Info.** You can add a number of standard bits of text based on the metadata of your image when this is selected. When Photo Info is active, you can click Filename to the right to give you a number of choices, as seen in figure 10-20, including the image file name, date it was shot, exposure, equipment used, and more when you select Edit. You can change the size of the text by clicking the number to the right of Font Size and choosing a new size (shown in figure 10-17).

This information is fairly specialized for most photographers, though if it is needed, it is also critical. A pro submitting proofs to a client is very likely going to include the file name. Any photographer testing new equipment will want to choose Equipment and perhaps Exposure so prints can be compared. Because the information that you can add to a print is so specialized, it is difficult to offer any real guidelines.

PRINT JOB

This section is very important for getting an optimum print from Lightroom. It is where you tell the program how to communicate with the printer so that the two speak the same language and is shown in figure 10-21. You will hear a lot of different ideas about how some of these settings must or must not be a certain way. Lightroom is designed to make the whole digital darkroom experience easier and not have a lot of absolutes, so I give you some ideas here on how to use Print Job simply and effectively. Because the individual settings of Print Job are so important, I am giving them to you in separate sections. I am not going to spend much time with Draft Mode Printing, however. This is not particularly useful for photographers. Why would you want to make a print at less than full quality? Still, there may be folks who just need a quick print at the proper size to use for evaluating a size, and this is what to use for that.

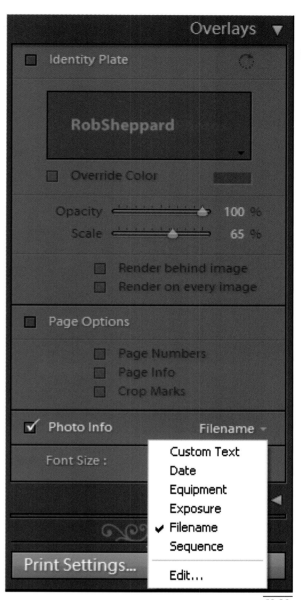

10-20

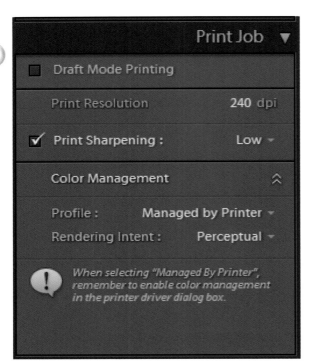

CHOOSING PRINT RESOLUTION

Print Resolution is the resolution of your image as it is sent to the printer. It is very important to understand that this is not the printer resolution and has nothing to do with printer resolution. The default of 240 dots per inch (dpi) is fine. You sometimes hear Photoshop users say that you should print at 360 dpi. That puts an unnecessary processing burden on your computer as your print file increases in size dramatically. An image at 360 dpi can add a huge amount of memory demand compared to 240 dpi. You can try printing at 240 dpi or even 200 dpi as your photos increase in size so that you keep the demands on memory lower. On most printers, you see little difference between prints of 200 dpi and 360 dpi. Some folks claim they can see a difference with a magnifier, but who do you know who hands you a print, and then a magnifier to see it better?

Some purists will tell you that dpi should not be used with image resolution, which is expressed as ppi or pixels per inch, in Photoshop. The idea is that dpi should be reserved for devices like scanners and printers and ppi for images. That might work except for two problems: First, scanner dpi affects the pixels in an image and directly correlates with the ppi of images; second, it is something totally different from the dpi of a printer. A printer's dpi tells you how ink is laid down on the printing paper and has nothing to do with pixels.

PRINT SHARPENING

Print Sharpening adds sharpening to the image for a print. You need to sharpen your photo for a print unless you sharpened it first in the Develop module. I recommend against sharpening it there. This is sharpening just for output as a print and is not applied to the photo otherwise.

Lightroom sharpens differently than Photoshop and uses different algorithms than either Unsharp Mask or Smart Sharpen. You can't use any formulas you used to use for Photoshop here. Lightroom is sharpening the image as it comes from a linear gamma space. Okay, I admit, I am not an engineer and I can't explain exactly what that means, but I can tell you that it means you need new formulas for using Lightroom.

Sharpening is always a subjective thing. The subject itself, the size of the print, the mood of the image, and the personal preference of the photographer all influence what might be used for sharpening. Print Sharpening offers three choices when you click the drop-down menu arrow, as shown in figure 10-22: Low, Medium, and High. I recommend you experiment with them using these guidelines:

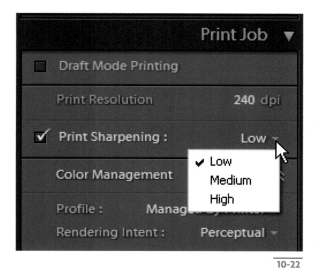

10-22

Immediately to the right of Color Management is a pattern of two up bracket arrows. Click them to turn on and off the warning seen below Rendering Intent in figure 10-23.

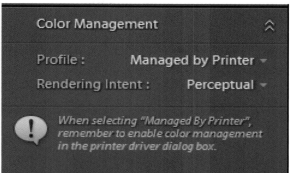

10-23

> **Low.** This is often a good choice for images of people, especially women and young children. It is useful for soft-focus or selective-focus images. Moody, atmospheric photos usually need less sharpening, too.

> **Medium.** This is a good choice for many subjects: groups of people, men, athlete portraits, flowers, gentle landscapes, and moody scenes with more detail.

> **High.** Reserve this for subjects that can handle it, such as architecture, landscapes with lots of textured rocks and other detail, dramatic abstract images, industrial scenes, and so on.

WORKING WITH COLOR MANAGEMENT

This is an important section that whole books have been written about. Lightroom is designed to be easy to use, however, so you really don't have to read a book about color management in order to use it well. One thing that I do recommend is that you ignore advice that makes you feel incompetent because you don't fully understand color management — you don't have to. Color management here is simply the way Lightroom communicates how it sees a photo to the printer.

Color Management gives you two controls, Profile and Rendering Intent, both with two choices. Here's how to use them:

> **Profile.** This is the paper profile of the printer and defines how colors are translated from the computer space to a specific paper. You have two choices: Managed by Printer and Other. With most advanced photo printers, Other generally works best and gives you optimum control, so I describe it first. However, you may find that some printers work better with Managed by Printer.

> > **Profile:Other.** Other gives you choices in paper profiles as shown in figure 10-24. You simply check the profile that matches the paper you are using. This is frequently the best way to go with high-end inkjet printers designed for pros. These profiles have been very carefully developed by the printer or paper manufacturer. They either come with your printer when you install it or you can add them later by downloading profiles from a paper or printer company Web site. However, Managed by Printer often works quite well with a printer and can be worth trying, especially with lower-priced inkjet printers.

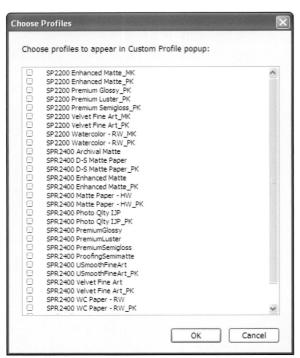

> **Rendering Intent.** You have two choices: Perceptual and Relative. Both work, but it is my experience that photographers generally prefer Perceptual. I would recommend you use it. Try Relative if you want to experiment.

> **Warnings**. If you have turned them on, as shown in figure 10-25, you will find some very useful warnings underneath Rendering Intent. The warnings basically remind you that you need to leave printer color management turned on when the color management is left to the printer, and turned off when a profile is used to control it within the computer. You turn printer color management on or off in the printer driver — where and how is dependent on the printer and the operating system.

10-24

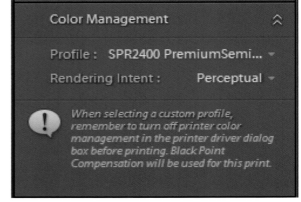

10-25

> **Profile:Managed by Printer.** Many Photoshop users often downplay this choice. Years ago, it was rarely the best choice. However, printers today are very, very good. Printer manufacturers want you to have a good experience printing. It is to their benefit when the printer software handles the paper profile automatically if the resulting prints are good. I find when working with a lot of photographers that this choice works well with the simpler and more mass-market photo inkjet printers. In addition, photographers occasionally find that no matter what they do, they cannot get the results they want with a paper profile on a particular printer. Yet if they select this option and let the printer take control, they often do. It can be worth trying a sheet of paper to see how it does.

USING THE TEMPLATE BROWSER

I am leery of many automated functions in programs for photographers. As a whole, photographers like more control over a photo than full automation allows. Luckily, Lightroom only uses its automated features, such as templates, as a way to get started, and you can tweak and modify any adjustments to the photo as needed. In addition, Lightroom enables you to remember consistent Print adjustments by creating your own, custom templates.

Print has a great set of templates for photographers. As you choose them, a graphic of their layout appears in the Preview above Template Browser. They include

> **2x2 Cells.** The 2x2 is not about inches but about a 2 × 2 grid of images printed on the page as shown in figure 10-26. By default, it is a vertical and vertical photos fill the cells. Horizontal images do not; instead, they only use the width of the vertical cell for their width as well. Change that with Auto-Rotate to Fit in Image Settings. Select multiple photos from the Filmstrip, and they appear automatically in the photo work area grid.

> **4 Wide.** This is a unique and dramatic layout for a page, as shown in figure 10-27, designed specifically for pro photographers' promotions. Each cell is a very wide, panoramic cropped format. In addition, photos come in sized to fill this width, meaning they are severely cropped (unless they are a panoramic photo to begin with). You can click and drag any photo up or down, or side to

side to better fit the crop to the content. This template with its extreme crop doesn't work with every photograph or photographer. At the bottom, your Identity Plate is inserted — simply double-click on it and you will get a dialog box to change it as needed.

> **Contact Sheets.** The Template Browser offers two templates for a "contact sheet," a printout that includes many photos with key information beside them, including photo information from the metadata such as the file name, the date the photo was taken, its title, and the copyright (change that under Overlays). The 4×5 Contact Sheet gives four columns wide by five rows high for a total of up to 20 photos per page as shown in figure 10-28. The 5×8 provides five columns by eight rows for a total of 40 photos per page. Only images that are selected in the Filmstrip or Library Grid view appear on the printed page.

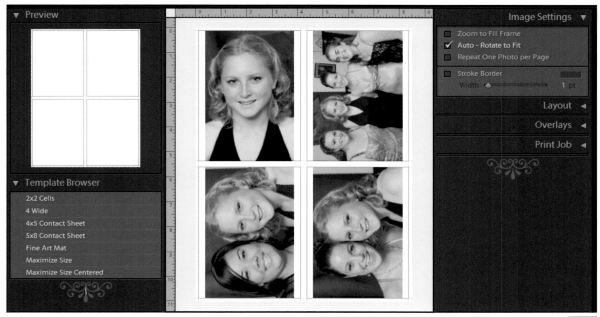

10-26

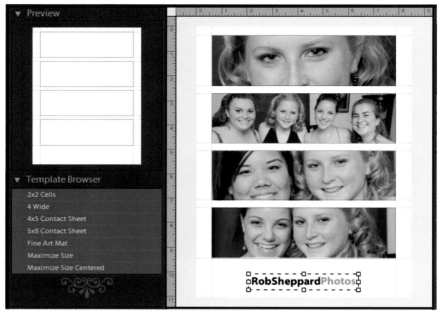

10-27

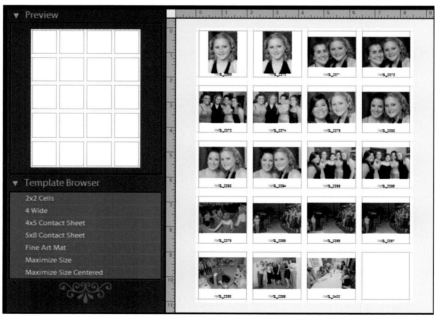

10-28

> **Fine Art Mat.** This template creates a cell to start that is approximately a square and is very slightly higher than it is wide as shown in figure 10-29. The size changes depending on the size of the paper. This cell is designed to make a photo smaller on the page and sitting higher so that you get an exhibition mat look. Verticals take up the center vertical portion of the cell, while horizontals take up the center horizontal part of the cell. You can get them to fill the cell by clicking Zoom to Fill Frame in Image Settings.

> **Maximum Size and Maximum Size Centered.** These two templates are very similar. Both bring in the photo to what Lightroom considers the largest size possible for the image on a given page with margins around the photo. Maximum Size puts a slightly different margin on the sides compared to top and bottom around the photo. Maximum Size Centered puts the same margin all around and is slightly smaller.

Use any of these templates by just clicking one. You can add your own templates at any time by making printing choices specific to your needs based on everything discussed in this chapter, including Page Setup and Print Settings. When you have them set, click Add at the bottom of the left panel and type a name for a new template. That's it!

CREATING CONTACT SHEETS

Printouts that show a group of photos (called "contact sheets" in Lightroom) are absolutely critical to the pro or even advanced amateur. They give you instant visual access to a lot of photos at the same time. You can use them for many purposes, including

> **A reference sheet that you can file.** You can put all of the images in your collections and shoots onto pages of printouts that you can file for reference by client, shoot, and so on, allowing anyone to quickly scan images without going to the computer.

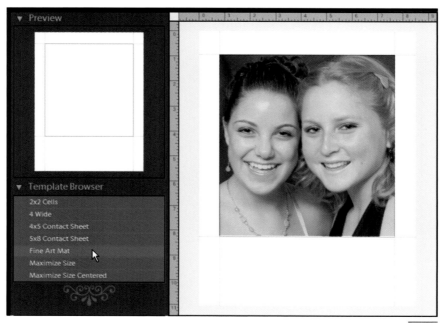

10-29

> **Selects reference sheet.** You might not want to put a printout of all of the images into a file for a client, for example, but you might want to put a printout of the key images or "selects" into it.

> **Index sheet for image submissions.** You can print out a sheet showing all of the images you have submitted to a client or other photo buyer that you can include with any media used for the submission or included with the invoice for reference.

PRO TIP

If you are a pro who is submitting photos to a publication, I highly recommend that you always print out a contact sheet with your submitted discs. This instantly puts you on the good side of the editor or art buyer. Many editors don't like disc submissions without photos because it means more time and effort out of their busy schedules to deal with a disc and their computer before they can even see what might be included. A contact sheet (or index print) lets them see what you have and which photos they want to look at quickly rather than forcing them to go through all of them.

The two choices for contact sheets in Lightroom, 4×5 and 5×8, provide enough images per page to fit most needs for this type of printing. However, you can change these quickly enough by going to Page Layout tools and choosing different numbers for the Page Grid. As you do that, you may find that the images get too close or too far apart. Correct that by changing Cell Spacing or Cell Size.

PRINT

After you make all of your adjustments, you are ready to print. You took care of Page Setup earlier. Now you need to set up your printer and print. This is one area where Mac and Windows operating systems differ completely. The Mac OS incorporates the printer

driver (the printer's software) into its own graphics and separates the options into different sections of a single Print dialog box, as shown in figures 10-30 and 10-31. The Windows OS accesses a unique printer driver dialog through the Properties button in the Windows Print dialog box, as shown in figures 10-32 and 10-33. Regardless, the choices you make for a print are essentially the same in both systems.

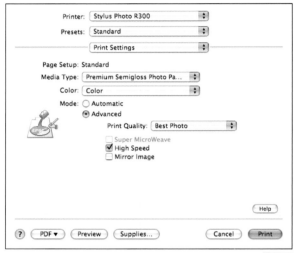

10-30

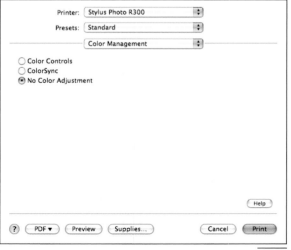

10-31

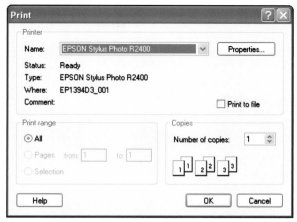

10-32

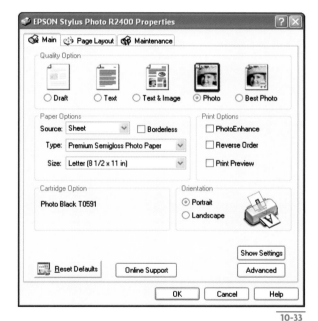

10-33

The important parts of the print sequence can also be accessed in Page Setup and Print Settings, but frankly, you can go right to Print if you want in Windows (on a Mac you cannot set paper size through Print Settings; you need to use Page Setup).

Some photographers prefer to set up printing separately from making the print, hence the choice. Here are the options you must confirm:

> **Number of copies to print.** This is pretty standard for all computer printing programs.

> **Color Management.** This goes right back to Color Management in Lightroom. If you selected Managed by Printer, you can pretty much stop at the printer driver screens shown in figures 10-30 and 10-32 and just select the Quality and Paper Type (this dialog box varies depending on the printer, but the choices will still be there somewhere). If you selected a paper profile, choose No Color Adjustment, as shown in figure 10-31 for Mac and 10-34 for Windows. To reemphasize an important point: You will see different layouts and arrangements of options in these dialog boxes with different printers, but the key choices are still there. Setting color management properly in the printer driver is critical, because you do not want the printer trying to readjust colors already adjusted for a paper profile by Lightroom.

After you make your choices, click Print and sit back while Lightroom and your printer make the print for you. In Chapter 11, you learn how to use Lightroom to go from a good print to a great print.

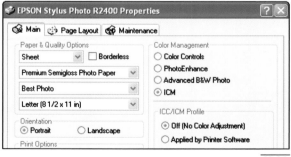

10-34

■ **I have heard that you should use an image resolution that is a fraction of the printer resolution. They say, for example, that you should use 360 ppi with an Epson printer because Epson prints at 720, 1440, 2880, and so on, so 360 is a simple fraction. Does that work?**

Logically, that might seem to make sense. After all, shouldn't the pixels in a photo somehow line up with the dots of an inkjet printer?

However, there are several problems with that theory. Modern printers print at variable resolution up to the maximum set. In other words, they might print a light area at a different resolution than a dark area, plus they may lay down different colors at different resolutions. So, if you want to work with an image resolution that is a fraction of the printing resolution, what fraction you will get is something that changes constantly depending on what color or tone is being printed.

Related to this, inkjet printers lay down ink with highly evolved patterns for color and tonality. These are so secret and are such prized possessions of printer companies that very few people actually have access to the algorithms that control this. From what I understand, these very sophisticated algorithms pay more attention to tonalities and color changes then they do to the actual pixels in an image. Plus, these patterns overlap ink dots in unique ways that don't always match pixels, either.

You talk about Lightroom's Color Management option as it relates to the printer and print. But what about the monitor? Doesn't this make the print match the monitor?

A lot of photographers are disappointed when the print doesn't match the monitor. In Chapter 11, you learn why having a consistent color for your monitor that can be interpreted by the print is important, but that thinking of actually matching a print to the monitor can be both misleading and very frustrating.

Color management, at any level, is about consistency first of all. You need to know that colors will be managed by the computer so that they will be interpreted correctly and consistently by every device used in digital photography, from the camera to the printer. While it is possible to even create profiles for a camera in order to better define its response to colors, it is rarely productive for most photographers. So, you set a color space, and then the computer with its programs recognizes it and interprets the colors correctly.

On a very basic level, obviously, you want the computer to interpret a red from the camera as a red and not a purple at worst or a red-orange at best. Then you need the computer to translate that red into a red that the printer understands and can duplicate. That may or may not be exactly the same red that appears on the computer screen, but it better be consistent and done as accurately as possible. That is what color management is about.

Chapter 11

FROM GOOD TO GREAT PRINTING WITH PRINT

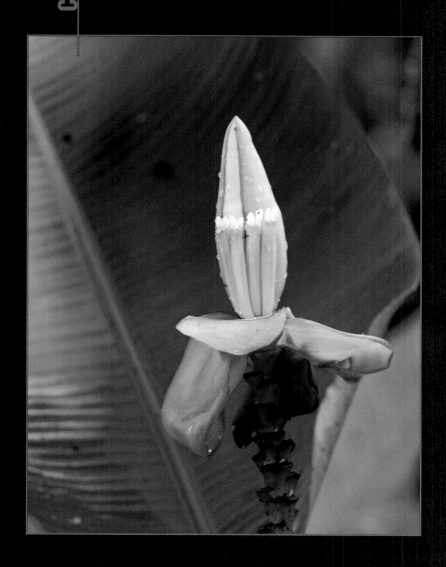

In the previous chapter, I covered everything you really need to know in order to use Adobe Photoshop Lightroom to create a good print from a digital image file. To refine your printing and get a better print, you have to make a lot of prints. I know of no other way to do this. Image printing is truly a craft, not just a set of "right choices" in a digital imaging program. It is about practicing with the program, learning the tools, and making the program conform to your expectations.

In this chapter, I help you make better prints by encouraging you to better learn the craft of printing through Lightroom. I am taking that further, though, and promising great prints. Of course, having a great subject or interpretation of that subject is up to you and can't be controlled by Lightroom. A great print, though, is one that truly expresses what your image and subject mean to you and that affects the viewer as well. I believe great prints are possible for anyone, but I repeat that this takes some time and effort to master.

MONITOR VERSUS PRINT

There is a pervasive, and I believe very misleading, idea that the best prints match the monitor. This idea can lead you in wrong directions as you strive for a great print. It is true that you should be able to get a good print that accurately interprets the colors and tonalities on your monitor, as shown in figure 11-1. Monitor calibration and attention to color management, as I describe in Chapter 10, helps you achieve that.

However, the monitor and the print are not the same. Here are some things to keep in mind:

> **The monitor displays colors from glowing RGB colors while the print represents its colors with flat CMYK colors.** These two color spaces are very different. RGB is the standard computer space using red, green, and blue. CMYK is an ink color space using cyan, magenta, yellow, and black, and is a smaller color space than RGB. No matter how well each works, they present colors in their own way, plus we react differently to glowing versus flat ink colors.

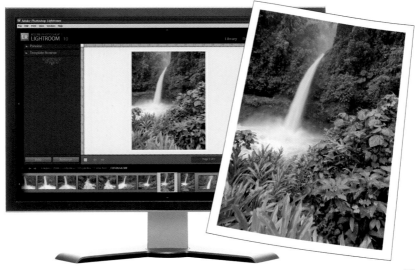

11-1

> **A print is seen in a different place than a monitor.** Surroundings always affect how we see the print, and print locations are never the same as a monitor's position.

> **The size of an image changes it.** If you make a small, 4-×-6-inch print, then a large 13-×-19-inch print, you will find all sorts of differences. Even compare the two images of the Costa Rican waterfall, La Paz, shown as a print and in a monitor in figure 11-1. You see color, contrast, details, and more quite differently when looking at different sizes. Yet a monitor is a single size and can never show the full range of sizes possible for a print.

> **A print is a different object altogether from a computer monitor.** You don't hold a monitor the way you do a print. You don't frame and move a monitor the way you do a print. These affect more than the physics of image handling — they affect your perception and your viewers' perception of the image.

> **No one ever asks a photographer to compare a print with what was displayed in Lightroom.** I have never seen computers set up at a gallery of photography so viewers could check to see if print and monitor match.

> **Viewers of a print need to respond to that print and make a connection through it to you and your subject.** It is possible that an evocative print might have no relation to the monitor image, which might be used for a different purpose than the print one.

This is not bad news! Getting a good print used to be so hard when you were working with labs that the promise of a perfect print made by computer seemed awfully seductive. Get the right program, use color management right, and you get a perfect print, right?

That path leads you into making a technically "correct" print, but not necessarily one that truly connects with your viewer.

WHY YOU NEED A WORK PRINT

Ansel Adams is considered one of the great print makers in photography. He died about 20 years ago, yet his influence on photography is still very strong. His prints are part of museum collections around the world, plus they sell at huge prices when any original print becomes available. How he worked and created those great prints offers some insight for getting your own great print from Lightroom. The name Lightroom is especially appropriate as it mirrors a darkroom, the place where Adams spent so much time making his images come to life on paper. Lightroom is the modern photographer's place for making digital images come to life on paper, too.

Adams was a master printer who had years of experience in the darkroom. He could "read" a negative and know what exposure to use with his enlarger when making a print from that negative. A lot of people would have been happy with such a print, and, indeed, they might have considered it a good one.

But Adams wanted more. He wanted a print that truly expressed his experience and feelings for the subject in the print as well as how he felt about the actual visual qualities of the print itself.

So, his first prints were always work prints. A work print was a common part of the film photographer's workflow in the darkroom. This was not meant to be anything final. It was a simple print that clearly showed what was in the negative (the original image capture) and offered insights to the potential of the image. In figure 11-2, you see a series of images to illustrate how an image might evolve from a work print (left) to a final interpretation (right).

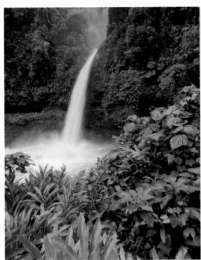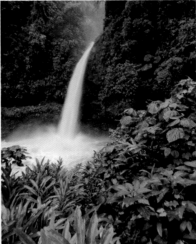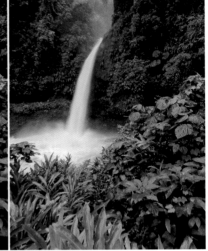

11-2

From that work print, Adams would begin to formulate a plan of work. What needed to be darker? What needed to be lighter? What areas of the photo were unbalanced? Where was it too light? Too dark? And so on. Based on this, Adams would make a new print, still considering that a work print, making revisions as to how the image needed to be adjusted to refine his vision of the scene. He would continue this for quite a while until he felt he had a master print that finally expressed his way of seeing.

It is true that in some ways, your monitor acts like a first work print. You should be evaluating what the image looks like, not simply what it looks like in Lightroom, but what it would look like if it were a photo hanging on the wall. That might seem obvious, yet I find many photographers don't do that. They adjust the photo until it looks good as a screen image on their computer. With experience making work prints, you can look at what is on the monitor and interpret it as a print. But to do that requires a different mental attitude. Once you start thinking that way, though, I guarantee you will start to see your photo differently before printing.

But sooner or later, you need to actually create a physical print that you use as a work print to evaluate what else is needed in Lightroom (or even if you need to do some work in Photoshop) to make this a better print, and, in the end, a great print.

One problem is that photographers sometimes see prints as simply a cost and don't want to "waste" paper and ink. An inkjet print costs far less than any traditional printing media from the old darkroom, especially when that print is in color. Consider the work print as an investment, a step toward truly wonderful photos and not as only a "cost."

EVALUATING A WORK PRINT

How do you evaluate any photo? How, exactly, can you define a good print? A great print? There is no question that these are very subjective. What is a good or great print to one person may be something else to another, but then that is true for any creative medium. What is important is not finding some absolute or perfect great print, but creating a print that truly reflects your needs, interests, and feelings about your subject. It might be difficult to define an absolute great print, but you will know it when you get it.

Getting to that print means making work prints, evaluating them, making adjustments to the image, printing out a new photo, evaluating it again, and so on until you get the print you want. There are some things you can do to evaluate your print to get you more quickly through the work print process, as shown in figure 11-3. Here are some things to look for:

> **Are your blacks printing properly?** Look at the darkest parts of the photo. Are there blacks where

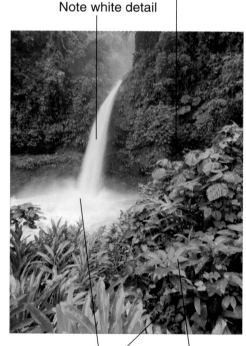

Check how blacks print

Note white detail

Check color in highlights and shadows

How do midtones look?

11-3

they need to be? Are the black areas too small? Too large?

> **Are your whites and highlights printing with the right detail?** If something should be pure white, then it should be that white in the print. If a highlight area should be registering detail, look to see if that detail is too light or too dark.

> **Check your midtones.** They can have a major effect on the look of a print. If they are too dark, the image can look muddy. If they are too light, the colors can be weak and pasty. I have often seen prints that had the right blacks, but in setting them, the photographer did not reset midtones and made the print look heavy and dark. Another problem is midtones that are too bright because the photographer tried too hard to show everything in the image.

> **Check your dark tones.** These are the dark areas of an image that have strong detail. When they are too dark, the image looks heavy. When they are too light, you often lose the feeling of dark in areas that should look dark, which plays havoc with the mood of a print.

> **Check your light tones.** These are the parts of a photo that have detail and are brighter than middle gray. If they are too dark, you will have a muddy, heavy-looking image. If they are too light, you can lose any feeling of substance in those areas.

> **Are your colorcasts correct?** Inappropriate colorcasts can make a photo look like a poorly adjusted television set. Skin tones can be sickly, neutral tones stained, and colors as a whole look like you are viewing them through some odd filter. Subtle colorcasts can be hard to see precisely, yet they can create major problems for a photographer, especially advertising photographers working with

products having defined colors or wedding photographers who had better have the right white for the bride's dress.

> **Is the color in the shadows and highlights different?** This is often the case, so make sure that both areas display appropriate colors. Does one look right but the other look wrong?

> **Check your sharpness.** Make sure sharpness is appropriate to the subject. Is detail sharp where it should be sharp? Is the image oversharpened, leading to a harsh look for the subject?

REFINING THE WORK PRINT

Lightroom's modular structure is the key to making a good print better. As soon as you notice an image doesn't quite work the way it should in the print, you can immediately go back to the Develop module, as shown in figure 11-4, and make some

adjustments. You are not limited by a darkroom's processing times like the traditional film photographer who works with an enlarger and processing chemicals. He or she could spend a day on a single print, but not because all that time is spent evaluating and changing prints. The time from when the enlarger comes on until the print is ready to be evaluated can take 20 minutes or longer per image.

Now, you can quickly make changes to an image, be ready to print again in minutes, and have a print in hand in less than five minutes. That helps many photographers feel freer to experiment as they fine-tune a print.

After reading what I discussed about image evaluation just before this section, you might have already started thinking how you can correct those things. Here are some ideas for doing just that, using the Develop module to refine your prints:

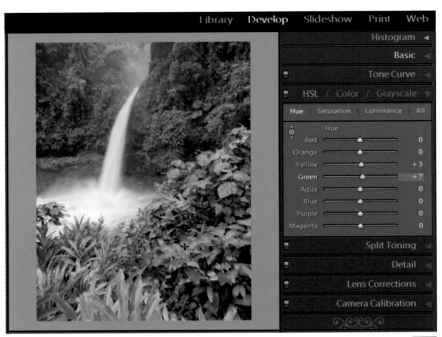

11-4

> **Weak blacks.** This is one area that I consistently see as a problem in prints. Check your blacks under Blacks in the Basic group of controls. Use the Alt/Option key to see where your blacks are.

> **Blacks cover too much or two little of photo.** Again, check Blacks in Basic. Use the Alt/Option key to see how much of the dark areas are truly black. You may be limited by your subject and exposure as to how far you can go. Try Basic ⇨ Fill Light to lift and open dark areas. You can also try the Tone Curve — use the click-and-drag direct control (fully explained in Chapter 6) so you can click directly on the dark areas and move the cursor up to lighten them.

> **Whites have no detail**. Don't try to get detail in places you need no detail, such as a bright sky behind a person or in specular highlights (bright reflections of light in the scene). If you feel you do need detail, check Exposure and Recovery in Basic. Your exposure might also give you no detail to bring out, and you will see this as you try to change Exposure. You can also work the Tone Curve — use the click-and-drag direct control again, this time to click directly on the light areas and move the cursor down to darken them.

> **Highlights don't have the right detail.** While you can use Exposure to affect this, you are usually better off going right to Highlights under the Tone Curve.

> **Midtones are off.** For slight midtone adjustments to a print, you may find that Brightness and Contrast in Basic work very well and you don't have to muck around in the Tone Curve. If you find, though, that the midtones just look muddy or heavy, especially if they seem to have some contrast problems, then you will probably need to make some Tone Curve adjustments.

PRO TIP

Consider blacks (and to a degree, whites) in your print to be like the framework of a house. Without that framework, no matter what else is done to a house, it will never be whole without the proper framework. Now, a building that is only framework won't work too well, either. You need the rest of the structure to make a real house. That's what midtones provide to a print. They make a photo complete and make it work as an image for a viewer.

> **Dark tones are out of balance.** Start with the Tone Curve and Shadows. This isn't the only place you can go, however. You may find that the dark tones have a color problem that affects their tonal appearance — try adjusting the Shadows part of Split Toning. Also, check out the HSL controls. Sometimes it isn't the overall tonality of the dark areas that causes the problem, but a specific color that makes up a large portion of the dark areas is too dark or light in tone. Then you can try changing its Luminance in HSL.

> **Light tones are out of balance.** Start with the Tone Curve by changing Lights first, then Highlights. Split Toning doesn't have as big an effect on light tones (the colors don't react as much), though changing Luminance for specific colors in HSL can be worth a try.

> **Correcting colorcasts.** You can try making slight changes in Temperature and/or Tint in Basic first. Next, try the White Balance tool and click in a number of areas in the image. Another possibility are the HSL controls, which enable you to tweak specific colors, such as those represented in the colorcast, by hue (to change their actual color) and saturation. You may have to work more than one color slider to get the best results. Split Toning can affect the color in highlights (those areas often show colorcast problems the worst), and then shadows when the colorcast is not consistent across the range of tones in an image.

> **Correcting color in shadows and highlights.**
> Shadow and highlight colors are nicely affected by changes in Split Toning.

> **Getting optimum sharpness.** You have to make many prints at different sizes to start to get an intuitive feel for sharpness in the print. Be critical of how sharpness affects your subject and the mood of the photo, and then increase or decrease Sharpness to fix any problems. You may also need to check Detail in Develop to be sure you have not sharpened twice (once in Develop and once in Print) and that Luminance and Color noise reduction controls are not set too high (or they will affect small detail in a photo). You can also try setting Luminance high if your photo looks sharp, but details, such as skin tone on a face, are too sharp.

USING VIRTUAL COPIES

Lightroom offers an interesting option that can be helpful in making prints called Virtual Copy. Right-click on the image (in the center or Filmstrip, it doesn't matter), and you get the context menu shown in figure 11-5, where among many of the other options in Lightroom you find a choice called Create Virtual Copy. If you are using a Mac, you must press Ctrl+click to see the menu (another reason to get a right-click mouse if you work with a Mac).

Choose Create Virtual Copy and Lightroom makes a file of instructions that duplicate any adjustments on the original image, plus adds a new image to Library and Filmstrip views with a little page-turn symbol at the lower-left corner, as seen in figure 11-6. The actual image file has not been duplicated so an insignificant amount of additional hard drive space is needed. Now you can adjust this virtual copy just as you would adjust the original image, but every adjustment is kept separate and connected only to this copy.

This can be very helpful in making prints. You can create virtual copies for different printing purposes. You might keep one simply for the original file you used to make the first work print, and then use others for variations of prints needed for different locations, sizes, or on different papers. You can group these copies into a stack (so less space is used on the screen) by selecting all versions, then right-clicking and choosing Stacking ⇨ Group into Stack. I don't use the Stacking command much, but you can stack any selected group of images this way.

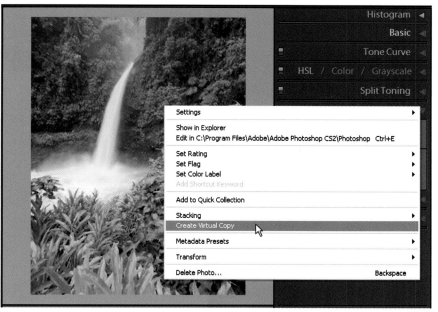

11-5

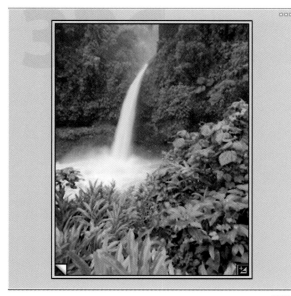

11-6

PRINTING MULTIPLE PHOTOS ON ONE PAGE

Often you will want to print several small photos on a single page, as shown in figure 11-7. Printing the same image on a single page is covered in Chapter 10. You might do this to give copies of images from a shoot that you promised folks who helped you with that shoot. It is far more efficient to do this as multiples on one page of paper rather than make a lot of small prints. Here's how to do this:

1. **Select your photos.** Either go into Library or Filmstrip to multiple-select the specific images. I sometimes find it helpful to put all of these into a Quick Collection and print from there.

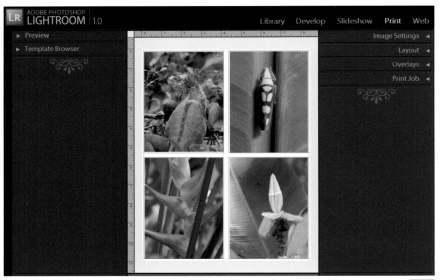

11-7

2. **Set the number of photos and adjust the cell size.** In figure 11-8, I simply used the 2x2 Cells option in the Template Browser, which makes it very easy to print four images on a page. If you need a different set of images, select the number of images per page by going to Layout and changing the Page Grid to the appropriate number of rows and columns, as shown in figure 11-9.

> **NOTE**
>
> A reminder for multiple photos of the same image: In Image Settings, select Repeat One Photo per Page. This fills all cells with your selected image. Also select Auto-Rotate to Fit.

3. **Set a specific size (if needed).** You must watch the Cell Size shown in figure 11-9 to know how big your images will print on the page. Lightroom does not crop your photos for any specific size unless you tell it to. You can crop the image in the Develop module to a specific format, or you can simply select Zoom to Fill Frame in Image Settings, and then set that specific size in Cell Size. If you can't make the photos big enough in Cell Size, you must change the Page Grid to something with fewer images.

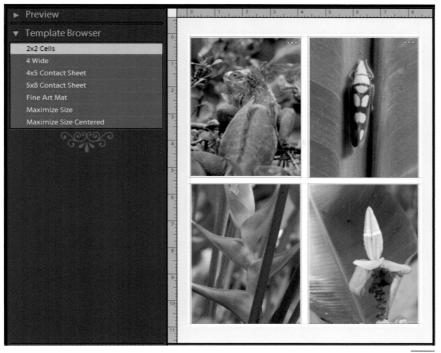

11-8

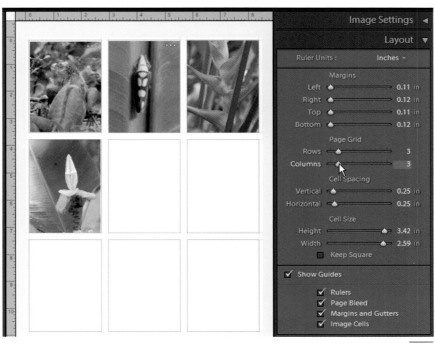

11-9

233

4. **Adjust Cell Spacing.** You may have specific needs on how you cut up your final print for the multiple copies. Or you may find you just need some sort of spacing so you can better see where one image begins and another ends. Adjust Cell Spacing to accomplish these things. And because all the controls are interrelated, you may have to also change Cell Size and/or the Page Grid again, or you can make a change to Margins.

5. **Print Crop Marks.** Go to Overlays and select Page Options. This makes Crop Marks available as a choice. Select it and Lightroom prints small marks on the page to help you use a paper cutter to cut the multiple images on the page into singles. You can see the marks if you look closely between the images in figure 11-10.

CREATING A PROMO SHEET I

As you saw in Chapter 10, Lightroom has some very flexible capabilities for making a contact sheet. Yet, a contact sheet is only one thing you can do with multiple images on a page. With a little thought and creativity, you can quickly do some attractive promotional pieces that you can print as needed. The easiest way to show you what is possible is to show you how to create a flyer or promo sheet that holds a group of photos.

A good place to start is with the 4 Wide template in the Template browser, as shown in figure 11-11. This is a really cool combination of images cropped to a panoramic format, with your Identity Plate at the bottom. You can't use this for all photos, obviously, because the crop is pretty severe. However, with the right images, this creates a classy, dramatic look for a promotional piece. Here's how you can use it:

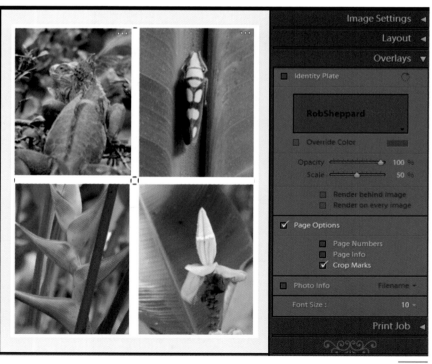

11-10

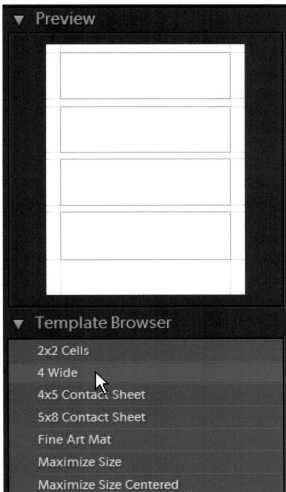

1. **Pick four interesting images.** You can go to your Filmstrip and work with a single collection or shoot. I recommend you go back to the Library module, add some photos for possible use to the Quick Collection, as shown in figure 11-12, and then use the Quick Collection for your image resource to do the flyer. In looking at photos for this grouping, remember that each one will be cropped severely to a short horizontal and that the four cropped images need to have some visual or contextual theme so that they look like they belong together.

PRO TIP

You can easily move images in and out of Quick Collection by clicking the little circle that appears in the upper-right side of images in Grid and Filmstrip views when you run the cursor over an image. You can also clear everything from Quick Collection from File>Clear Quick Collection or Ctrl/⌘+Shift+B.

2. **Bring them into the template.** In the Print module, choose 4 Wide in the Template Browser. Then multiple-select the four images you want from the Filmstrip. If you put just four into a Quick Collection, you can select them all by pressing Ctrl/⌘+A. They now all appear in the grid, as shown in figure 11-13.

11-11

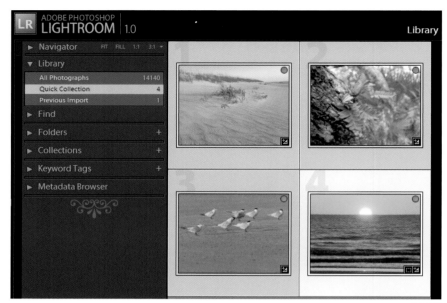

11-12

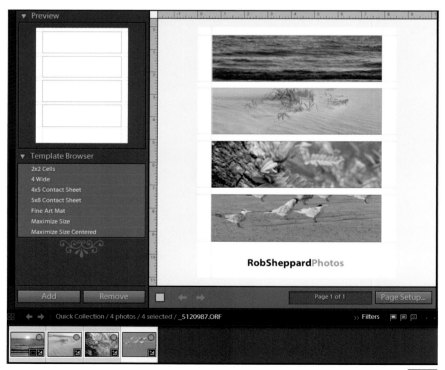

11-13

3. **Move photos within frame.** Click and drag to move the images up and down within the crop area to find a part of each that works best with the shot, as shown in figure 11-14. You can't move it side to side because Zoom to Fill Frame is automatically selected in Image Settings, so the photos are zoomed to the full width of the crop.

4. **Arrange the photos.** Here it gets a little tricky. You can't simply click and drag photos around on the page. Yet, the order in which you shoot the photos is the order they appear on the page. You get around this by going to the Filmstrip. After first deselecting all (click in a space where photos aren't), you can rearrange photos in the Filmstrip by clicking and dragging photos, and that order will show up in the central image when you select them again, as shown in Figure 11-15. This is a good reason for using Quick Collection because you will only have a few images to deal with as you rearrange them.

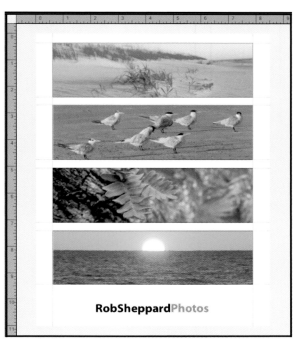

11-15

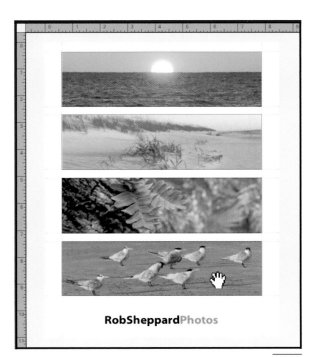

11-14

5. **Edit the Identity Plate.** The Identity Plate really finishes this printed piece nicely. It appears at the bottom of the page. You can change it as you change any Identity Plate in Print as I describe in more detail in Chapter 2 (double-click the Identity Plate that appears to edit it or use Overlays). You can even add a Web site or phone number, as shown in figure 11-16. There is a trick to this because the Identity Plate Editor is really pretty basic and has a small text space. Reduce the size of your text so it fits while you work on it, which is what I did in figure 11-17. Then press Enter/Return to insert line breaks, and press the space bar to insert spacing. When done, select all and set the text to the size you really want it (though not all sizes work properly with two lines — you may also have to resize the text box on the photo). You can select different parts of the text for different sizes, too, though that can be challenging.

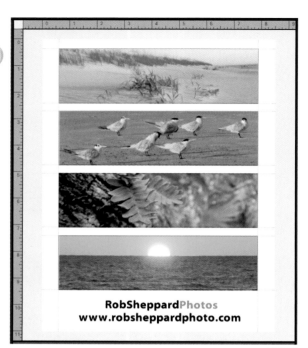

11-16

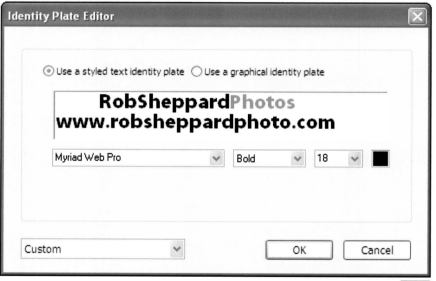

11-17

PRO TIP

The text editor for Identity Plate is pretty basic and somewhat awkward to use for the purposes I describe here, but you can do it. If you have trouble doing it as described, you can also create (and edit) the text in a word processor like Microsoft Word, select the text, copy it, and then paste it into the preview area of the Identity Plate Editor. Or you can create a graphic in Photoshop, save it, and then import it as a graphic into the Identity Plate.

6. **Position the text.** Click and drag the Identity Plate to the position you want it. Sometimes you will find it looks best perfectly centered, but other times it looks best at the right or left side, lined up with the grid line that marks the edge of the photos.

CREATING A PROMO SHEET II

Another way of creating a promo sheet, one with more photos that are not arbitrarily cropped, is to use another Contact Sheet template such as 4x5 Contact Sheet or 5x8 Contact Sheet, and then include an Identity Plate. As a photographer who also has worked a long time as a magazine editor, I can't really recommend those numbers. It puts too many photos on a page for a promo sheet. They are fine for a contact sheet as a reference, but they make the images too small for any editor or photo buyer to really see them adequately. Here's what I recommend:

1. **Decide the number of images to go on a promo sheet.** I recommend nine images by using a four-row, three-column grid setup in Layout, as shown in figure 11-18. That gives a total of 12 spaces, but the bottom three give a space for the Identity Plate. This puts a good number of images onto the page, keep them large enough to view easily, offers decent spacing for the photos, and presents a nice-looking page.

2. **Choose a group of photos for that promotion.** Again, I find the best way to do this is to use the Library module and put your photos into the Quick Collection. Pick a group of photos that look good together and that show off your work. Use the Quick Collection while still in Library to compare, contrast, and arrange images to be sure they work together, as shown in figure 11-19.

3. **Vertical or horizontal?** I suggest keeping your photos for a given page all horizontal or vertical. It is possible to mix them, but because you can't change the design of the page, the mix never quite looks right if the images are all oriented the same direction; that is, both horizontals and verticals read correctly). If you mix horizontal and vertical photos that are sized equally, they will not be oriented the same, so you will have to rotate your page in order to view individual images. That's not a good look to send to an editor.

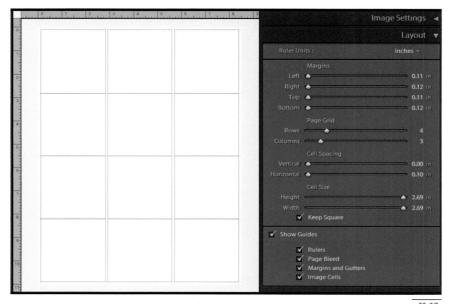

11-18

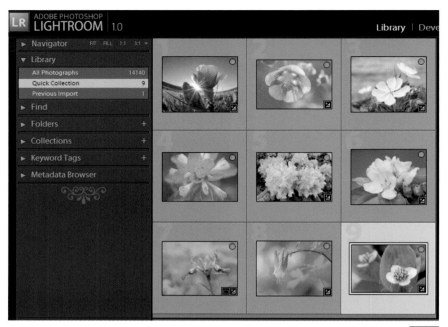

4. **Set up the use of the photos.** Go back to Print, and select all of your photos so they now appear in the grid. Select Zoom to Fill Frame, as shown in figure 11-20. This keeps the cells filled and makes the overall "design" of the promo sheet look its best. At this point, though, the images are all cropped to a square, which may or may not work for your photos. Images can be moved within that space, but not all photos look good as squares. The lines in the design shown in figure 11-20 are guides and will not print.

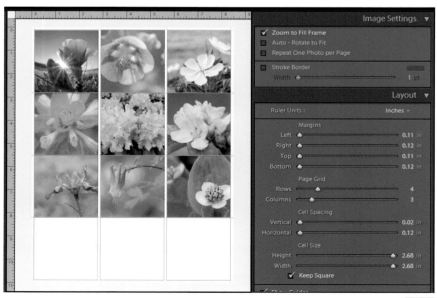

5. **Refine the arrangement of photos.** Go down to the Filmstrip to click and drag photos into new places that work better together, as shown in figure 11-21. A hint: If you can't click and drag, it means your photos are all selected. You need to deselect them by clicking off the photos in the Filmstrip or pressing Ctrl/⌘+D.

6. **Adjust the cell size.** If you don't like square images, you have to change Cell Size in Layout. Deselect Keep Square and move the Height slider until you like the look of your photos. You might also want more space between the photos — you can do that in Cell Spacing, as shown in figure 11-22.

PRO TIP

Experiment with cell spacing. You can get a very interesting look with groups of photos butting up against each other (0-inch horizontal spacing for vertical photos; 0-inch vertical spacing for horizontal photos) that create rows of linked photos. You can also try the "block" look with 0-inch spacing all around.

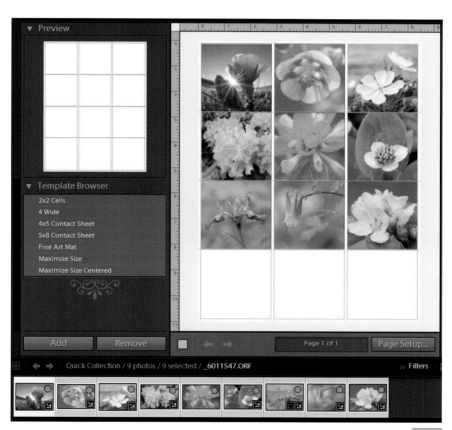

11-21

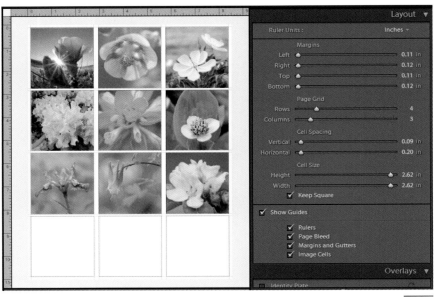

7. **Add and edit the Identity Plate.** In Overlays, select Identity Plate. It is placed at the bottom of the page in the empty cells — drag it to where you like it best, as shown in figure 11-23 (the guides have been turned off). Edit it as needed

(double-click on the frame). As I note in the first Promo Piece section, a very classy way of doing this is to create a text-based Identity Plate with your name and Web site or phone number.

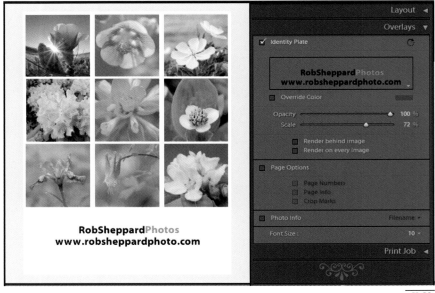

Q & A

Making a lot of prints, especially work prints, seems costly and wasteful. I realize that I can't just use a cheaper paper so I don't waste the good paper on them. But what can I do to make this more efficient?

Early on in the transition to digital printing, the idea of using cheaper paper came up a lot, as prints could be expensive. Now that paper and inks cost much less, your idea that this is not a good idea is right. In general, you want to only use the paper you want the final print on as that is the only way to truly evaluate what an image will look like. Papers do change the look of colors, contrast, and tonalities.

So what can you do? Here are a few ideas:

> **Stop bad prints as soon as you see they are off.** Most printers have a stop button. If you see the print is too dark, too light, off-color, and so on, stop the print from continuing. This can happen because you set the printer driver wrong (and we all do that at times — you go through the process too quickly and forget a key step, such as turning off color management in the printer driver). By stopping the print, you obviously use less ink. In addition, you often get a large bit of blank paper that you can use again for a work print or, at least, a small print.

> **Print small images at the start.** You will need a full-size work print at some point because you need to see how the image looks at its final size. However, creating a small print for initial evaluation gives you a quicker print using less ink, and, even, smaller paper (or at least you can print more than once on the same larger sheet by putting it in the printer again in a different orientation).

> **Crop images for test prints.** Often there is a critical part of a photo that you can print to get most of the information you need for the final image. Go to Develop, crop the photo to a strip through that area, and then just print it. You can shift the strip to the right or left on the page using the Page Layout tools and run the paper through the printer more than once. Because all work in Lightroom is non-destructive, this cropping doesn't hurt anything, so you can "uncrop" the photo for full-size work prints and the final print without hurting anything in the image.

The promo sheets sound like a neat way of creating a group of photos. Could you put the Identity Plate over a photo or a group of photos for a different design? And what about other uses than strictly marketing?

The first part of this question brings up a great idea: using a photo as a background for the Identity Plate. This can be a standard, iconic photo for your business, for example, that you can use on all promo sheets. You simply need to import it into a folder in Lightroom in order to use it. You could also build the text and photo together in Photoshop so it would be imported as a graphic.

The biggest thing to consider about using a photo behind the Identity Plate is that the photo has to be subordinate to the text or logo in that plate. You don't want a strong photo that competes with the plate, or why bother doing this? You can make an adjustment to a photo to make it lighter, darker, or less saturated (even black and white) so that the text or graphic shows up better against it. If you decide to use such a photo a lot with that adjustment, you might consider exporting it as its own file, then reimporting that adjusted photo back into Lightroom just for this use behind the Identity Plate.

The second part of the question brings up many possibilities for how you can use these promo sheets. They are simply a quick way of neatly grouping photos together, and then with the Identity Plate, adding some text. Maybe these ideas will stimulate more based on your specific situation:

> **Article query.** Put together images that support an article idea, and then put something about the idea along with your name and contact information in the Identity Plate and use this to support a query letter to a publication.

> **Organization flyer.** If you photograph for a community organization, whether it's your church, soccer league, or kids' school, consider gathering some of those images into a group that you can use together to support the organization, using the Identity Plate to identify the organization.

> **Graduation announcement.** What if the group of photos shows off your senior's past year's activities? I shoot all digital and photograph both images for my work as a writer/photographer and as a dad, so it would be pretty easy to gather a series of photos for that announcement, using the Identity Plate for information about the senior.

> **Family story.** You take a great vacation with your family, but then the photos rarely get seen. Make a selection and put them onto a promo sheet form using the Identity Plate to identify the location of the trip.

Chapter 12

THE WEB MODULE

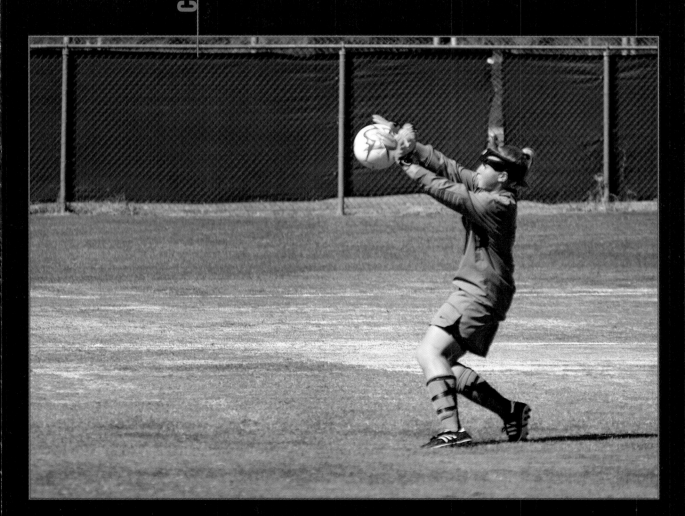

Photoshop and other imaging programs often have a Web component to them, but few have such a strong and easy-to-use section like Photoshop Lightroom's Web module. The Web has become an extremely important place for photographers and their images. For pros, it has become pretty much a necessity as shown in figure 12-1 (which was made in Lightroom). Even amateurs are using it extensively as a way of displaying images to friends and relatives across short and long distances.

Let's be straight about this, though. This is not the program for anyone doing extensive Web work. The Web module follows the concept of the rest of the program — making digital photography easier and simpler for the photographer. And it does exactly that for Web galleries, a standard need for photographers, but it won't give you the tools to create a complete Web site. Still, a lot of photographers have their Web site designed professionally, and then upload new photos regularly. The Web module is designed to make that task easier and more efficient for a non-Web designer . . . the photographer.

This is not to say that there is nothing here for the photographer who is more sophisticated in his or her Web use. The Web module does offer anyone a quick and easy way of creating both HTML and Flash picture galleries for Web use.

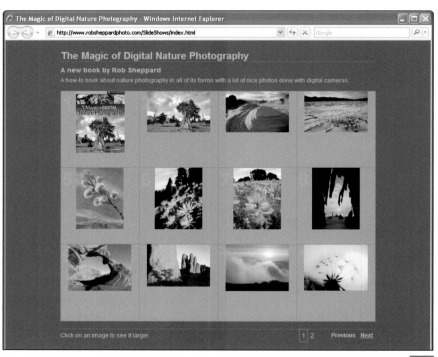

12-1

WEB MODULE LAYOUT

Like all other Lightroom modules, the Web module has its main adjustments on the right, its presets on the left, and a work area in the center as shown in figure 12-2. Here's what you find in this module's interface:

> **Center work area.** As usual, this shows you what you are doing in a Web gallery with photos. In this module, you see only the complete Web page as it is being constructed. You immediately see how your photos will show up in the Web gallery based on what is in the Filmstrip, including links

to different Web views of the photos. If you remember, Print calls the active image area a "cell," which the Web module continues (however, there is a big difference between Print and Web in that Web uses all the images in the Collection selected, while Print uses only selected images in the Filmstrip). The bottom has a very simplified toolbar. Images in the central area are active like on a Web page — if you click on a small photo, the interface changes (how it changes depends on the type of gallery). Or, if you see Previous or Next buttons (links), you can click them and the photos change.

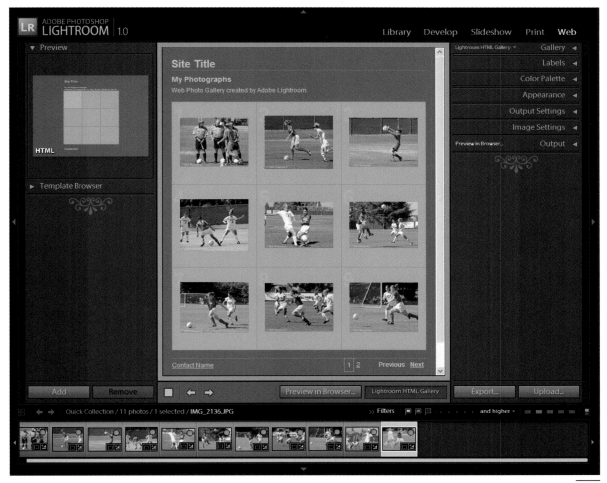

> **Right panel.** The standard of Lightroom, the right side panel holds the controls. Here is where you change how your photos appear on a Web page: the information that is included with the page as well as individual photos, the size of the images, and so forth. At the bottom are Export and Upload buttons to move your Web gallery out of Lightroom.

> **Bottom Filmstrip panel.** This is the standard photo display area that allows you to arrange the photos in the gallery.

> **Left panel.** Once again, here is a Template Browser, plus a preview area that shows what the galleries look like as you move your cursor over the presets. At the bottom are Add and Remove buttons for the Template Browser.

||| PRO TIP |||

For a lot of Web gallery work, you don't need the filmstrip at the bottom or the presets at the left. Close those panels to give more space for your work area, the actual Web page as it develops.

CHOOSING YOUR WEB GALLERY TYPE

The first step you will always do is to choose the Web gallery style, which will be either HTML (Hypertext Markup Language) that looks like what is shown in figure 12-1 and figure 12-3, or Flash as shown in figure 12-4. Notice that in the Flash example, you can see small images and a larger image at the same time. In HTML, you see an index view first (figure 12-1), then click on an image to get a large image (figure 12-3). In the HTML gallery, you move from image to image using the Previous and Next buttons (Index takes you back to the index view). In Flash, you always have a larger image that is a slide show. In that area you have playback-style buttons to play a slide show or move from image to image.

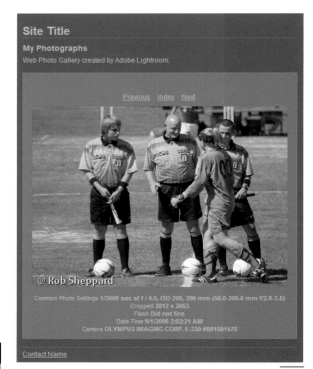

12-3

Note that in the large photo view seen in figure 12-3, you see a lot of metadata. This comes in as a default in all HTML galleries, but can be turned off entirely or in part in the Caption setting of Image Settings explained later in the chapter.

The type of gallery selected influences everything else, so you need to know right away which one you want to work with. You make this choice at the top of the right panel as shown in figure 12-5. Some readers might wonder why I would say that you need to choose right away given the Web module, like the rest of Lightroom, is non-destructive, simply providing instructions for adjustments, not the actual adjustments. You can change anything at any time, including the Web gallery style; however, I don't recommend changing your mind about the Web gallery once you've chosen. The reason is that you are dealing with a graphic treatment of Web pages and radically different visuals for HTML and Flash designs. These visuals are affected by everything included in their layout,

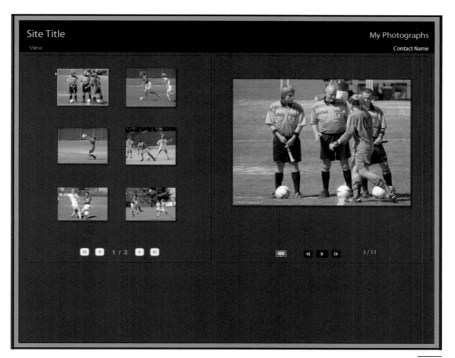

12-4

from the colors to the text used. I really believe that your best-looking page comes from making an early decision about which style best fits you, your

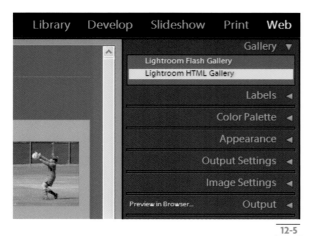

12-5

personality, and your needs, and then choosing all modifications to it based on that specific style.

HTML and Flash are different uses of Web sites and the browser. HTML is the traditional authoring language for Web sites. All Web sites use it. It defines and structures how a Web site looks, acts, and interacts with the visitor. It allows for many designs, but not for a lot of activity in that design.

Flash, on the other hand, lends itself to some lively uses of images on the Internet. With this technology, slide shows and fun actions with photos becomes very easy to do. Flash technology is one of the primary tools for adding animation and interactivity to Web pages. You won't be doing that in Lightroom. In this program, Flash is primarily used to animate the Web gallery.

There are advantages and disadvantages to each. Think about these things:

> **Flash is lively and modern.** It can make your Web site seem more up-to-date and "hip." You can display the photos in different arrangements, all based on a Flash slide show. The gallery even allows viewers to get a full-screen slide show. It is quite appropriate for a sequenced presentation where the images have some sort of order or story.

> **The HTML gallery is tried and true.** It lets you show off a larger number of photos immediately, then access individual shots as larger views by clicking on any one. The HTML design works quite well for dealing with something more like a light table presentation where you see images as individuals. It has a conservative look to it, too, which can be important for certain businesses. But probably the most important thing is that it can be read by all Internet browsers. With Flash-made Web sites, you need a plug-in inside your Internet browser in order to read it, and some people simply don't have it.

So for the simplest gallery that everyone can see, go with HTML. On the other hand, if you want something a little more hip and modern, go with Flash.

I know there are photographers who want a recommendation as to which is best. Which style should they really use? That's not a recommendation I can give. A gallery style is not simply about computer technology and software code. It is also a distinctly visual graphic that affects the personality of your Web gallery. That makes it a very personal decision. The nice thing about Lightroom is that you can quickly compare each style with your photos inserted, making it easier to see the differences.

SETTING UP THE GALLERY PAGE

Once you have a gallery chosen, you typically modify the gallery page look next. The controls are in Custom Settings in the right panel. However, if you are like me, Web page galleries are not something you do every day, so you might like some inspiration here. That's why in this module, I highly recommend you go to the Template Browser first. You can find a lot of ideas there, ideas that can be used as is or customized for your specific needs.

NOTE

If you included a copyright in the adjusted metadata when you imported your photos, you see a copyright notice on the images when working in the Web module.

CHOICES IN THE TEMPLATE BROWSER

You get a lot of choices to start in the Web module's preset template browser as shown in figure 12-6. Most photographers can also use the Template Browser to create new presets for Web galleries that are unique. Each template shows up in the preview as you move your cursor over it.

Each template uses a specific set of colors with either a Flash or HTML gallery. Here are your choices (the text shown is simply the default text — changing text is discussed later in the chapter):

> **Blue Sky.** This Flash option uses a nice blue set of tones with a white background, as shown in figure 12-7, for a Flash gallery showing images on the left with the slide show in the center.

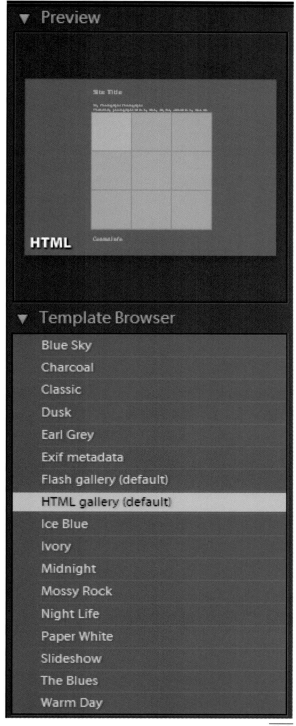

12-6

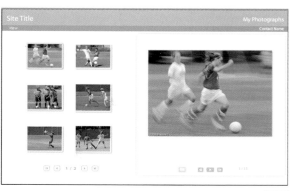

12-7

> **Charcoal.** This is very close to the default HTML option and uses neutral tones around the images as shown in figure 12-8, set up first as a grid of 3 × 3.

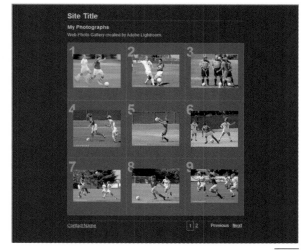

12-8

> **Classic.** This Flash option is basically a white design with cool grays for the colors used and a left filmstrip to go with the slide show in the middle as shown in figure 12-9.

251

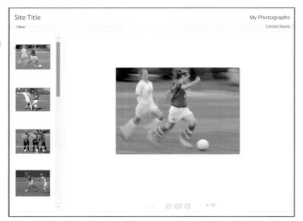

12-9

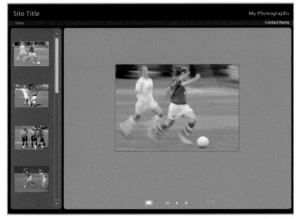

12-11

> **Dusk.** This HTML option has a dark tone to it, using mostly blues as shown in figure 12-10. The Identity Plate is included automatically and there is a grid of 4 × 3 images.

> **Exif metadata.** This is a simple gray HTML design that automatically includes selected metadata in the larger view as shown in figure 12-12.

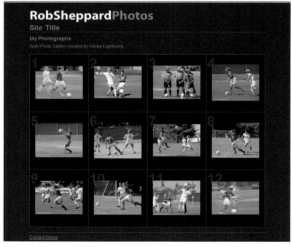

12-10

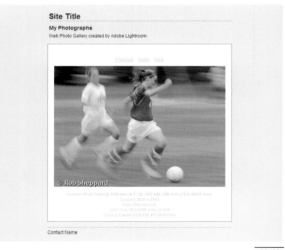

12-12

> **Earl Grey.** This Flash option is a black and gray design as shown in figure 12-11. The slide show is at the right, a filmstrip at the left.

> **Flash gallery (default).** This Flash option uses a very dark setting as shown in figure 12-13 that makes the right-side slide show look like a show in a darkened room. The filmstrip is on the left. This and the default HTML design are what appear when you first open the Web module.

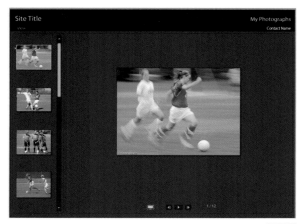

12-13

> **HTML gallery (default).** This is a very basic HTML gallery that uses middle and dark gray tones to set off a grid of 3 × 9 images as shown in figure 12-14.

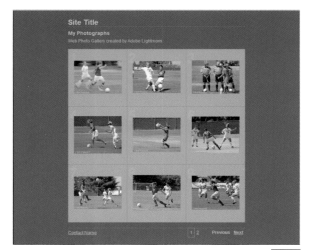

12-14

> **Ice Blue.** This is a mostly white HTML design with low-saturation blue accents as shown in figure 12-15, and uses a long 5 × 3 grid.

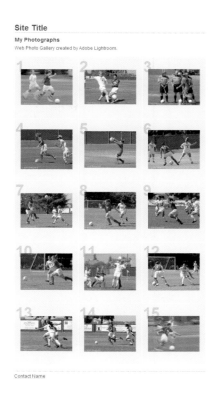

12-15

> **Ivory.** This is another very simple, white HTML design where the photos seem to float on the background as seen in figure 12-16.

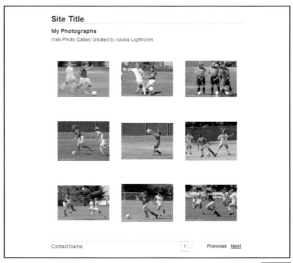

12-16

> **Midnight.** This option is the reverse of Ivory, presenting images in a very simple, pure black HTML design where the photos seem to glow through cutouts in the page as shown in figure 12-17.

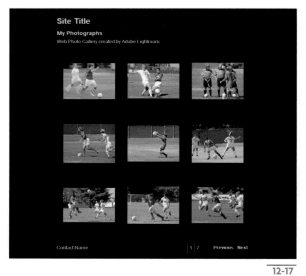

12-17

> **Mossy Rock.** This Flash option is colored as you would expect from a mossy rock, green, as shown in figure 12-18. The color is so strong that it limits what you can use with it.

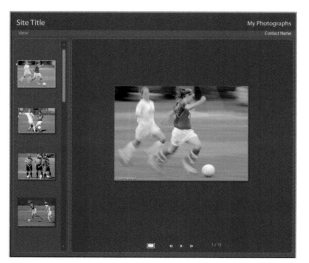

12-18

> **Night Life.** This option is really the HTML Midnight option done in Flash — a very simple black design that makes images look like they are glowing as shown in figure 12-19.

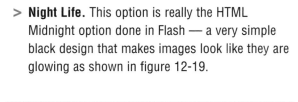
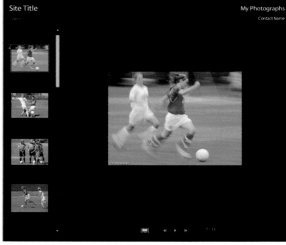

12-19

> **Paper White.** This is the HTML Ivory option done in Flash — a very simple white design where photos seem to float in the space as shown in figure 12-20.

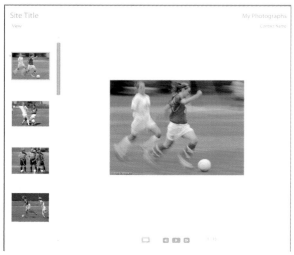

12-20

> **Slideshow.** This Flash option is pure slide show with no filmstrip and the image is displayed large against a black background as shown in figure 12-21.

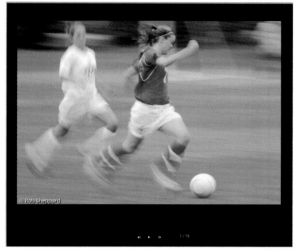

> **The Blues.** This Flash option is strongly colored like Mossy Rock, this time in blue as shown in figure 12-22. The color is, again, so strong that it limits what you can use with it.

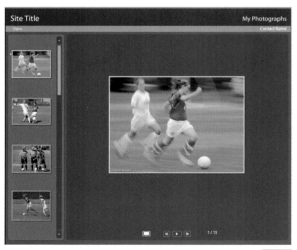

> **Warm Day.** This Flash option uses some strong colors as accents; though the background itself is warm neutral, as shown in figure 12-23, it is not overpowering. Still, the colors used in the accents are so strong that they may limit what you can use with it. The filmstrip is on the bottom.

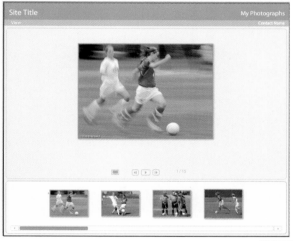

These presets may give you exactly what you need right from the start for your Web gallery. Seeing the options here as an overview should help you better compare them, too. If they don't exactly meet your needs, they should at least give you ideas of things that you might try.

If you do modify the look of any of these templates, or you create a Web page look that you really like, you can save it as a preset for the Template Browser. You do this quite simply — once you have completed your work gallery, click the Add button at the bottom of the right panel. This adds a line to the presets and high-lights the words Untitled Template. Just type in a name for your preset and this information is now retained within Lightroom. You can go back to this same gallery setup at any time with new photos.

To delete any preset templates, click that option to highlight it, and then click the Remove button at the bottom of the panel.

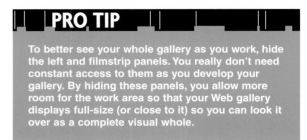

ORGANIZE YOUR IMAGES

Once you have a basic look for your gallery, you need to organize your photos. You can change colors of background, title bar, text, and so forth, but since your images are really the stars here, I believe you should consider their order now. It is especially important to choose a first photo with impact as that is the one that every viewer of the gallery sees first, either as the top-left photo in an HTML gallery or the first image in the slide show.

Click and drag photos in the Filmstrip to move them from place to place. Once you have a first image then look at how the rest fit together. This is especially important in the Flash gallery as there is a slide show there that shows images one after another. You can use some of the ideas discussed about slide shows in Chapter 9 to help organize images for a Web gallery.

MAKING TITLES FOR YOUR GALLERY

For a Web module gallery, you get a number of different places to add information to the page in the Labels section of the right panel as shown in figure 12-24. Before you start typing in information, think a bit about what you want to say on your Web page. You are best served if you choose what you want to put into the text areas before you start typing. I say that because there are five distinct places in Labels for information: Site Title, Collection Title, Collection Description, Contact Info (which should always go on a pro's site) and Web or Mail Link. How you use these text areas should be organized to get the best impact from your gallery. How do you want to use this information? What do you want to put where? The Site Title could relate to your overall Web site or it could be something specific for the gallery. The Collection Title might refer to a specific grouping of images, a description of the subject (Mountains of California), or even a specific client job. The Collection Description gives you the option to include a bit more about your collection — but exactly what? And can you say it in a brief set of words?

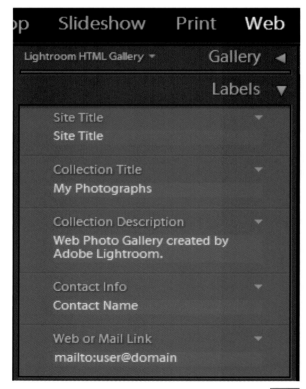

12-24

Here's how to use Labels once you have decided what information you want to give to your viewers:

> **Site Title.** This first entry enables you to add a dominant title to your gallery as shown in figure 12-25. You can use a name appropriate to your work, your Web site, or maybe your business. You want to have visitors to this gallery always remember who you are and associate your photos with you. Click the text either under Site Title under Labels or click the text itself on the Web page being built in the central work area as shown in figure 12-24. Keep the title simple, with only a few words. Press Enter/Return to accept the words.

> **Collection Title.** In this section, you can give more information to the viewer about the collection of images seen in the gallery as seen in figure 12-26. Put whatever makes sense. I recommend something that quickly explains what the viewer is seeing such as "Portfolio," a shoot name such as "London," or even "Recent Photojournalism Assignments." Keep it simple, however, because you don't want viewers to struggle with reading text in this position.

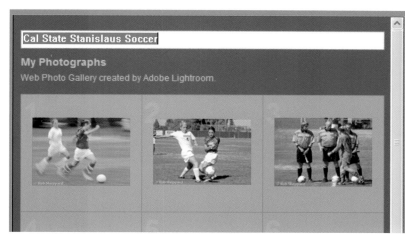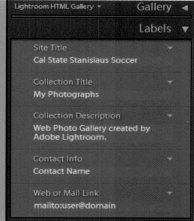

12-25

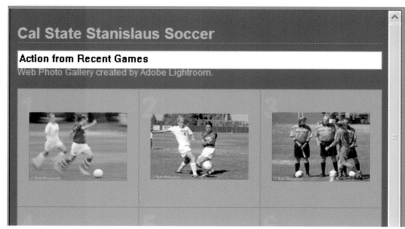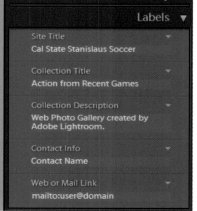

12-26

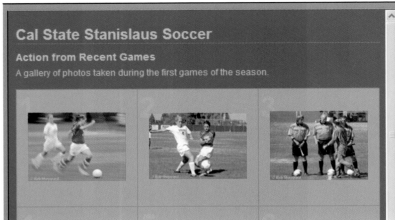

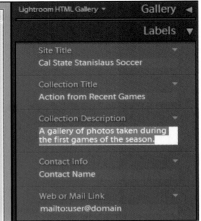

12-27

> **Collection Description.** Now you can get a bit wordier to explain what is seen on this page. You could describe the work in terms of a specific job or give more information about a location than you included in the Collection Title as shown in figure 12-27.

> **Contact Info and Web or Mail Link.** Having worked at several magazines as an editor receiving photos from photographers all the time in many forms, I have to tell you that Contact Info is extremely important. Too often photographers forget this on printed promotional materials, and then continue to forget it on their Web sites. Pros should find these choices, as shown in figure 12-28, a valuable reminder to add contact info to their Web sites at all times. Web or Mail Link info does not show up on your Web gallery, but is linked from the Contact Info if a visitor clicks on that.

As you do work on a Web gallery in this module, Lightroom remembers your choices. If you click the arrow to the right of each title, you get a drop-down menu of what you have used for it. This can be helpful as you work to make changes on the gallery.

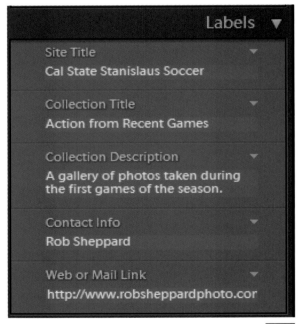

12-28

CHANGING COLORS

The next section of the Web module deals with the colors of elements on the Web gallery. This is a very straightforward section as shown in figure 2-29. To stay consistent with the gallery, I am going to illustrate these with the HTML design. Flash galleries use the colors in the same ways. Here's how to work the choices:

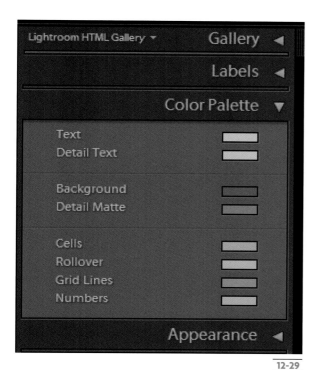

12-29

> **Text.** Click the little rectangle to the right of Text to choose a new color for the main text of the gallery. A Color Picker dialog box appears that allows you to pick almost any color or tone. You need color that makes the text readable, yet you don't want something too obtrusive. This is one place you can sometimes add some color to the page without causing competition among a variety of colors. One idea is to use a color here that is complementary to your logo when it is used as an Identity Plate. Whatever the color you use is, however, it needs to work with the background color (which is explained later), so you may want to choose a background color first.

> **Detail Text.** This is a minor use of text as seen in the red letters of figure 12-30, but can be a place to add a small bit of color to the page. I am not suggesting using red here — the color is only for illustration so the text areas show up better.

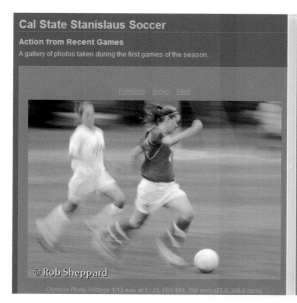
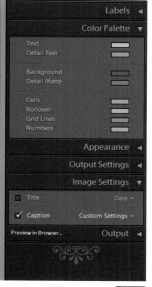

12-30

> **Background.** This color shown in figure 12-31 (the color is again for illustration) is set in the same way as the Text color — click the little rectangle to the right of Background to open a Color Picker dialog box. Background and cell color are two interrelated and very important choices for your Web gallery. This is what sets off the entire gallery page, and, in many ways, is what your viewer sees first. It is possible to use a more vibrant background color and a neutral cell color, because the cell color is what actually surrounds the photos. However, I recommend you choose saturated colors very cautiously. They don't always display properly on a Web site and can really distract from the real reason for your gallery page — the photos. I suggest you try neutral

tones or light colors with low saturation. I think it is a nice effect to have a background different from the cell color so that it acts like a frame to the images.

> **Detail Matte.** This is another more specialized use of color. It shows up with detail views such as that shown in figure 12-32. Color is set the same way as other options.

> **Cells.** As mentioned in Background, this is one of the key areas of color. Though you see it brightly colored in figure 12-33 for illustration, I recommend you use neutral colors so as not to compete with the photo colors. This is a very important part of Color Palette because it changes the color directly around your photos.

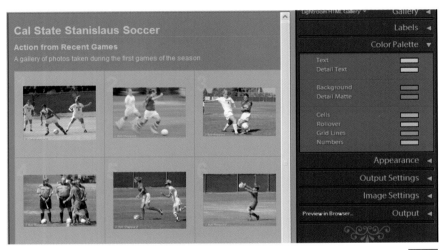

12-31

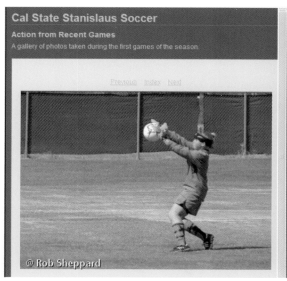

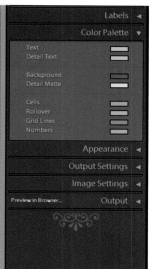

12-32

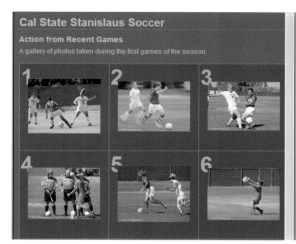

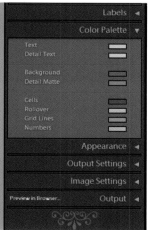

12-33

> **Rollover.** The Rollover color (the color that high-lights the cell when you roll over an image with your mouse to select it) can be many colors because this is only temporary. In fact, it can work well to use a brighter color for this as seen in figure 12-34 so it is obvious which photo is being selected (however, don't overdo the brighter color idea).

> **Grid Lines.** Having a bit of color for the Grid Lines can add a nice touch as shown in figure 12-35 — the lines aren't big enough to really compete with your photos.

> **Numbers.** I advise you to be cautious about making the numbers anything other than the default color. They are right by the photos and big enough to be a serious distraction if too bold in color or tone.

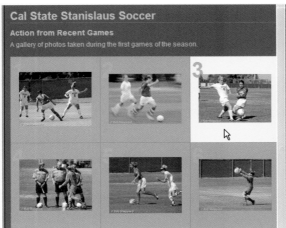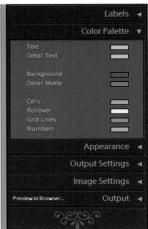

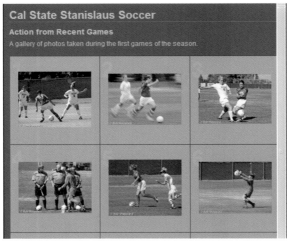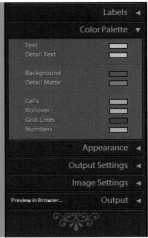

12-34

12-35

CHANGING APPEARANCE

Appearance enables you to change three things on the gallery — the rows and columns in an HTML gallery, the layout of filmstrip and slide show in a Flash gallery, and the use of your identity plate. These are very helpful tools in refining the look of your work. Here's how to use this set of tools:

> **Number of Columns and Number of Rows.** This section shown in figure 12-36 allows you to change how many of your images show up on the page when in an HTML layout — just run your cursor over the grid to see new cells highlighted and click when you see something you like. The default numbers of three columns and three rows are good for a Web gallery. You can increase both columns and rows, but this doesn't fit more images in the viewing area. It adds images to the page, which results in many viewers having to scroll the page to see them all.

PRO TIP

Be careful of adding too many images that are hard to really see by your Web site visitor. I can tell you from experience as a magazine editor, that images start to get lost in the viewer's mind as the numbers go up. They just compete with each other. I suggest choosing a number of cells from 9 to 12 for most purposes.

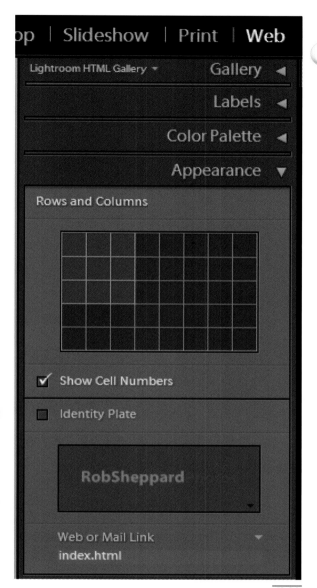

12-36

> **Layout.** When you select a Flash gallery, you can choose from four different layouts as shown in figure 12-37 when you click the drop-down menu at the right of Layout. These include Scrolling, Paginated, Left, and Slideshow Only. Scrolling is a very popular way of dealing with images in Flash. In this form, you have a large photo on display in the top half of the page, while all other photos in the gallery appear as thumbnails in a scrollable filmstrip at the bottom as shown in figure 12-38. The viewer selects the top photo by clicking any image in the filmstrip. In all Flash layouts, the large photo can also become a slide show of all of the gallery images when the viewer clicks a play button, or the user can click the other "step" buttons to step through the gallery images one at a time.

The Paginated option changes the look so that now the large image is in the right half of the page, and the gallery photo thumbnails are in the left. The gallery thumbnails are now grouped in pages as shown on the left in figure 12-39. Left is very similar, but uses a scrollable filmstrip on the left. The last view is Slideshow only and no thumbnails are available as shown in figure 12-40.

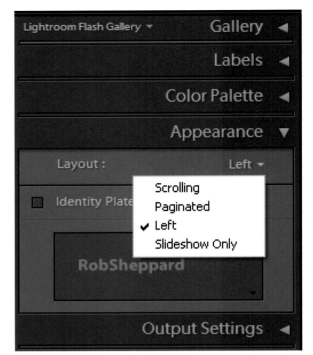

12-37

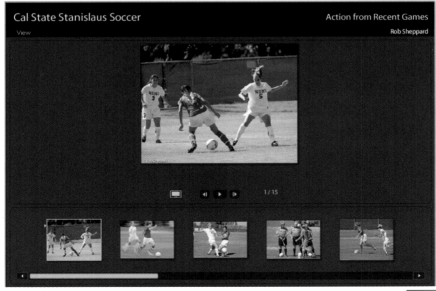

12-38

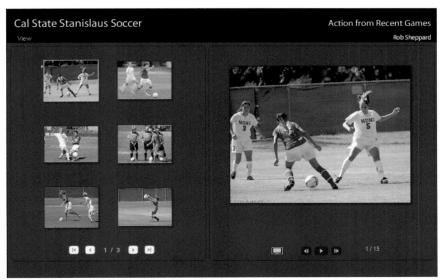

12-39

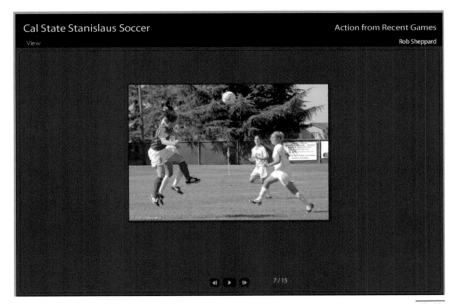

12-40

> **Identity Plate.** This option puts the Identity Plate either on or off your Web gallery page. It is placed at the upper left, over the site title text as shown in figure 12-41. I describe Identity Plates in detail in Chapter 2.

> **Web or Mail Link.** This option, which is only available when using an HTML gallery, lets you make your Identity Plate a live link to another part of your Web site. This is a good place to put your home page for your Web site so a viewer can instantly go back to your home page by clicking the Identity Plate.

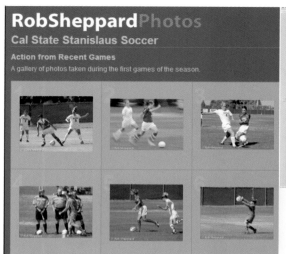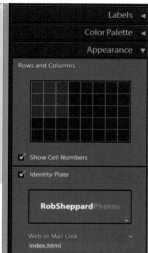

The Importance of Color for the Web Gallery

The effect of your Web gallery on a viewer is strongly affected by color, which I touched on earlier. Having seen a lot of photographers struggle with selecting colors that appear around or near a photo, I thought it might be helpful to emphasize a few ideas in a separate section to summarize and complement what I said earlier in the chapter.

> **Choose colors carefully for areas that are physically close to the actual photos.** As I mentioned, neutral colors are good because they do not compete with your photos. Black and white are extreme and can make a gallery look harsh, though. Try shades of gray. Then try unobtrusive colors that are low in saturation. Avoid really bright colors — they are extremely difficult to use without the bright colors competing too strongly with your photos.

> **Choose text colors for readability.** I've seen people try to get cute with odd colors for text. Text needs to be legible or what is its point? Select colors for text that contrast with the colors or tones that the text is read against. Avoid highly saturated colors as they can be hard to read.

Be cautious in the use of blues as they can make text look out of focus for many people.

> **Use grid and line colors for accents.** As the lines around the active areas of the gallery or grid lines are not large, you can use all sorts of colors for them without too much of a problem. Try colors that contrast with the neutral colors of the rest of the gallery page to enliven it. However, watch for unintended effects when certain line/background color combinations are used — lines can look too vibrant, almost like they are vibrating.

Choosing Output Settings

The Output section of the Web module is a really simple little section that affects what your photos look like in the gallery. The JPEG Output Settings offers two options — Preview and Quality. Preview affects the size of the image when it is displayed large on the page — compare figure 12-42 and figure 12-43. While larger images look great, they can slow down the download of pages from your Web site. Quality changes the compression of the JPEG files used for the gallery; a lower quality setting gives smaller image files that download faster.

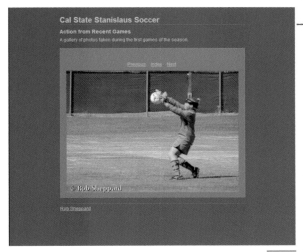

12-42

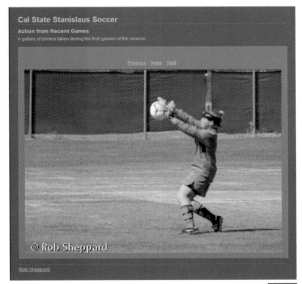

12-43

Add Copyright Watermark adds your name with the copyright symbol as seen in most of the figures in this chapter. It finds your name from the metadata you added to the photos when they were imported into Photoshop Lightroom.

USING IMAGE SETTINGS

Image Settings set up text that appears with the larger photo display in your Web gallery. The text does not appear with thumbnails; it only appears with the large slide show image of a Flash gallery or the large images that appear when a viewer selects a thumbnail in the HTML gallery. The text you type appears the same with all photos as they are enlarged — you do not have the ability to change text per photo in the Web module.

You have two choices for text: Title and Caption.

> **Title.** At the right of Title is a drop-down arrow that gives the choices seen in figure 12-44: Custom Text, Date, Equipment, Exposure, Filename, Sequence, and Edit. These are all pretty much exactly as the names suggest and come largely from the metadata. Choose Edit and the Text Template Editor dialog box appears. It contains a lot of choices for what appears in this title as shown in the dialog box in figure 12-45. Many of these options, to be honest, are very specialized and unlikely to be used by the average photographer.

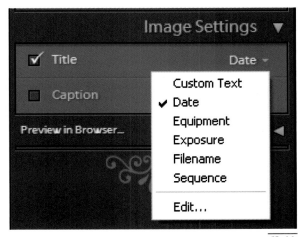

12-44

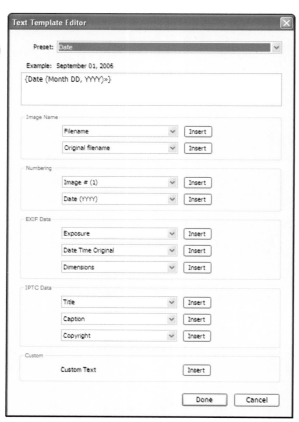

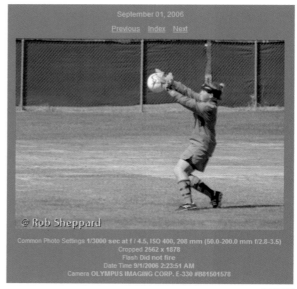

12-46

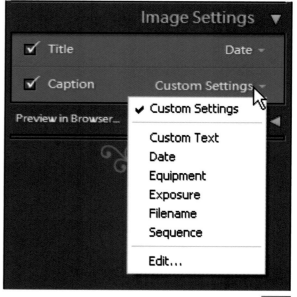

12-47

PRO TIP

If you want unique captions for your photos, you can use IPTC caption information. Image Settings do allow you to select that in IPTC data. This can be caption info that you added to the metadata of your image back in the Library module or you can go back to that module and add the caption info now.

> **Caption.** In the Web module panel, check Caption and the metadata uploaded with your photos now appears with your photo as shown in figure 12-46. You can control what appears here by clicking on the drop-down menu as shown in figure 12-47.

Working with Output

The Output section of controls is fairly straightforward as shown in figure 12-48. It is where you tell Lightroom how to deal with the Web gallery you are working with, including the settings for uploading it to your Web site.

Preview in Browser enables you to see what your gallery page actually looks like in an Internet browser. Click the phrase, and your browser is launched, and your Web gallery appears on it.

FTP Server tells Lightroom where to upload your gallery. You have to click the drop-down menu arrow and then select Edit to set this up. The Configure FTP File Transfer dialog box is shown in figure 12-49. Here you name your preset, put in your server address, name, password, and so forth, to allow an upload to your Web site. When you have set this up once, a preset name automatically appears that you can choose in the future.

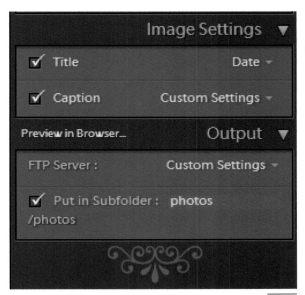

12-48

Configure FTP File Transfer

Preset: Custom

Server:

Username: Password:

☐ Store password in preset

Server Path: Browse

FTP Port: 21   ☑ Use passive mode for data transfers

OK   Cancel

12-49

Using the Export and Upload Buttons

Export and Upload buttons are at the bottom of the control panel side of the Web module as shown in figure 12-50. Export enables you to save your Web gallery on your hard drive. It saves either a Flash or an HTML file, depending on the form you choose.

Upload uses your FTP presets and server output path you put into Output. This enables you to send your page directly to your Web server and get it onto your Web site. Even if you do go directly to your server from Lightroom, I recommend you always save (Export) your Web gallery first. This just protects you so that the work you put into the gallery is saved and you can at least use it directly from that file in case you go on to other things in Lightroom and go out of your Web gallery, yet later you discover the FTP transfer didn't do what you expected and the gallery did not go to your site properly. If you really like your gallery design, I also recommend you save it as a preset in your Template Browser.

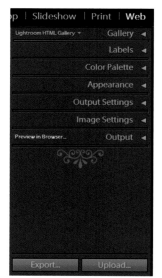

12-50

Q & A

I am not much of a Web expert. I have someone who knows the Web who is doing my Web site. I don't fully understand all the FTP business with Output. What do you suggest I do?

This is very common. A lot of photographers do not do their own Web sites and are not familiar with the information in Output. They are busy taking pictures and not spending time doing Web sites! I am no Web site expert, either. I have a Webmaster who handles that detail for me. Still, I like the gallery options in Lightroom — they make it very easy for a photographer to quickly create his or her own gallery without waiting for help.

Once a gallery is done, I would do one of two things:

> Talk to your Webmaster (the person doing your Web site) and get the appropriate information from them. Just tell them what Lightroom asks for in the Output section, FTP Preset, and ask how you can best use that to work with your Web site.

> Save your gallery and send that "file" (actually a folder of files) to your Webmaster to upload.

What if I don't like the fonts for the Web gallery? How can I change them?

Unfortunately, at this point in the development of Lightroom, you can't. This isn't all bad. The fonts used are a simple, easy-to-read typeface that displays well on a Web page. Most photographers aren't Web designers, so offering a lot of choices in the Web module is probably counterproductive and Adobe was smart to avoid that. If you really do know how to design a Web page and select fonts properly, then Lightroom's Web module is probably not the software you should be using.

I am still undecided. Should I use the HTML or Flash gallery? They both seem to have advantages and disadvantages, but I am thinking mostly from a visual perspective. They show images quite differently. Which do you think affects viewers more?

That's really a hard question to answer. It is based on such personal, subjective ideas. You really have to look at several things in making this decision:

> **Your existing Web site.** Which type of gallery seems better suited to the tone and personality of your Web site? Try opening your Web site in your browser, and then go back and forth between the Web gallery in Lightroom and your Web site to see how they look together. You can use Alt/⌘+Tab as a keyboard command to go back and forth between these programs without using your mouse and a toolbar.

> **Your audience — who is most likely going to view your gallery?** If you expect a lot of hip designers to visit, maybe the Flash gallery is better. On the other hand, if you know that photo researchers from book publishers are visiting, they may prefer the HTML gallery because of the way it presents more images to them.

> **Your photos and the subject matter.** You may find that some photos really go together nicely in a slide show format, making the Flash gallery ideal. On the other hand, another group of photos might be such stand-alone images that they never quite work when blended into a slide show, so the HTML gallery will be better.

> **Your personality.** You may just like the way a slide show looks on your Web site. If this is the case, obviously the Flash gallery is the better choice. On the other hand, you may be the type of person that prefers images to stand alone as single pieces of art and so the HTML gallery is the way to go.

Part III

THE PHOTOSHOP PARTNERSHIP

Chapter 13: Going Between Lightroom and Photoshop

Pro Glossary

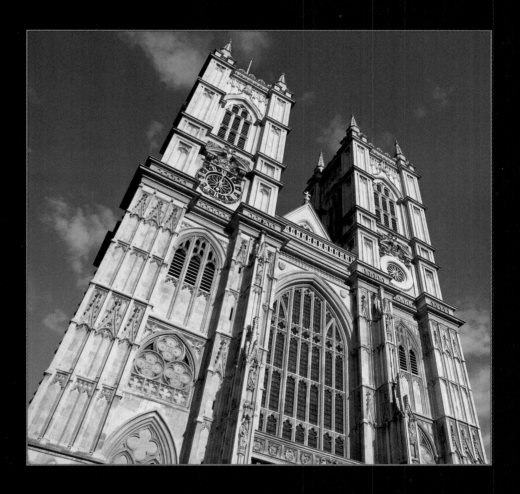

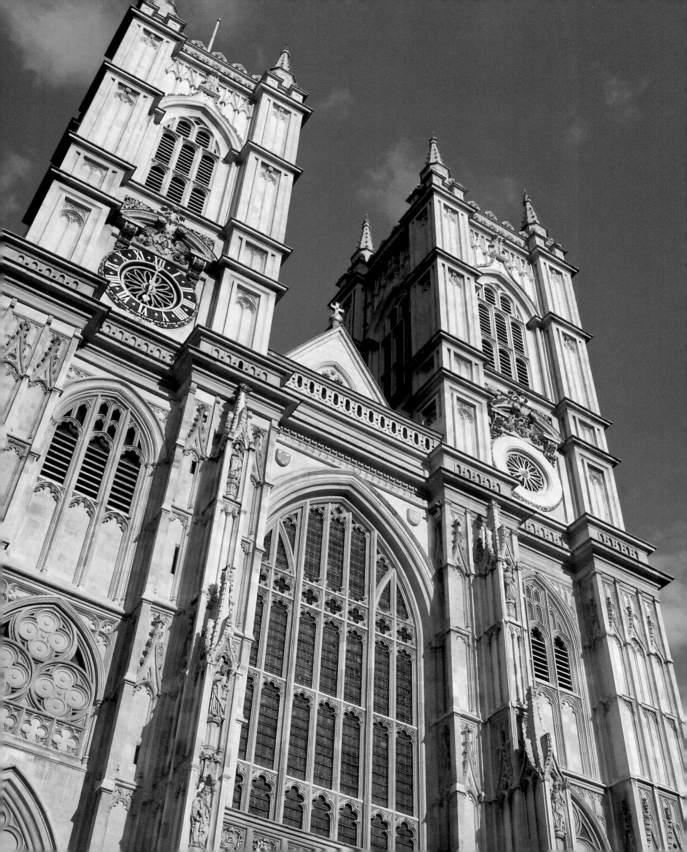

GOING BETWEEN LIGHTROOM AND PHOTOSHOP

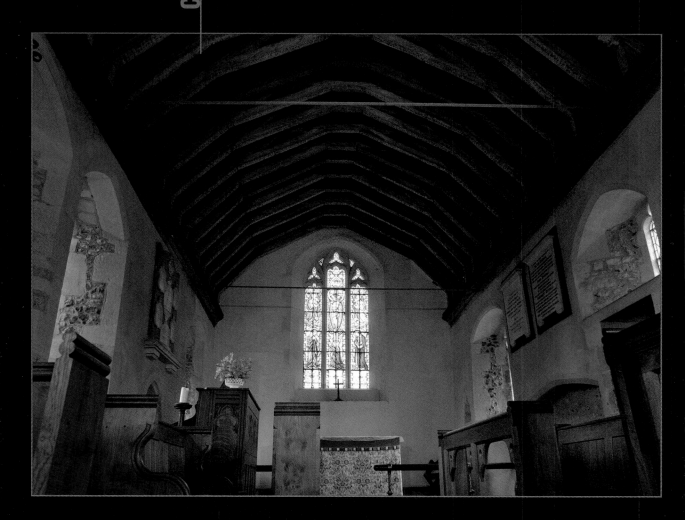

As I worked on this book and learned to master Adobe Photoshop Lightroom, I got a lot of questions about Photoshop itself from photographers who knew I was doing this. The big question was, "If I have Lightroom, do I still need Photoshop?"

That is not a simple question or an easy one to answer. "It depends" is rarely a satisfying answer, yet in this case, it really is true. While some find Lightroom can replace Photoshop, I believe most photographers will find Lightroom is an excellent complement to Photoshop, and that the two programs need to be part of their digital arsenal. Probably most photographers will go back and forth between the programs simply as needed — sometimes never using Photoshop for one group of photos, and then using it for all of another group. Some photographers may even find that Lightroom does so much for them that they only need Photoshop Elements for occasional work in layers.

Adobe makes it easy for these programs to work together — in fact, that is part of the reason that Photoshop is included in the official name, Photoshop Lightroom. But remember that Lightroom and Photoshop are designed for very different purposes. Lightroom is a program for dealing quickly and easily with a lot of photos, and then working on them fluidly from one to another. It is not a program for doing detailed work on individual photos whereas Photoshop is. Photoshop was designed from the start to deal with single images and for very concentrated, meticulous work on them. Bridge was later developed to try to deal with multiple photos, but it really was an add-on patch rather than something integrated into the program from the start. Many photographers feel that Bridge, while it is helpful, is slow and clunky compared to other programs on the market even in the latest version packaged with Photoshop CS3.

For now Photoshop is the detailed image processor that includes layers and layer mask controls;

Lightroom is the multiple photo organizer and overall image processor. In this chapter, I discuss some of the possibilities of having Lightroom work together with Photoshop. For the Photoshop power user, this chapter is pretty basic.

However, I know that many Lightroom users are not sophisticated Photoshop users and want some guidance in going to and from Photoshop. That's what this chapter is designed to do. This is not a course in Photoshop, so I am not covering every specific command or the location of controls. If you are not sure of some of them, there are many excellent Photoshop books on the market that can help.

MOVING BETWEEN LIGHTROOM AND PHOTOSHOP

Lightroom is set up to move a photo to Photoshop (or any other program, such as Photoshop Elements) pretty easily. You can be in any module with a photo selected (in Library, Develop, and Print, that includes the central work area and Filmstrip; in Slideshow and Web, it includes just Filmstrip). Then simply right-click the photo (yet another reason to get that right-click mouse for Mac users!) to get a menu, as seen in figure 13-1. Among these choises is Edit in Adobe Photoshop CS2 (the reference to CS2 will change when CS3 is officially on the market by mid-2007). In Library and Develop, press Ctrl/⌘+E or choose Photo ➪ Edit in Adobe Photoshop CS2.app or Edit in Other Application if you don't have Photoshop CS2.

PRO TIP

I know I constantly nag Mac users to get a right-click mouse. Sure, you can Control+click to substitute for the right-click, but why do this when the right-click is so easy and convenient? Right-clicking gives you context-sensitive menus in so many programs.

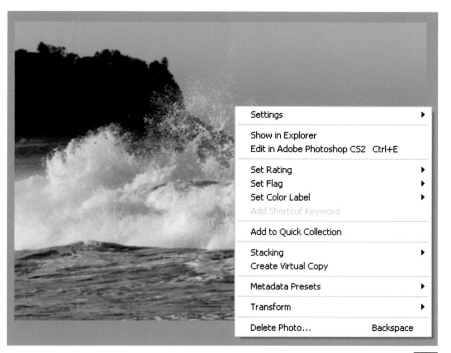

13-1

The Edit Photo dialog box appears, as shown in figure 13-2, although it looks slightly different depending on if you are working with a RAW or non-RAW file. The dialog box provides three choices for non-RAW files: Edit Original, Edit a Copy, or Edit a Copy with Lightroom Adjustments. The first two are grayed out for RAW files so you only get one choice: Edit a Copy with Lightroom Adjustments. I will explain each, starting with the last one because it is common to all types of files:

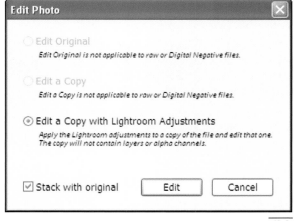

13-2

> **Edit a Copy with Lightroom Adjustments.** This is the last option in the dialog box, but is probably the one that is used most often. I believe it is the best choice for most photographers. In figure 13-2, you can see the other choices are grayed out. Because the selected file is a RAW file, and the first choices are not applicable. The small type continues with "Apply the Lightroom adjustments to a copy of the file and edit that one. The copy will not contain layers or alpha channels." For RAW files, this basically means that the image is converted from RAW, and a copy is saved in the folder with the original and exported to Photoshop. RAW files go to Photoshop as 16-bit images. For non-RAW files, the image is processed and saved as a copy and then exported to Photoshop. Remember that all Lightroom adjustments are non-destructive (that is, they do not affect pixels), essentially like adjustment layers. To move an image from Lightroom, those adjustments must be actually applied to the image. If you select Stack with original, the copy is stacked in Lightroom with the original (it appears as a numbered stack in Grid and Filmstrip views).

> **Edit Original.** This choice is a little misleading. When dealing with the true original image as captured by the camera, I can't recommend ever using this. To me, the original, no matter what the format, should never be touched. If you have a choice to immediately use a copy for editing, why would you go to the original? The original file goes to Photoshop for editing and no adjustments you make in Lightroom are applied. Now, if you have a copy of the image (likely because you have already done the Edit Copy with Lightroom Adjustments) and saved that Photoshop file with layers, you would choose this option for that file. This is why the choice is misleading, because in that case you really aren't working on the original, but Lightroom considers that file the "original"

because you are using it directly without making a copy.

> **Edit a Copy.** This can be an alternate way of using Lightroom with JPEG files. It allows you to use the program as a very efficient cataloging and organizing program, and then go straight to Photoshop with a copy of the original. However, I am not sure this is the best way to d this. Why not use the nondestructive power of Lightroom to do the basic adjustments to the file and then send a copy of the processed image to Photoshop?

With any of these choices, Photoshop is launched (if it isn't open) and the image opened into it. The image is renamed with "Edit" added to the original name, as shown in figure 13-3, and saved in the same folder as the original as a PSD file. It also is added automatically to the Lightroom Folder where the original is cataloged, so if you access that folder, you find both the original and the new PSD file (assuming you do not select the Edit Original option). If you then use Save As in Photoshop to save the image with a different name into the same folder, it also automatically is added to the folder and appears in Lightroom. This is a nice feature so that you don't have to remember to add processed images into Lightroom later.

PRO TIP

Lightroom and Photoshop have an interesting relationship when you select Edit Copy with Lightroom Adjustments. The copy that Lightroom creates and places by your original file (or stacked with it) is directly linked to Photoshop. Any changes you make to that file (including adding layers) show up in the copy file as soon as you save that file in Photoshop. You cannot save it to another location or change its name. You have to save it as it is, with the name that Lightroom gave to it, but this is a way of linking Photoshop and Lightroom adjustments directly. You can even reopen that image later using the Edit Original option as noted above and go back into Photoshop for any further adjustments needed there.

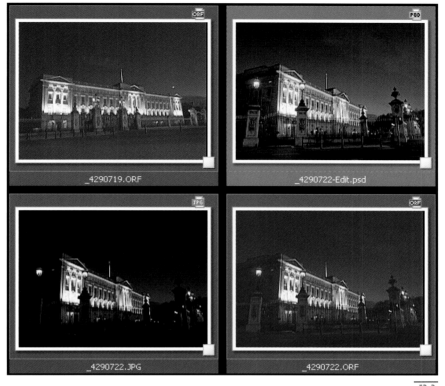

_4290719.ORF

_4290722-Edit.psd

_4290722.JPG

_4290722.ORF

13-3

HELPING PHOTOSHOP COMPLEMENT LIGHTROOM

You can obviously do anything to an image brought into Photoshop that Photoshop Lightroom is also capable of. I believe, however, that this may be counterproductive. When possibilities are endless, choices can seem overwhelming. Plus, Lightroom has stream-lined many functions nicely, so why not keep that in mind when you go into Photoshop and keep adjust-ments there focused to what Photoshop does best?

So for most images, you will go to Photoshop for very definite controls. I suggest thinking specifically about what is missing in a photo so that you enter Photoshop focused on a distinct task for your image. The following list of Photoshop image adjustments complement Lightroom for the photographer and make the use of both programs stronger. While it is by no means complete, I offer the list as a checklist of

sorts that you might use to identify your needs in Lightroom and focus your work in Photoshop.

> Layers

> Layer masks

> Local changes

> Balancing an image

> Sophisticated selection effects

> Cloning

> Complete set of healing tools

> Blur tools

> Correcting perspective

> Correcting distortions

> Controlled black and white effects

> Filters

I could spend a book on these techniques (and I actually did in *Outdoor Photographer Landscape and Nature Photography with Photoshop CS2*, Wiley, 2006). In this chapter, I want to offer a perspective on working between Lightroom and Photoshop by summarizing some of these adjustment tools in the context of these two different programs.

LAYER BENEFITS AND USING LAYERS

Layers are not possible with Lightroom. In a sense, you are adding layers of information on how to process an image file when you use the Develop module, but you can't access these layers, nor can you see them. The isolation of controls that layers gives you is a strong benefit of Photoshop and a major reason why you might finish processing an image there.

In doing workshops around the country, I hear from a lot of photographers that layers give them problems. While layers are an extremely important part of Photoshop, and many people consider them to be the ultimate advantage of the program, they are certainly not very photographic. Or at least they don't seem to be. If you know and are comfortable with layers, you can skip this section. But if you aren't, this section is an overview of what layers can do for you.

You see a photo of an Alaskan flower, a nagoonberry, in figure 13-4 with seven layers. It illustrates very well why you might go to Photoshop after Lightroom. If you are not comfortable with layers or you need a review, you might find this figure anything from obscure to intimidating.

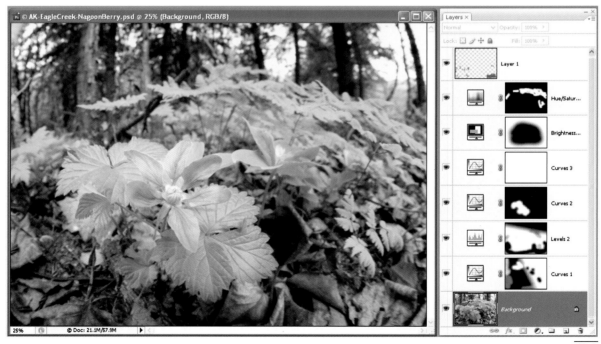

13-4

I like to tell photographers that they already know a little about layers, information that you can translate directly to figure 13-5. Think about if you put a stack of mail on your dining room table — some bills in standard-sized envelopes, a larger envelope promoting some credit card offer, a magazine or two, and some miscellaneous, mostly worthless, flyers. You know what I'm talking about.

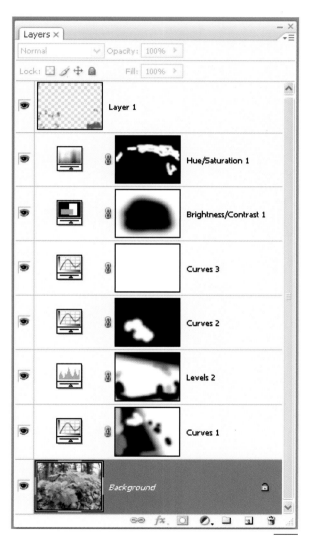

13-5

That mail stack is a pile of layers. You can affect any part of the stack without changing any other part (except its position, probably). You can write on a part of an envelope sticking out from the pile and have that writing appear nowhere else but that envelope. You can remove a magazine without removing other parts of the stack. You might not be able to read the blurbs on the cover of a magazine at the bottom because it is covered by other "layers" above it.

If you deconstruct that pile and write down each envelope, bill, flyer, magazine, and so on, in order, top to bottom, on a piece of paper, you have the equivalent of the Photoshop Layers palette (illustrated in figure 13-6). That palette works just like the stack of mail. You read it from the top down; opaque things on top block your view of things underneath. The same thing happens with the Photoshop Layers palette.

I will deconstruct the photo and its layers so you can see how the layers apply unique and specific controls to the image. Layers are generally added to a layer stack from the bottom up, just as you usually put letters in a pile, so I start from the bottom. Figure 13-7 shows the photo fresh from Lightroom with its blacks and whites set properly as well as its midtones. However, the light causes a visual imbalance, changing the scene to something rather arbitrary in tonalities, rather than the way the eye sees it. The flower is too dark, while the background is too light. In part, this happens because I photographed the flower with an extreme wide-angle lens up close, which means I shaded it slightly.

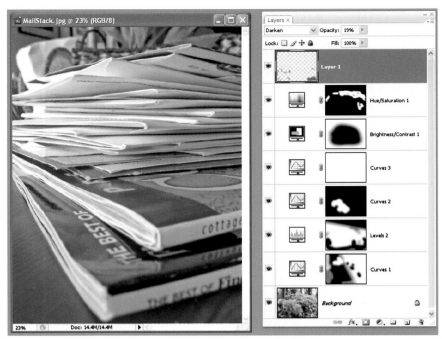

13-6

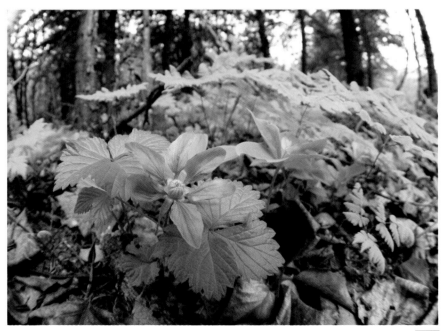

13-7

In figure 13-8, I add an adjustment layer. I use Curves to darken the background, then use the layer mask to limit the darkening to the background and some localized areas. This is shown with its layer mask detail in figure 13-9 — blacks block the effect of the layer, white allows it, and grays are in between (I explain layer masks more fully later in the chapter). This photo is becoming better balanced. The layer control with the layer mask restrictions is impossible in Lightroom.

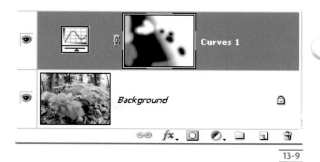

Curves 1

Background

13-9

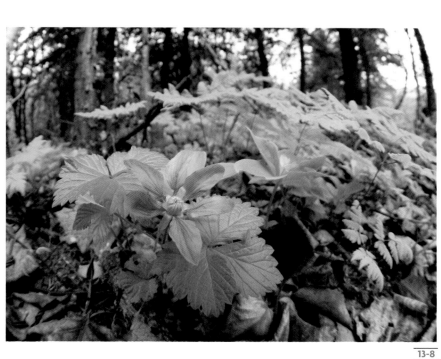

13-8

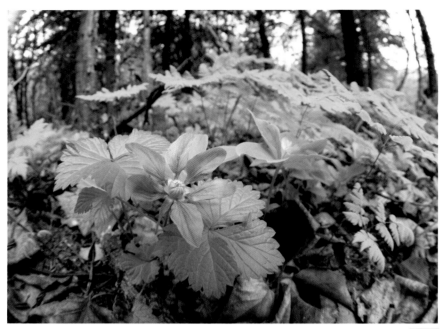

13-10

I add another adjustment layer because the greens of the leaves are now too dark over the whole image, yet I don't want the bottom or top of the photo to get brighter, too. I use a Levels adjustment layer to create the new tonalities shown in figure 13-10 and use its mask to limit the changes to mainly the leaves as reflected in the layer mask shown in figure 13-11.

The next layer brightens the flower and the leaves near it with a Curves adjustment layer. You can clearly see the change in figure 13-12. The layer mask in this case is really limiting, as shown in figure 13-13 — you can see only a small area of white is in a large field of black. This means that only the area over the flower and nearby leaves can be affected by the change in Curves.

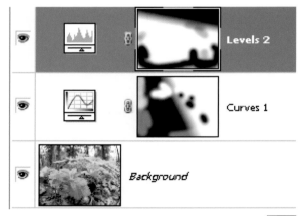

Levels 2

Curves 1

Background

13-11

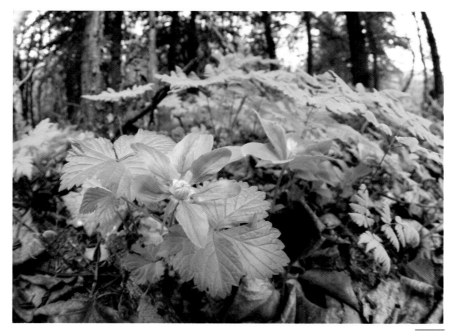

13-12

The fourth layer is a bit subtle for the printed page so I do not show a full image here. This is a Curves layer that just darkens some of the darker midtones slightly and shows up in a print. No layer mask is used, as shown in figure 13-14.

I add another adjustment layer — this time Brightness/Contrast, as shown in figure 13-15. Brightness/Contrast is a blunt and coarse adjustment tool; it is not something for general use, but is perfect for this purpose, which is to darken the outside edges

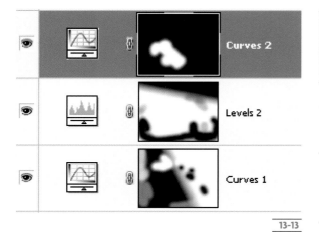

Curves 2

Levels 2

Curves 1

13-13

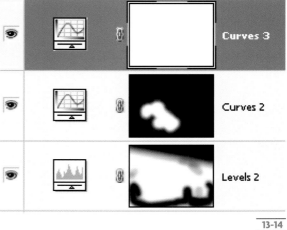

Curves 3

Curves 2

Levels 2

13-14

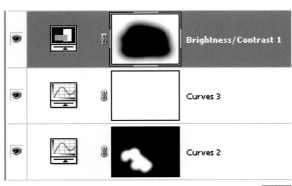

of the image as shown in figure 13-16. This is a traditional technique used by classic darkroom workers such as Ansel Adams and W. Eugene Smith. They darkened down the corners and edges of a photo to give it more dimension and keep the viewer's eye from wandering off the image. You don't want or need the control of Levels or Curves to do this in Photoshop — in fact, they don't create the same traditional darkening effect, and Brightness/Contrast does. I simply use the Brightness slider to darken the image and then a layer mask to limit that adjustment to the outside edges and corners.

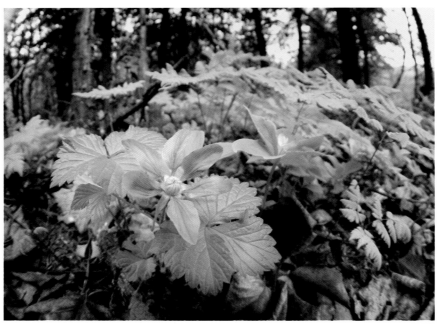

13-16

Going Between Lightroom and Photoshop

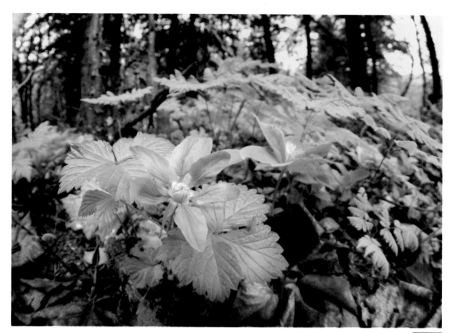

13-17

In the sixth layer, I use a Hue/Saturation adjustment layer to change the color of the background leaves. The saturation and hue of the green leaves behind the main subject are competing with it and need to be toned down, as shown in figure 13-17. This is not a big change (I am not trying to make the leaves something other than what they are), but in a print it really makes a difference. You can see from the layer mask, as shown in the Layers palette in figure 13-18, that the area controlled by the layer (the white) is very restricted.

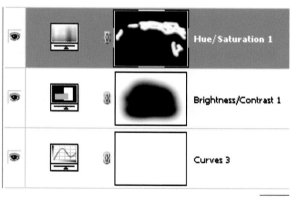

Hue/Saturation 1

Brightness/Contrast 1

Curves 3

13-18

The last and top layer is a pixel layer. There are a few places in the old leaves that are too light. They did not darken properly with the right color when using any adjustment layers. I picked a color from a dark leaf with the eyedropper, which puts it in the foreground color. I then use a paintbrush and paint over those areas on a new layer, as shown in figure 13-19. I change the layer blending mode to Darken and reduce its Opacity until it looks right. The result is seen in the final image shown in figure 13-20 (which has also been sharpened).

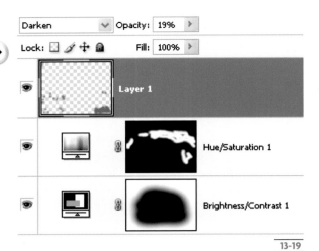

Using layers is a matter of applying them step by step, as shown by this example, each time affecting one thing on the image. I do not try to make a layer do multiple things — that makes it harder to control the effects in that layer. You can see from this example how much control you can get from layers.

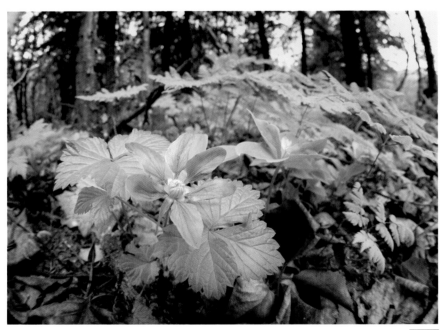

13-20

WORKING WITH LAYER MASKS

A very important part of this image, as you saw in figure 13-9 through figure 13-20, is the layer mask. This is a hugely valuable part of using layers because it offers you control in Photoshop that cannot be achieved in Lightroom. Yet it is also one of the most consistently confusing parts of Photoshop for many photographers. It is extremely helpful to understand layer masks, however, and I strongly recommend spending some time learning them. In this section, I give you enough information to get you started with layer masks (and to see how valuable they can be) so you can practice on your own.

A *layer mask* is an invisible layer control that allows some, all, or none of a layer and its effects to work. Masks have been long used by advanced darkroom workers, publication printers, and Hollywood to block part of an image so something unique can be done in the blocked area with a different visual. You may know that many movies of imaginary locations use a computer-generated scene, for example, to represent that location in the distance while the hero and heroine appear in the lower part of the image. The actors are often in common California hills, but a mask blocks the hills in the background so the computer-generated scene can replace it, resulting in a fantastic image that has no real-world connection.

You can do exactly that in Photoshop with layer masks, and, in this section, I explain how to use them to control how changes to an image are applied through layers.

The layer mask is represented in the Layers palette by the white box (layer mask thumbnail) to the right of the layer thumbnail, as shown in figure 13-21. It is actually an invisible mask on the image itself (though you can make it visible). When the mask is being

used, the layer mask thumbnails have black and white patterns in them, as shown in figure 13-22. These patterns show the actual mask being applied to the layer.

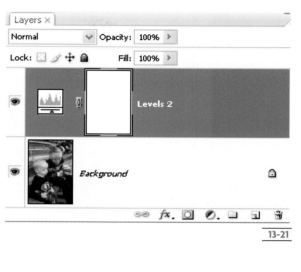

13-21

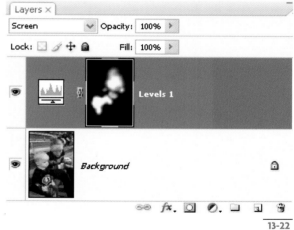

13-22

In a layer mask, black creates the masking effect, while white acts like it is the transparent area around a traditional mask. As a photographer, you may find it helpful to keep several things in mind about the effects of black and white in a layer mask:

> Black blocks anything that a layer might do. This could be an adjustment layer making the photo lighter, darker, more saturated, less saturated, and so on. No matter what the control, black blocks it from changing the photo.

> White permits anything that a layer might do.

> Gray partially allows a layer to act (or partially blocks the effect).

> Some photographers like to remember this: Black conceals, white reveals.

Here's another way of thinking about a layer mask. If you use an adjustment layer to change an image, the layer mask, in a sense, sits between that adjustment layer and the photo. When the layer mask is black, it is as though it creates a very dark shadow on a sunny day. You can't see what is happening in that dark area, therefore preventing the adjustment layer from working. When the layer mask is white, it is like the shadows are gone and all appears in the bright light. The adjustment layer now can work.

In the photo of the two kids at a hockey game that appears in this section, you can quickly see the effects of a layer mask. Figure 13-23 shows the image with its overall, Lightroom processing. Figure 13-24 shows the effect of adding a layer to lighten the dark face of the girl and the shirt of the boy, but without anything in the layer mask (shown in figure 13-21). This makes the whole image lighter, but it should not be.

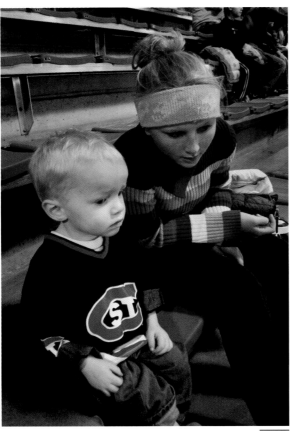

13-23

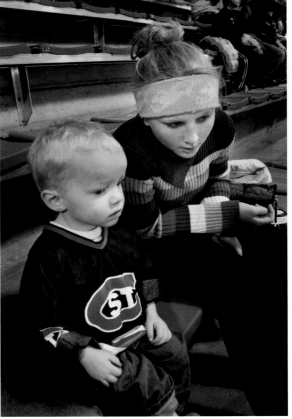

13-24

In figure 13-24, the effect after black is filled into the layer mask to block its overall effect (choose Edit ⇨ Fill ⇨ Black), and then white is painted over the girl's face and nearby dark areas. This reveals the adjustment layer's effects, but only in the areas of the mask that are white. Figure 13-25 shows the actual layer mask (Alt/Option+click on the layer mask icon reveals the mask).

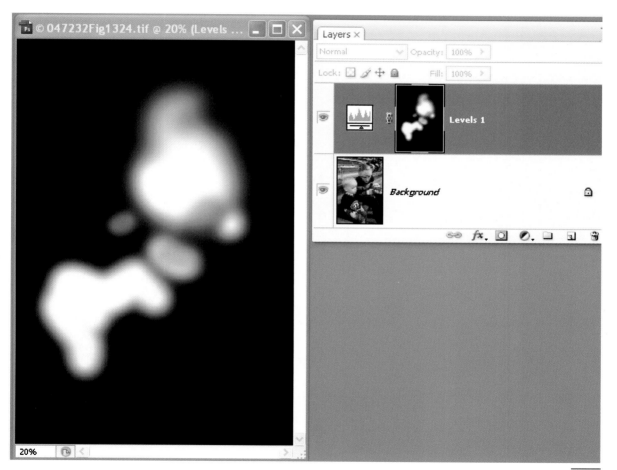

13-25

A great advantage of a layer mask at this point is that it is infinitely changeable with no adverse effects on your photo. You can fill it with black at any time to block the effect overall. You can fill it with white at any time to reveal the overall effect if your mask work is going in the wrong direction. You can also go back and forth between black and white to refine where an effect is concealed or revealed as much as you want.

LAYER MASKS WITH PIXEL LAYERS

In figure 13-26, a layer mask is used to limit the effect of sharpening a pixel layer back to the nagoonberry from Alaska. There is no point in sharpening the whole scene because only the flower and leaves in the foreground are actually sharp. When you sharpen out-of-focus areas, you often introduce unwanted artifacts of the sharpening. By sharpening a layer, you can use a layer mask to limit where the sharpening occurs, something that cannot be done in Lightroom.

You can add layer masks to a pixel layer either through the menu (choose Layer ➪ Layer Mask ➪

Reveal All or Hide All — reveal is white; hide is black) or through the layer mask icon at the bottom of the Layers palette (the little gray rectangle with a white circle in the center). In this case, I want to remove any evidence of this sharpened layer, and then paint its effects back in only on the flower and nearby leaves. If you press Alt/Option while clicking the layer mask icon, you get a black mask.

Then I simply use a white paintbrush to bring the sharpening back to the flower. This selective sharpening technique can be very useful in many situations, and it can be especially helpful in low- or available-light photography where noise can be high. This enables you to avoid sharpening the noise where it does not need to be sharpened.

You can paint in and out the effects or appearance of any layer, from pixels to adjustments, simply by using a layer mask. For example, you could put two photos together on a page, using separate layers for each, overlap them, and then blend them together with layer masks. That's exactly how you do a panoramic image.

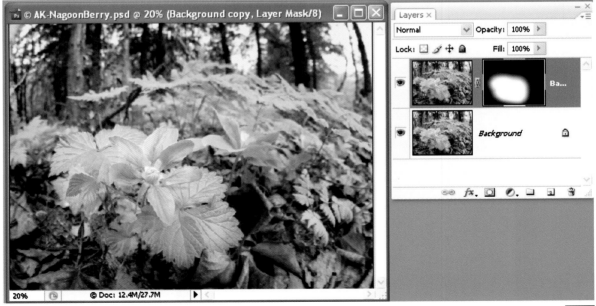

13-26

LOCAL ADJUSTMENTS

Using adjustment layers and layer masks gives you a lot of control over small areas of a photo. This is often called *doing local control or adjustments*. Ansel Adams used to talk about using dodging and burning for adjusting the exposure and contrast of local areas in a print that would not affect the overall exposure or contrast of the image. This was an important part of the work of many famous darkroom workers from nature photographers like Adams and Edward Weston to photojournalists like W. Eugene Smith.

Photoshop has Dodge and Burn tools that even look like the tools used in the traditional darkroom. However, they really don't work as well as true dodging and burning in the darkroom for large areas of an image. By large areas, I mean something more than a spot or tiny fraction of a photo. Local adjustments are needed whenever you must affect part of a photo without changing the whole image, so this can mean a large fraction of a picture, as well as very small parts of it. This is what I did in the previous examples showing layers and layer masks.

The Photoshop Dodge and Burn tools provide you with far less control than you can get with an adjustment layer and the layer mask. You can adjust and readjust an adjustment layer, plus alter the layer mask as much as you want to give you exactly what you want, where you want it. This is simply not possible with the Dodge and Burn tools. Perhaps you have heard of using a dodge and burn layer, a gray-filled layer set to the Overlay mode — the gray is neutral in Overlay. In it, you can darken (burn) or lighten (dodge) that gray to make areas of the photo lighter or darker. This still has less control than an adjustment layer with a layer mask and is far less flexible. In addition, using the Burn tool can cause splotchy patterns over large areas no matter how you use it.

Local control extends to more than image brightness and contrast. That's a great thing about using adjustment layers and layer masks. You can use exposure, contrast, and color controls. You can color correct a

part of a photo, for example, without changing any other part of the image. This can come in very handy if you shoot a scene with the available light there and the lighting sources are mixed. The human eye-brain connection compensates for this, and you don't see the strong color difference that the camera, unfortunately, captures. You cannot correct this in any overall adjustment. However, you can correct the overall scene the best you can in Lightroom, and then go to Photoshop and add a special adjustment layer to correct the problem color. You then use the layer mask to control that correction to only the problem areas.

BALANCING AN IMAGE

We see the world differently than a camera does. This affects everything photographers do when they take a picture. All sorts of techniques and tools are used to better control how the camera captures the world, the use of flash, white balance, graduated neutral density filters, different focal lengths, reflectors, and so on. The great *LIFE* magazine photographer Andreas Feininger once said that the uncontrolled photographic image is a lie compared to the photographer-controlled image because uncontrolled photography captures reality in arbitrary ways that don't necessarily match our experience.

One area that is a common problem with digital photographers is the brightness balance in an image. Many photos can come straight from Lightroom and look great from the processing done there. However, some will not be visually balanced to match the composition. Perhaps a graduated neutral density filter should have been used, but it wasn't, so the sky is too bright in relationship to the ground. Or maybe a person in a group gets hit with a slightly stronger light than the rest of the group, which is no problem when you look at the group in person, but is definitely a problem in the photo.

Lightroom cannot help. It has no controls to enable you to visually balance the brightness, contrast, or color of an image if there are differences across the composition. So, this is a key use for Photoshop.

An example of this appears in figure 13-27. This image of a 13th-century country church near Marlsborough, England, has had all of the correct overall adjustments made to it. But the bright walls on the left and right take away from the composition, which is based on the ceiling and the central stained glass window. When looking at a scene like this in real life, few people notice the brightness of the walls. Their eyes compensate for what they see and focus on the central window and ceiling.

But in the photograph, the brighter side walls take the eye away from the center altar end of the church. True, the contrast and color of the window attracts the eye, but the photo becomes more a three-point composition — window, left side, and right side — rather than focusing around the window area as it should. And it is also true that you can lighten dark areas with

Fill Light or by using the Tone Curve, but these adjustments affect the whole image.

In figure 13-28, you can see a Curves adjustment layer has been added to brighten the center area of the church. If you look at the layer mask thumbnail, you note that it is allowing the brightness in the middle and not allowing it on the sides (except the dark wood at the bottom right). This is a virtual version of the classic dodging (lightening) technique in the traditional darkroom.

You can see a Brightness/Contrast adjustment layer is added in figure 13-29. I have to briefly comment again on why I use Brightness/Contrast for such darkening effects. I use it precisely because it is a coarse tool that darkens everything. I don't want the variable tonal changes that Curves or Levels gives. With one slider, I can make everything darker or lighter.

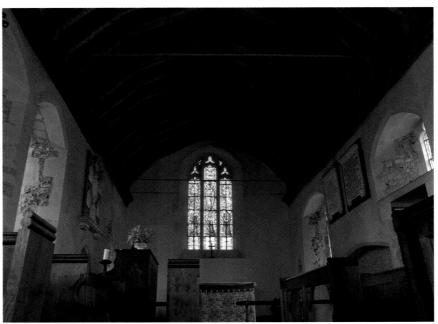

13-27

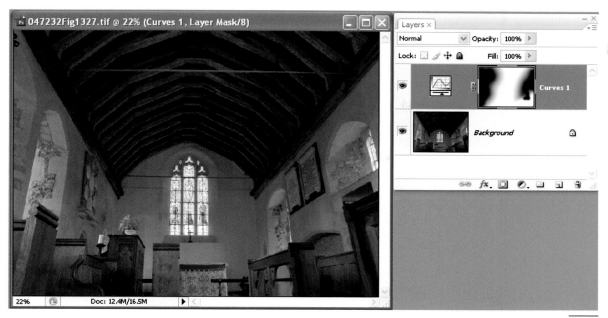

13-28

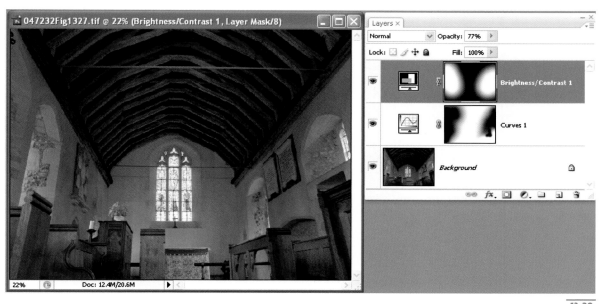

13-29

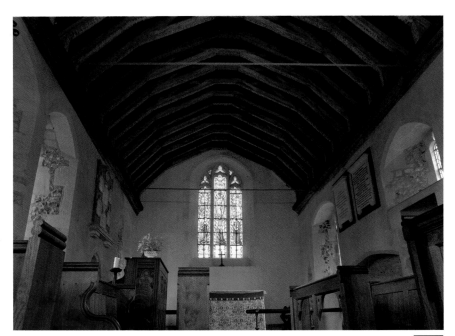

In this case, I darken the photo so that the side areas become more subordinate to the center of the image. I then use the layer mask to isolate this darkening to the sides of the church. Look at the difference this makes to how you look at the final image shown in figure 13-30. This controls the viewer's eye by visually balancing an image to better represent what was seen at the location. This is what balance is all about.

USING THE CLONING TOOL MISSING FROM LIGHTROOM

Lightroom has a healing tool that helps remove things like specks in the photo from sensor dust. It does not have a cloning tool, which along with layers, offers much more control over dealing with problems in an image that need to be removed. There are many things that can use the help of this tool (and its cousins, the healing brushes): flare artifacts, unseen distractions along the edge of the photo, and so on. Maybe the next version will have this tool. Until now, you've got to go to Photoshop for this one.

You can use cloning to radically change a photo, but I am not a big advocate of that. I like photo fantasies that are meant to be just that — fairies in flowers can be great fun. However, there are better techniques for doing this than cloning. When simple image-processing programs exploded a few years ago (and since then have largely disappeared), marketing people used to promote the cloning tool by adding a third eye to a portrait's head — possible to do, but hardly something worth doing except as a party game.

You do cloning using the Clone Stamp tool in Photoshop. It is important for cleaning up good images. Many photographers use this tool, but have problems with cloning artifacts. Cloning artifacts are details that begin to show up from cloning that did not originally exist in the photo. They appear purely from the cloning. The most obvious examples are repeating patterns or duplicate details. These are a sure sign of poorly done cloning and people do notice.

Removing Spots

The Remove Spots healing tool in Lightroom can be found at the bottom of the center work area in the Develop module. It mainly is used to remove specks that appear from sensor dust. It is simple to use: select the tool, move the cursor over the speck and click. Then move the cursor to a spot that you want to heal from. There are two choices, Clone or Heal — Clone duplicates the information from the "from" spot, while Heal compares the information and blends it with the original. You change the spot size with the slider. I can't recommend this for a lot of healing or cloning work. Because it is working non-destructively, it puts all the requests into memory and can really put a drain on your computer processor and memory, slowing down Lightroom considerably. Photoshop is much more flexible and controllable for this type of work.

Figure 13-31 is a summer beach scene near San Diego, California. The sun is important to the composition and gives a strong feeling of being at the beach on a sunny day. However, a nasty, bright bit of flare shows up at the bottom, as shown in figure 13-32.

That area is really treacherous for using a cloning tool because of the pattern there (which also makes the healing tools difficult). Here's how to use the Clone Stamp tool:

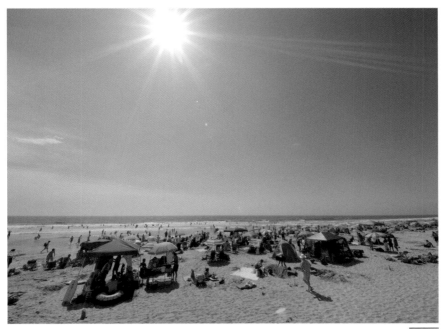

13-31

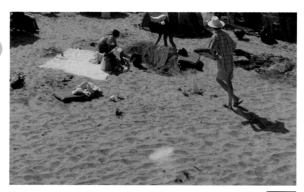

13-32

1. **Enlarge the area to the location that has the problem, as shown in figure 13-33, and select the tool in the toolbox.**

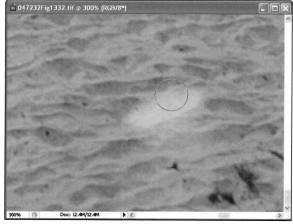

13-33

2. **Choose a brush size appropriate to the area in which you are working.** The Photoshop Clone Stamp tool is a brush tool and you can size it in the Options bar (below the menus) so that it is close in size to the area that needs to be cloned out, also shown in figure 13-33. Choose a soft-edged brush.

3. **Start with the brush at 100 percent opacity and lower the opacity to help blend in a cloned area when needed.**

4. **Clone to an empty layer, as shown in figure 13-34.** Add a layer before beginning cloning by clicking the Add Layer icon at the bottom of the Layers palette (the second icon from the right). Cloning to a layer gives you a lot of flexibility to clone because you cover the original problem, not change its pixels; plus you can use layer masks for refinement of the cloning work.

5. **Start with the brush at Aligned and Sample All Layers.** In the Options bar below the menu headings, you see these two options that you can check on or off (in general, leave everything else at the defaults). Aligned makes your cloning point follow your cursor at the same distance and angle from the start of your cloning, even if you release the mouse button (or move the graphic tablet pen from the tablet). Sample All Layers lets you clone to your new layer. You only turn this off when you need to keep your cloning limited to one layer (both the clone from and clone to points).

6. **Set your clone from point (the place where there is detail you want to copy over the problem) by pressing Alt/Option and clicking with the cursor at that point.**

7. **Move your cursor over the problem and start cloning by clicking your mouse (or using your graphic tablet pen).**

The problem is hidden in figure 13-35, but there are some new problems due to the cloning. Notice the three ridges in the center that are identical — this is a cloning pattern artifact that will always draw attention to your cloning work. Here are some tips on getting the most from the Clone Stamp tool and avoiding such problems:

Going Between Lightroom and Photoshop

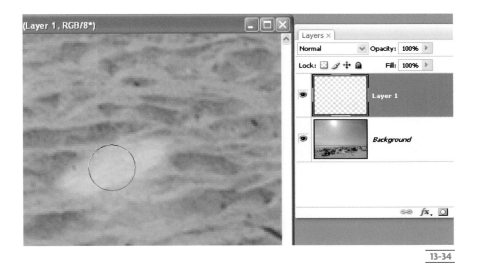

13-34

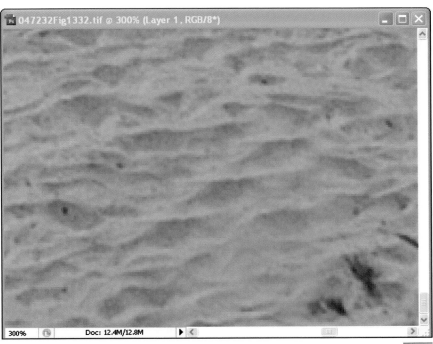

13-35

> **Be quick to use the Undo command (choose Ctrl/⌘+Z).** If you find you picked the wrong clone from point and your cloning starts out looking off, stop immediately, undo what you've done, and try a new clone from point. Do not try to make the cloning work by continuing to clone when it looks off from the start.

> **Avoid cloning with a single click and drag of the mouse (or pen).** Unless you have a very small spot (like a dust speck), you will not blend and merge the cloned area with its surroundings if you just click and drag. Do it in multiple clicks.

> **Change your brush size as you go.** Keeping the same brush size as you clone tends to aggravate cloning artifacts.

> **Change your clone from point as you go.** This is especially important for larger clone areas, such as flare removal. Keep finding new spots to clone from (Alt/Option+click) around your cloned area. This is another technique that really helps you avoid cloning artifacts.

> **Clone into cloning artifacts.** Break up a cloning artifact by setting a new clone from point and using a smaller brush size, and clone directly into the artifact. This is how the problem seen in figure 13-35 is corrected, as shown in figure 13-36 (in this small an area, the cloning work looks fine — some photographers will want to go further with cloning on areas that are more prominent in a photo).

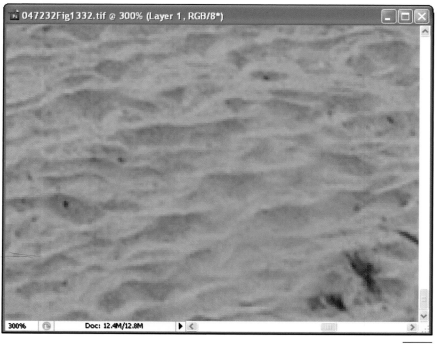

13-36

Q & A

Suppose I work on a photo in Lightroom, then export it to Photoshop and work on it there with those tools specific to Photoshop. What if I decide I need additional adjustments that I can do in either program? Which one would be best to use?

This is not a simple question to answer. There really is no quality difference if you use adjustment layers in Photoshop. The answer depends largely on workflow. If you are working on an image that is going to go straight to a client or other single use, it might be best to finish the image in Photoshop. This takes less time and you are done.

However, if you need to keep that image consistent with a group of photos (from a given Folder or Collection, for example), it is probably best to go back to Lightroom. That is certainly easy given the photo was automatically saved into the Folder it originally came from when it was saved from Photoshop. Once there, you can adjust the image to match the others, or even use those adjustments and copy or synchronize them to other photos. You can do this in Photoshop, but it is much harder to do because Photoshop is not designed to handle multiple photos.

When I discovered Lightroom, I thought I had found exactly what I needed. I really didn't like spending so much time in Photoshop. Now you are telling me that I need to use Photoshop to complete my photos. What happened to the simplicity of Lightroom?

The great thing about photography, I think, is that it fits so many different needs and personalities. Photoshop is not for everyone, nor is Lightroom. Both programs are simply tools that can help photographers achieve whatever their photographic goals are. If one tool gives you what you need without you having to use the other, that's no problem.

I do know that many photographers start feeling guilty because they are not using a certain technique, workflow, file format, and so on, that they heard they "should" use. I believe that photography should be fun. As soon as the "shoulds" start taking over, you quit having fun. That's not good.

Don't be intimidated by any expert into thinking you have to do something that expert's way. I know the feeling. As I started learning Photoshop years ago, I would hear things that I "had to do" in order to "do Photoshop" right. Sometimes they worked just fine, sometimes not. Yet, even if I found a certain way of working really fit my needs, I sometimes felt uneasy because that was not what the experts of the time said I should be doing.

I admit that this helped me learn a whole range of techniques. But the "guilt" was totally unnecessary. To this day, I get into disagreements with experts who want every photographer to do something their way. I just can't support that idea. Photographers are different, unique, and all have needs and attitudes that are not satisfied by one-stop shopping. I really believe you have to find the way that works best for you.

If it means experimenting with lots of ways of working, that's great. If it means stopping experimenting when you find what works for you, that's also great. Your photography is yours, and so should your workflow with it be. Have fun and stick with what seems to best fit your needs.

PRO GLOSSARY

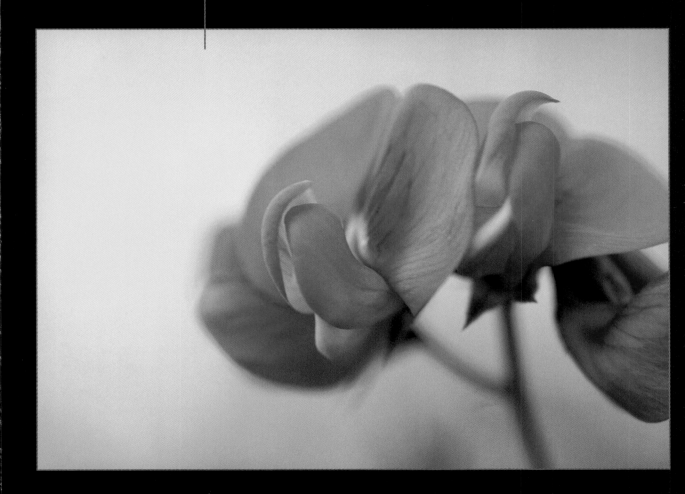

Adobe RGB A working color space based on the standard computer RGB colors created by Adobe Systems. It includes a wide gamut of colors that makes it a very flexible color space for use in Photoshop.

Algorithm Computations, formulas, and procedures — the software-based steps or instructions used in digital devices and programs to process data.

Anti-aliasing Using software to soften and blend rough edges (called aliased).

Archival storage Using external, nonmagnetic media such as DVDs and CDs to store information long term.

Artifact A defect in an image or other recorded data created by the tool used to record or output; something in an image that did not exist in the original scene but was inadvertently added to the photo by the technology.

Aspect ratio The proportion of an image comparing the height and width.

Background color The color chosen in Slideshow for the background behind the image.

Batch processing A way of making one or more changes, such as brightness or color adjustments, to a group or batch of image files all at once.

Bit The smallest unit of data in a computer.

Bit depth This refers to the number of bits required to represent the color in a pixel. With more bit depth, more colors are available. This increases exponentially (in base 2). True photo color starts at 8-bit but has limited adjustment range; 16-bit color offers a much larger amount of data that can be adjusted.

Browser 1) A program that's used for examining sites on the World Wide Web; 2) A software program designed to show small, thumbnail images of digital files.

Cast shadow A virtual shadow that appears like it is under a photo, making the photo look like it is floating over the background; often called a drop shadow.

CCD (charge-coupled device) A common type of image sensor used in digital cameras. The CCD actually only sees black and white images and must have red, green, and blue filters built into it in order to capture color.

CD-ROM (Compact Disc-Read-Only Memory) A compact disc (an optical medium) that contains information that can only be read. It cannot be updated or recorded over.

Cells Units on a page that hold images for prints and Web galleries in Lightroom.

Chip Common term for a computer-integrated circuit; the place where the data in a computer is processed.

Chroma The color component of an image; it includes the hue and saturation information of color.

Clone Stamp tool Photoshop's cloning tool; this brush-based tool lets you copy small areas from one spot and clone them (paste them) over other places in the image; often used to cover up or fix problems or defects in the photo.

CMOS (complementary metal-oxide semiconductor) A common type of image sensor used in digital cameras. Like the CCD, a CMOS sensor typically sees only black and white images and must have red, green, and blue filters built into it in order to capture color. CMOS sensors use less energy than CCD chips.

CMYK (cyan, magenta, yellow, black) These are the subtractive primary colors and the basis for the CMYK color space. They're used in so-called four-color printing processes used in books and magazines because they produce the most photo-like look for publications.

Collections A basic form of image organization in the Library module that allows you to create unique groupings of photos.

Color noise Noise in a digital image that has a strong color component to it; commonly found in dark areas in long exposures. Also known as chromatic noise.

Color Picker A color palette dialog box that allows you to pick colors based on hue (the actual color), saturation (the intensity), and tonal value (from black to white); it appears when you click on color option boxes in Slideshow, Print, and Web modules.

Color space Models of color that are based on a range of colors that can be interpreted by a particular digital device from camera to printer. This is its color space. There are many color spaces, though the two main ones used for photography are RGB and CMYK. Within those spaces are subsets of spaces such as Adobe RGB 1998 (larger) and sRGB (smaller).

Color wash A graduated color background used behind images in Slideshow; it blends two colors equally from top to bottom, side-to-side, or any other angle.

Continuous tone The appearance of smooth color or black and white gradations, as in a photograph.

Copy This Lightroom command copies adjustments from one photo that can then be applied to another.

Copyright A legal term that denotes rights of owner-ship and, thus, control over usage of written or other creative material. Unless otherwise noted, assume all images are copyrighted and can't be used by anyone without permission of the photographer.

Compression The use of algorithms to reduce the amount of data needed to save a file in a smaller form.

DPI (dots per inch) Resolution of a computer periph-eral as a measurement of the number of horizontal or vertical dots it's able to resolve in input or output. This is confusing because dpi for a scanner is the same as ppi of an image, yet both are different from the dpi of a printer. Dpi for a printer refers to the way ink droplets are laid down on paper.

Drop shadow A virtual shadow that appears like it is under a photo, making the photo look like it is floating over the background; in Lightroom, it is called a cast shadow.

Dye-sublimation Printing technology that results in continuous-tone images by passing gaseous color dyes through a semi-permeable membrane on the media surface.

Dynamic range The difference between the highest and the lowest values, as in the brightest highlights and the darkest shadows, in an image.

EVF Electronic viewfinder.

Export Sending photos out of Lightroom; this means the image is fully processed as a finished file based on Lightroom's adjustments.

EXIF data Special metadata added to a photo file by the camera that includes such things as shutter speed, aperture, ISO setting, and so forth. EXIF stands for Exchangeable Image File.

Exposure 1) The combination of shutter speed and f-stop used in a camera to control the light hitting the sensor or film; 2) A specific control in Lightroom that affects highlights.

File format How the data that makes up an image is defined and organized for storage on a disk or other media. Standard image formats include JPEG, RAW, PSD, and TIFF.

Filmstrip 1) A linear sequence of images; 2) The bot-tom panel of Lightroom.

Filter In traditional photography, this refers to col-ored optical glass or plastic sheet that goes in front of the lens and affects how the image is captured.

FireWire A very fast connection (meaning lots of data transmitted quickly) for linking peripherals to the computer; also called IEEE 1394 and i.Link.

Flash A multimedia system designed to create pro-grams of slide shows and more for computers, pro-grams that showed much interaction among the visual elements, yet could be stored and played back from a small file size; originally developed by a company called Macromedia, which was later bought by Adobe.

Folders Folders are the groupings of images as imported into Lightroom.

FTP server Stands for File Transfer Protocol; it is a standard for transfer of images from one computer to another, typically used to transfer large files (such as photos) to a server, hence, FTP server.

Graphics tablet and pen A way of controlling your cursor's movement and actions by using an electronic tablet that senses where its graphic pen is moving; an alternative to the mouse.

Gray scale (or Grayscale) A black-and-white image composed of a range of gray levels from black to white.

Guides Lines that appear in a work area to guide or structure the placement of an object, sizing, and other changes to a photo but are not part of the image; they can be turned on or off.

Histogram A very important tool for reading the exposure of a photo that is a graph of pixels at different brightness levels in the photo, with dark tones represented toward the left, bright tones to the right, and midtones in the middle.

History An interactive chart of the actions taken on your photo in the Develop module; it gives the photo's history, so that you can see what you've done and back up to earlier actions.

HTML Short for Hypertext Markup Language, HTML is the standard language used for instructions that structure text and images to create Web pages.

Hue The actual color of a color.

Identity Plate A unique and customizable text or graphic element that can be added to Lightroom in place of the program logo and can be used with prints, slide shows, and Web pages.

Import Bringing photos into Lightroom; the identification and recognition of image files so that they can be brought under Lightroom control.

Inkjet A digital printing technology where tiny droplets of ink are placed on the paper to form characters or images.

Interpolation A way of increasing or decreasing the apparent resolution of an image by using algorithms to create additional pixels in an image by smartly filling in the gaps between the original pixels or by smartly replacing them in order to get to a smaller file size.

IPTC data A set of writable metadata that is based on a standard that can be readily used by pros and publications; IPTC stands for International Press Telecommunications Council.

JPEG (Joint Photographic Experts Group) A file format that smartly compresses image information to create smaller files; the files are reconstructed later. JPEG files lose quality as compression increases. Technically, JPEG is a compression standard rather than a file format (the term JPEG really refers to the standards committee), but through common use it has come to mean a file format.

JPEG artifacts Image defects due to file size compression that look like tiny rectangles or squarish grain. This appears from high compression levels or multiple compression of a single file.

Keywords (keyword tags) These are unique words that can be attached to images in their metadata so that specific images can later be easily found from a search for keywords.

Layer mask A special part of a Photoshop adjustment layer that allows you to turn the layer effects on and off by painting in white or black, respectively. It can also be added to pixel layers.

Layers Separated elements of a Photoshop digital image in which each part has its own isolated plane or level.

LCD (liquid crystal display) A display technology used for computer monitors as well as small monitors that act as viewfinders and playback displays for digital cameras.

Lens aberration A defect in the optical path of a lens that creates optical artifacts such as color fringing that can affect color definition and sharpness of a lens.

Levels A key tonal adjustment tool in Photoshop; this uses a histogram and three sliders under it to affect the image the left is for dark areas, the middle for middle tones, and the right for bright areas.

Lights Out A Lightroom mode that darkens the whole screen except for the selected photo being worked on (accessed by pressing L).

Lossless compression Any form of file size reduction where no loss of important data occurs (redundant data is lost).

Lossy compression Any form of file size reduction technique where some loss of data occurs.

Loupe A single-image view in Lightroom that can be magnified with a single click on the image; loupe is a name for a magnifier.

Luminance noise A special type of noise in a digital image that looks like sand across the image — a dark/light pattern without colors in it (other than the original subject colors).

Metadata This means information about information; for photos, it refers to data stored with an image that describes exposure, camera type, copyright, and so on. Lightroom allows much additional information to be written to the file in the metadata.

Navigator A small preview image that lets you see the whole photo when the central work photo is magnified, then move around in it; it is also used as a preview of certain adjustments.

Noise An artifact of the digital technologies, largely the sensor, that shows up in the photograph as a fine pattern that looks like grain or sand texture.

Overlays Details about a photo, including text and rating stars, that Lightroom adds to the exported image in a slide show or a print.

Paste In Lightroom this pastes copied adjustment information to new files.

Photosite The individual, actual photosensitive area on a sensor that captures the brightness for a single pixel in the image. There is one photosite for every pixel in the original image.

Pixel Short for picture element (pix/picture, el/element). The smallest element of a picture that can be controlled by the computer.

PPI (pixels per inch) A way of measuring linear resolution of an image and refers to how the pixels are spaced, meaning the number of pixels per inch in an image, often used interchangeably with dpi.

PSD file The native file format for Photoshop and Photoshop Elements. It allows the saving of layers, layer masks, and more.

Quick Collection Lightroom's semi-automated way of grouping images together quickly though temporarily.

RAM (Random Access Memory) The computer's memory that's actually active for use in programs; comes on special chips. Anything in it is temporary and disappears when a program is closed or the computer is shut down.

RAW file An image file that is minimally processed after it comes from the sensor in a camera. Data comes from the sensor and is translated to digital in the A/D converter; that data is then packaged for the RAW file. A RAW file is not generic for all cameras; there are actually proprietary files made by each camera manufacturer.

Resolution The density of pixels in an image or the number of pixels or dots per inch in an image or that a device, such as a scanner, can capture.

RGB The primary color system of a computer based on red, green, and blue, the additive primary colors. Computer monitors (CRT and LCD) display RGB-based screen images.

Saturation The amount of brilliance or intensity of a color; how colorful or dull a color is.

Sensor The light-capturing part of a digital camera, usually a CCD or CMOS chip.

Snapshot A stage in image adjustments in the Develop module remembered by Lightroom; it is a snapshot of what the image looked like at that point in processing.

Split Toning Coloring of an image so that the shadows and highlights are colored differently.

sRGB A common color space in the RGB color system that is more restricted than others.

Stacking The grouping or arrangement of images in the Filmstrip or Library so that different images sit on top of each other in a virtual stack.

Stroke A fine line around a photo that acts as a thin border.

Sync metadata and sync settings Sync in Lightroom is used to synchronize settings among a series of individual photo files; sync metadata matches metadata among those files, while sync settings duplicates adjustment parameters.

Thumbnail A small, low-resolution version of an image that is used for browsing many images at a time.

TIFF (Tagged Image File Format) An important, high-quality image format common to most image-processing programs.

Tonal range The difference in brightness from the brightest to the darkest tones in an image.

Tone Curve An adjustment for tonal values in an image that offers a great deal of flexibility. It appears first as a 45-degree angle line running up to the right in a graph. When that line is clicked on and moved, it changes tones in the image. The upper part of the curve is light, the bottom dark. Moving the curve up lightens tones; moving it down darkens tones. It is possible to move parts of the curve in different directions.

Unsharp Mask (USM) The name is misleading because it is based on an old commercial printing term; it is a highly controllable Photoshop adjustment used for sharpening an image and includes three settings: amount, radius, and threshold.

USB A standard computer connection for linking peripherals to the computer; Hi-Speed USB 2.0 is very fast, comparable to FireWire.

Vibrance Similar to the Saturation control, vibrance also affects the intensity of colors, but uses a different algorithm.

Vignetting The darkening or lightening of the outer part of an image due to the way the photograph was shot (either the lens used or special vignetting techniques employed).

Watermark In Lightroom, this is a copyright text with the photographer's name that is added to images in Web galleries.

White Balance A special digital control that tells digital cameras how to correctly represent color based on the color temperatures of different light sources. All digital cameras have automatic white balance; most also let photographers adjust it manually.

index

F

G

Index